mathematical sociology

Prentice-Hall Methods of Social Science Series

Editors

Herbert L. Costner
Neil Smelser

mathematical sociology

Robert K. Leik
University of Massachusetts

B. F. Meeker
University of Maryland

Prentice-Hall, Inc., Englewood Cliffs, New Jersey

Library of Congress Cataloging in Publication Data

Leik, Robert K
   Mathematical sociology.

   (Prentice-Hall methods of social sciences series)
   Includes bibliographical references and index.
   1. Sociology—Mathematical models. 2. Sociology—
Methodology.   I. Meeker, Barbara Foley, joint author.
II. Title.
HM24.L425   301′.01′51   74-22271
ISBN 0-13-562108-9

© 1975 by *Prentice-Hall, Inc. Englewood Cliffs, New Jersey*

All rights reserved.
No part of this book may be reproduced in any form or by any means without permission in writing from the publisher.

Printed in the United States of America

10 9 8 7 6 5 4 3 2 1

Prentice-Hall International, Inc., London
Prentice-Hall of Australia, Pty. Ltd., Sydney
Prentice-Hall of Canada, Ltd., Toronto
Prentice-Hall of India Private Limited, New Delhi
Prentice-Hall of Japan, Inc., Tokyo

table of contents

preface   xi

CHAPTER 1

model building: the tie between theory and data   1

What a Mathematical Model Is   2
Models in Sociological Theory   2,   Models in Data Analysis   3,
Models in Mathematical Form   4

The Theory-Model-Data Triangle   9
Mapping   11,   Two Approaches to Mathematical Form   12,
Four Types of Models   14

Some Comments on the Uses of Mathematics in Sociology   15
Benefits of Mathematical Sociology, or Why Bother?   15,
Costs of Mathematical Sociology: Is It Really Worth It?   17

CHAPTER 2

a power-function model of status 20

Translation into Mathematics 22
Questions About the Choice of the Model 22

Development and Tests of the Model 24

Extensions of the Model 29

Evaluating the Model 32

Conclusions: Benefits and Costs of Mathematics 35

Problems 36

CHAPTER 3

the distribution of acts in small groups 38

Translation into Mathematics 40, Developing the Model 42, Evaluating and Extending the Model 44

Problems 51

CHAPTER 4

graphs, matrices, and structural balance 53

Translation into Mathematics 55
Formalization of the Theory 55, Basic Concepts of Graph Theory 56, Translating from Theory to Model 58, Development of the Model 58

Other Mathematical Representations of Balanced Structures 61
Matrix Representation 61,
Set-Theory Representation of Balanced Structures 64

Tests and Extensions of the Model   65
Application to Sociometric Data   65,   Modifications of the Model   66

Evaluating the Model   72

Problems   74

CHAPTER 5

kinship and clique structures   75

Kinship Structure Models   76
The Substantive Problem   76,   Translating from Data to Model   78,
Development of the Model   81,   Testing the Model   84,
Evaluation of the Model   84

Analyzing Cliques and Status Structures   85
The Substantive Problem   86,   Translation into Mathematics   86,
Developing the Model   89,   Evaluating the Model   92

Summary   93

Problems   94

CHAPTER 6

identifying causes in structures   98

Marginal Analysis Using Partial Differential Equations   99
Translation into Mathematics   99,   Moving from Theory to Model   101,
Translation into Mathematics   101,
Substantive Extensions of the Model   105,   Evaluating the Model   107

Some Final Notes on Structure Models   110

Problems   116

CHAPTER 7

time series data and diffusion   117

    Curve Fitting with Time Series Data   118
Translation into Mathematics   122,   Estimation of Parameters   125,
Interpreting the Model   126

    Process Models: Diffusion   128
Translation into Mathematics   129,
Further Development of the Model   135

    Problems   138

CHAPTER 8

computer simulation and renewal processes   140

    A Computer Simulation of Interpersonal Choice   140
Translation into Mathematics   144,
Testing and Extending the Model   149,
Incorporating the Idea of Social Pressure   151,
A "No-Host" Model   153,   A Final Attempt   154,
Other Implications and Other Models   156

    A Model of Birth Control Processes   158
The Substantive Problem   158,   Translation into Mathematics   158,
Efficiency of Abortion as Birth Control   161,
General Use of the Model   162

    Problems   163

CHAPTER 9

markov processes and occupational mobility   165

    A Brief Introduction to Markov Processes   165
Ways of Representing Markov Processes   166,
Aggregation and Equilibrium   169

Markov Models of Mobility   171
Developing the Model   172,   Estimating the Parameters   173,
Revising the Model   176,   Development of the Revised Model   177,
Estimating Parameters   178,   Testing the Model   180,
McFarland's Mobility Model   182

Problems   185

CHAPTER 10

value conflict in two-person interaction   187

Theory and Data   188
Experimental Procedure   188,   Results   190,
Translation into Mathematics   192,   Estimating the Parameters   193,
Test of the Model   194

Revised Model   195
Estimating the Parameters   198,   Testing the Model   201,
Interpreting the Values of the Parameters   201,
Evaluating the Model   203

Problems   204

Appendix to Chapter 10   205

CHAPTER 11

discrete-state continuous time models   208

Translation into Mathematics   210

Estimating Parameters   215
Panel Data   215,   Cross-sectional Data   220

Comments on the Model   224

Problems   224

CHAPTER 12

working with mathematical models   225

Questions about Variables   227
Order 227, Continuity 228, Level 229, Randomness 230, Treatment of Time 231

Questions about Relationships   232
Causality 232, Form 233

Key Questions for Model Building   235

General Philosophical Considerations   236

Inspiration for the Model Builder   238

index   239

preface

This book provides an introduction to working with mathematical models in sociology. The major focus is on purposes, approaches, and alternatives in developing and using models. The first chapter discusses general aspects of mathematical models and their relationship to theory and research; the twelfth, concluding chapter provides a series of guideline questions which should help determine the type of model building or application appropriate to the job at hand and a discussion of some general issues in model building. Chapters 2 through 11 are grouped into two categories based on the distinction between structural models (those not involving time) and process models (those that do involve time). For each of fourteen different models we discuss the sociological problem, the way the model was developed to handle the problem, and some suggestions about further development and extension of the model. Particular attention is given to the basis for and appropriateness of decisions made in developing the model. Other ways of handling the problem and other uses of that type of model are also noted. Statistical models are not covered in this book, except as they appear as part of one of the models—for example, in testing for goodness of fit.

This book will serve as a text for advanced undergraduate and for graduate level courses, and as a guide and reference work for the nonmodel-builder who wishes to understand more about the applicability of mathematics in the discipline. We have emphasized the process of building and using models as part of the general sociological enterprise by discussing a wide variety of mathematical and sociological approaches.

The mathematics involved in the various models includes linear algebra and matrix operations, some calculus and simple differential equations, and basic probability theory. We also assume approximately intermediate-level statistics as a background. Although the discussions can be read by someone without some of this background, it would be misleading to suggest that no mathematical knowledge is required; some familiarity with the kinds of mathematics indicated will be needed to understand and use the models.

*mathematical
sociology*

CHAPTER 1

*model building:
the tie between theory
and data*

Numerous contributions to the sociological literature, especially in recent years, might be categorized as mathematical sociology. The purposes of such work are diverse: attempting to formalize theories, finding systematic patterns in empirical observations, even playing "what if" games with sociological ideas. The range of subject matter and the kinds of mathematics used vary widely as well. It is evident from commentaries on the place and utility of mathematics in sociology that there is no agreement on how mathematics should be employed We contend that the use of mathematics in theoretical development, in analysis of data, and in the integration of diverse substantive areas of sociology is not only desirable but necessary to the long-range progress of the discipline. This does not imply that all sociologists will need to do mathematical work, but it does mean mathematics can make contributions to the field that no other approach can.

what a mathematical model is

Models in Sociological Theory. In substantive research a sequence of kinds of work must be fitted together to produce a useful contribution. The first part of the work (and, by the time the full cycle of research is completed, the last part as well) is theoretical. Particular questions related to the current substantive knowledge must be formulated so that productive research can be undertaken. Ultimately, new information from the research must be related to these questions so that general conclusions can be drawn.

A major advance in theoretical work in sociology in recent decades began with what is called axiomatic theory.[1] We need not discuss it in any detail here, except for one aspect that is salient to our discussion. Axiomatic theory requires that each concept and each relationship be carefully stated in terms of previously defined concepts or relationships. The initial, basic concepts and relationships are "given" in the sense that they remain undefined in the logic of the theory being developed. A few assumed relationships defined for a few primitive concepts allow logical deduction of a larger set of implications for the subject under consideration. The resulting theory is much "tighter" than the purely discursive theories found in classical sociological examples. This means that tests can be more rigorous and findings more readily fitted together to form the fabric of theoretical sociology.

There are two parts to constructing an axiomatic theory. One involves being certain that the substantive concepts and relationships are appropriately represented in the axiomatic theory. This concerns what might be called the external validity of the theory. The other involves the theory's purely logical form. The logical form consists of dichotomous variables and quite simple statements about the relationships between them. This purely logical part may be considered a *model*, which is applied when called for by a particular theory-development problem.

If we substitute more complex variables and more complex logic for handling the relationships between them, we still have a model—that is, an abstract logic system used to represent the substantive theory which we wish to develop. The translation from substantive area to model will still have to be worked out. The difference will lie in the extent to which the model being applied can accommodate subtleties in the substantive area. Presumably, as the model becomes capable of more subtle and varied treatment of any substantive problem, the external validity of the theory increases.

The most general, varied, and subtle type of formal logic available is mathematics. It represents, in all its diversity, the great variety of ways people have developed for handling complicated problems of correctly

---

[1]For example, Hans L. Zetterberg, *On Theory and Verification in Sociology* (Totowa, N.J.: The Bedminster Press, 1965).

deducing statements from assumptions. Problems that appear quite different can sometimes be treated by exactly the same mathematical formulation. In such cases the general mathematical approach can be worked out in detail in the abstract, without regard for the problems which it might resolve. Then, as someone working with a substantive problem turns to mathematics, he can employ the entire model that has been developed, simply by translating his theoretical concepts into the mathematical variables and showing that the mathematical relationships match reasonably well the basic relationships in his theory. Having done so, he then may use all the detailed consequences of the mathematical model by translating them into substantive terms. If the model is sufficiently well worked out, he may not have to do any actual mathematics himself. If not, he may contribute both to his own work and to any other work requiring that type of model if he is able to provide new detail in mathematical form. Whether or not a particular researcher contributes mathematical results, his task of theory development is greatly eased if he has available a range of mathematical models to work with.

Models in Data Analysis. The second step in sociological work (for purposes of our discussion, at least) is the actual data-producing research effort. Without observations of the reality with which the theory is concerned, there can be no way of knowing how valid that theory is. Speculative philosophic debate may be good sport, but scientific knowledge rests on demonstration that the speculation fits the reality. Which data are gathered is properly a question of which data are needed to answer the specific theoretical questions being considered.

Because we wish theories to be general, whereas data are inevitably limited by problems of time, money, and access to situations which allow research, there arises a third kind of work—that of determining the extent to which specific data can be related to general statements. Traditionally this is the function of statistical analysis. Performing a statistical analysis means using a kind of mathematical model. Ordinarily, people trained in the application of routine statistical procedures do not think of what they are doing as fitting data to an abstract model, then relating that model to the general theoretical questions they started with. It may help, however, briefly to consider such a view of statistical analysis.

Suppose we wish to find out whether more education produces (or at least is in some way related to) greater income. For simplicity and convenience, we determine the incomes of 100 people with doctoral degrees, 100 people with bachelors degrees only, and 100 people with high school education only. Also, for convenience, assume that these samples have about the same average age, the same kinds of occupational fields, and so on, so that other variables are not confusing our results. Now, if we compute the average income for the three educational groups, and find that they differ as expected, have we answered our general theoretical question adequately? Unfortunately, no, because there is no guarantee that our three sets of people really represent the great numbers of people in those three categories. Even though our data show, for example, higher incomes for those with doctorates, we may have gotten unusually well-paid doctorates in that sample, or unusually ill-paid people in the other samples.

The properly trained student will now reflect: "What we need is a statistical test." Fine! Ideally, analysis of variance (one way) will suit the task. The computations are not very difficult, and in fact there are ample computer programs to do the job. What is likely to be overlooked except in the most cursory way is that analysis of variance, or any other test, rests upon an elaborate system of reasoning. *If* samples are randomly drawn (mathematically random, not just haphazard), and *if* they are statistically independent of each other (again a precise mathematical assumption), and *if* the variance (a mathematical statement of variability) of income is the same for the three populations of cases from which the samples were drawn, then it can be derived mathematically that there is a specific probability that the sample means will differ a given amount even if the population means are the same. Using all that complicated reasoning, the researcher can deduce the chance that his results are happenstance. To do so requires that he assume—or, more properly, that he demonstrate—the validity of all those assumptions for his piece of research.

Fortunately, most researchers do not need to go through the mathematics underlying statistical testing. They can simply use the *model* developed by statisticians, determine whether their work meets the requirements of that model, then reap the benefits of someone else's mathematical efforts. Let us now substitute a more general problem. Rather than deducing strictly sampling consequences, suppose we wish to be able to deduce whether our data fit theoretically anticipated trends, system interrelationships, consequences of unmeasurable variables such as mental states, or other complex patterns. We need some way of reasoning from the observations to the level of theory. Just as with the sampling question, mathematical models can perform that reasoning function. In fact, it is reasonable to consider statistical procedures as one type of mathematical modeling.

Models in Mathematical Form. We have pointed out that most sociologists are already familiar with some kinds of models, using them in theory construction and data analysis. Let us examine in more detail what a model in mathematical form is like. In general, mathematical models are constructed of equations specifying precise relationships among a set of variables. At the risk of sounding trivial, let us begin by noting that an equation is simply a shorthand set of directions. It contains operators, such as $+$, $-$, $\times$, from arithmetic, and something which is supposed to be operated upon. The equation $Y = a + bX$ states "multiply X by b (the operator "$\times$" being understood by convention), add the value of a, and set Y equal to that amount." It makes no difference what X, Y, a and b stand for as far as the meaning of the equation in a mathematical sense is concerned. That is why a mathematical model can be completely general.

Certain conventions used in writing equations, however, would lead most people who are used to algebraic expressions to assume that X and Y are basically different from a and b. The former are what are called *variables* and the latter *parameters*. In the simplest usage, the parameters of an equation do not change even though a large number of different sets of X and Y values may be associated by that equation. For example, suppose that X indicated how many years of education someone received before seeking regular employment, Y stood for the average income he could expect to earn, and the parameters had the values of $a = \$1,900$ and $b = \$740$ per year. We could then predict that someone with no formal education would earn an average of $1,900, someone who completed high school (12 grades) would earn $10,780, someone who finished a B.A. degree (four years of college) would earn $13,740, and someone who had four years of graduate training would earn $16,700 on the average. Note that the values of a and b were the same for all four cases considered, although X and Y varied.

It is likely that the equation above would not give very good prediction. For one reason, the effects of education on income simply are not the same for males as for females. Other divisions of the population also get unequal return for their investment in formal school (for example, visible minorities such as blacks). What does such a problem imply for adequate treatment of the relationship between education and income?

Aside from throwing out the entire idea of expressing the relationship mathematically, we could recognize the need for a unique set of parameters for each special population (male-white, female-white, and so on). The value of $b = 740$ meant that for each additional year of formal education a person could gain an average of $740 income. If some parts of the total population realized only half that much profit from additional education, then their b value would be just 370. Also, not every part of the population would have the same baseline. Wealthy individuals may be able to assume, say, at least $100,000 income regardless of formal education because of family stock holdings. The value of a would therefore be very much higher than it was for the general population.

What has happened to the idea that parameters do not vary? In the illustration above we have found that parameters may indeed vary, but only from one set of cases to another (from one population to another). For any set of cases which are to be treated as being from the same population, the values of the parameters should stay fixed, at least for this example. If

6 Mathematical Sociology

the same kind of equation ($Y = a + bX$) holds for all populations, with just the values of the parameters changing, then we have one basic relationship between education and income, with special variations on that relationship, as defined by the parameters. The entire set of equations will be from a single "family" of equations; they are all "linear" equations.

Table 1-1 shows what happens to the parameters of the income-education relationship when categories of sex and racial-ethnic status are examined separately. The data are from the 1970 census. For convenience of illustration, we treat the data in simplified form by using mean income and mean education for each of five educational levels (highest used is college graduate) for persons who worked 50 to 52 weeks in 1969. Because of this simplification, the parameters in Table 1-1 may vary slightly from other analyses of the same data, but they should show comparable changes between subpopulations.

The parameters for white males are essentially those used for illustration earlier. Parameters for other populations show considerably different values. Looking first at the values of b (increment in income to be expected by one additional year of education), we find that education for white males is far more profitable than for any other category. Also, with the exception of blacks, males find education more profitable than do females. In fact, white females have less than half the gain from a year of school than do white males. These b values could be interpreted as indicators of relative status in that they show the extent to which one's investment will, on the average, be rewarded by the system.

The values of a seem to present a different story, but they need to be interpreted in light of associated b values. Although it looks as if black and Spanish-speaking males do better than do white males, remember that a implies expected income if there is no education at all. At three years of

Table 1-1

Linear Relationships between Income and Education, by Sex and Racial-Ethnic Categories

POPULATION		PARAMETERS (NEAREST DOLLAR)	
Sex	Race-Ethnicity	a	b
Male	White	1,885	741
	Spanish-speaking	2,501	511
	Black	2,306	413
Female	White	1,127	362
	Spanish-speaking	1,390	316
	Black	−485	445

education, the expected income for white males exceeds that of all others, and it continues to do so by an increasing margin. As will be seen shortly, the linear fit does not do very well, and all values of a in Table 1-1 are artifacts of this poor fit.

Just what *linear* means in a graphic sense warrants brief comment. Assuming that the equation used above was valid, we could say that a given increase in amount of formal education would raise income by a specific amount. It would not matter whether we looked at six years of education versus seven years, or 20 years versus 21 years; we would still expect an income increase of $740. If a graph were made that showed an income of $1,900 for no education, and then exactly $740 more for each added year of education, all points of the graph would fall on a single line. Such a straight-line graph is a linear relation. If the points did not fall on a straight line, the relation would be nonlinear.

The question of linearity or nonlinearity is a question of the form of the equation. Whatever the form is, if that form is retained but the parameters changed from one population to another, there will be produced a family of curves which all look alike in general shape even though they do not give identical predictions (that is, match up the same pairs of X and Y values). Actually, that statement might need some qualification, but it will do for now.

The relevance of parameters and the form of the equation in which they occur lies in the possible substantive interpretations. For example, we found that the value of b differed from one population to the next, and we might interpret such variation (in Table 1-1) as indicating that the sex-by-racial-ethnic categories have differential opportunity in the social structure. That single parameter in a simple equation could be of considerable theoretical importance. We might find, on closer examination of the data plotted on a graph, that there is a definite curve rather than a linear relationship. An equation such as $Y = a + bX^n$ might be needed. If n takes on the value of 1, then we are back to a linear relationship; but if n is greater than 1, then later years of education will be more profitable than were earlier years. On the other hand, n less than 1 but still positive would mean that later educational advancement produced diminishing returns in expected income. The former case occurs for all of the populations of Table 1-1. It produces an accelerating curve. The latter (decelerating curve) could indicate a population which has a job ceiling even more pronounced than that affecting minorities and women according to the 1970 census.

Figure 1-1 shows the curve of income by education (omitting those with more than four years of college) for the populations of Table 1-1. All curves show acceleration but in different degree and from different starting points. It is obvious that a straight line does not do justice to these data.

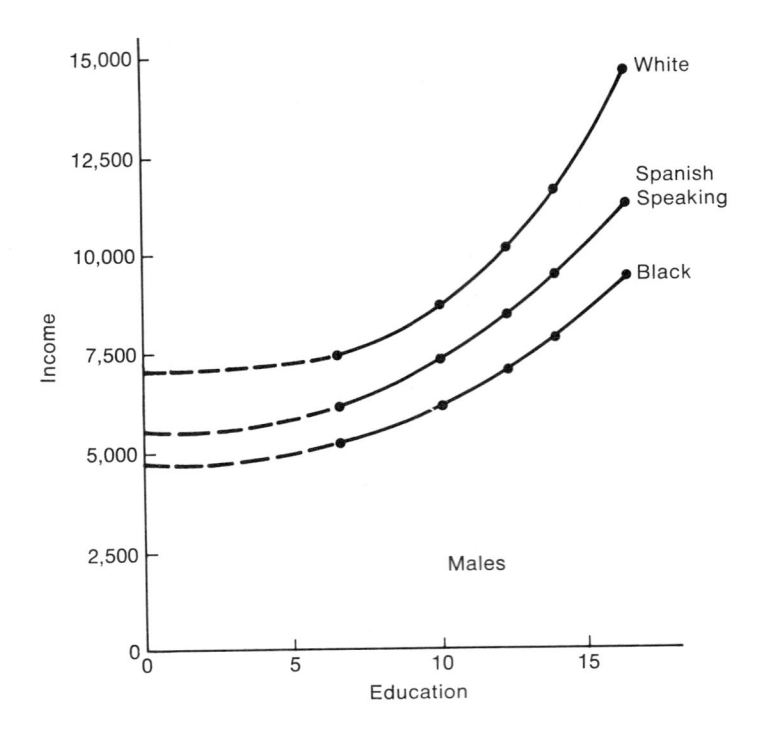

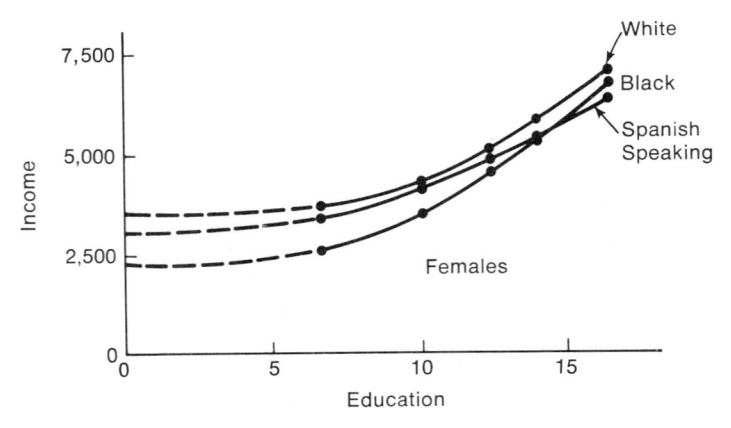

W = white; S = Spanish-speaking; B = black

Source: 1970 census

Figure 1-1

Income by education, sex, and race-ethnicity

Table 1-2

Income as a Power Function of Education

POPULATION		PARAMETERS		
Sex	Race-Ethnicity	*a*	*b*	*n*
Male	White	7,202	.29	3.68
	Spanish-speaking	5,615	4.26	2.59
	Black	4,779	4.42	2.50
Female	White	3,610	.53	3.20
	Spanish-speaking	3,190	6.69	2.25
	Black	2,358	2.52	2.71

The power function is $I = a + bE^n$.

Using the equation $I = a + bE^n$, as suggested before, and estimating parameters separately for the six populations provides the data in Table 1-2.

The parameters a and n in Table 1-2 are the most useful from a theoretical viewpoint, with b simply adjusting the X^n term to an appropriate scale for predicting income. With a power of 1.0 (linear model), b ranges from 316 to 741. As the power increases, the associated values of b rapidly decrease. The power, n, indicates how rapidly income accelerates with added education. Here it is evident that whites of both sexes enjoy an advantage over nonwhites, with white males again having the greatest acceleration of earnings.

As before, the parameter a provides the intercept of the curve (or the baseline income expected for someone with no education). The values of a in Table 1-2 are much more reasonable than those of Table 1-1 because the power curve almost perfectly fits the data points ($r^2 > .995$ for the five points for each of the six curves). Notice that, for each racial-ethnic category, males have approximately double the baseline income that females have. Furthermore, whites of both sexes have higher bases than do Spanish-speaking people, who in turn have higher baselines than do blacks. Thus the parameter a provides clear evidence of differential earning opportunities by sex and by majority-minority status, whereas the parameter n indicates differential gain through higher levels of education.

the theory-model-data triangle

The foregoing comments involve some theoretical interpretations of a mathematical equation fitted to census data. The links from theory to model to data lead to the idea of a *theory-model-data triangle* as shown in Figure 1-2. At

```
                    ─── (I1, D1) ───→
        Theory  ←─── (I2, D2) ───         Model
             ↖                          ↗
               (I4)              (I3)
               (D4)              (D3)
                 ↘              ↙
                      Data
```

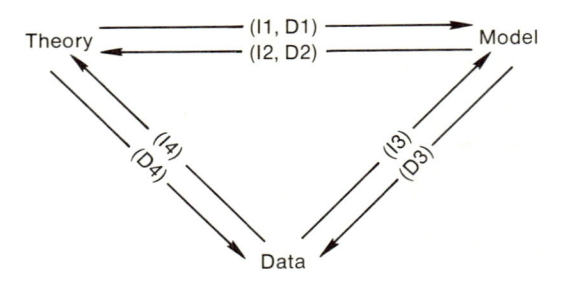

Inductive Modes:
    I1—Mathematical generalization of theory.
    I2—Substantive interpretation of mathematical patterns.
    I3—Mathematical generalization of empirical patterns.
    I4—Substantive interpretation of data.

Deductive Modes:
    D1—Formalization of theory.
    D2—Derivation of substantive hypothesis from mathematical patterns.
    D3—Mathematical prediction or extrapolation.
    D4—Substantive prediction.

The term "substantive" implies reference to a particular area of interest such as social mobility, small group interaction, and the like.

Figure 1-2

The theory-model-data triangle

the substantive theory point of the triangle we are concerned with various general propositions about the interrelationships of sociological variables such that we can predict and explain social facts. At the data point of the triangle we are concerned with observations of those social facts, whether by interview, questionnaire, field observation, laboratory observation, experimentation, or other source of information about social relationships. Much has been written about the relationships between theory and data, such as the requirements of operationalization of a theory. This aspect of the triangle need not detain us further.

The third point of the triangle represents mathematical models in general. As indicated, special cases may be statistical models. The term *model* indicates that the mathematics are neither substantive theory nor variables derived through observation. The model is a set of statements in mathematical form involving abstract variables which may be equated for theoretical purposes with substantive variables in whatever field is being examined. The values of those variables may be considered representative of the kind of data to be expected if the linkage between substance and model is appropriate. A model is in this sense strictly general—that is, devoid of any empirical or theoretical content. It operates as a kind of logical machine, which may be of use for either of the other points of the triangle if adequate correspondence between theoretical terms and mathematical terms or between observational procedures and mathematical terms can be established.

Mapping. Establishing the rules of correspondence between mathematics and either theory or data is often called *mapping*. Mapping *to* a mathematical model requires stating in what way theoretical or observational variables and relationships can be expressed in mathematical form. For example, religious affiliation or sex category are variables which are called nominal, meaning they imply no ordering of categories (more, better, higher?) and no specific distances between categories (male $+ X =$ female?) Any model to which we wish to map variables like religious affiliation or sex category will have to contain appropriate nominal variables. Otherwise the mapping is questionable and any conclusions of doubtful utility.

Inevitably such mapping will require simplification. Actual data may show a not-quite-linear (straight line) relationship between two variables. For convenience of working with a simpler model, the abstract relationship may be treated as linear. Of course this will entail the same problem of whether conclusions from the model are applicable to the real problem. Model building and borrowing therefore must be a careful compromise between precise correspondence (no simplification at all, but grave difficulty in actual use) and maximal simplicity (great generality but doubtful validity in any particular case). Objections to mathematical sociology often emphasize the loss of interesting and sometimes vital detail as a consequence of simplification. To some extent, we have just suggested, the utility of models will depend upon the net gain obtained by power and precision as opposed to the loss through simplification. This net gain will vary by type of theory, type of research, and ingenuity of researcher.

Mapping *from* a mathematical model to substantive theory or to empirical data requires the same kind of rules of correspondence that are needed for the reverse. Mathematical form, however, typically provides greater freedom of mapping to a variety of theoretical or empirical questions. Either direction of mapping will require careful answering of a series of questions about, on the one hand, the theory or data, and on the other, the model. In the last chapter we will attempt to specify the questions to be asked when mapping either to or from a model. Depending upon the starting point and the source of answers to these questions, a variety of approaches to mathematical sociology will be suggested.

It is generally stated that going from substantive theory to expectations about data which are implied by that theory represents deduction, whereas moving from observations to constructing theoretical generalizations that encompass those data represents induction. Both inductive and deductive modes will be evident in the use of mathematical models as well, with both modes appearing between the model and substantive theory and between the model and the data.

Two Approaches to Mathematical Form. We have noted that mathematical models are constructed of equations specifying precise relationships among the variables under consideration. Because equations take many forms, it will be necessary to choose among various kinds of operations for relating the variables. Either of two approaches could be chosen in deciding what form the equations in a model should take.

Assuming that one or more sets of data were available, it would be possible to specify simply that equations would have the form best suited to describing those data as accurately as possible. We would therefore be interested in what has been called "curve fitting." Any type of equation which did a good job would be suitable. The consequence, in part, would be a relatively accurate model in terms of reproducing empirical observations. Statistical procedures used in regression analysis do exactly this type of job, especially if a general curve rather than just linear regression is considered.

The alternative criterion for establishing the forms of equations is to require that the operations and the parameters have directly interpretable connections with any substantive theory guiding the work. If there is no explicit theory, at least operations and parameters should be easily related to the field under study. The consequence of such a criterion would be that the model would be intuitively more compelling than one which had only an obscure relationship to the meaning of the subject matter.

Note that the first alternative emphasizes the data-model side of the triangle. As suggested, this emphasis leads primarily to statistical analysis procedures. Because they form a part of the overall field of models, statistical procedures will be discussed briefly throughout the book as special cases of different types of models. The main difficulty with such procedures is that they have only minimal relationship to substantive theory or intuitive understanding. Most sociologists, using only statistical methods to examine their data, are still asking *whether* variables are related, regardless of form or interpretation of parameters. The typical significance test should be only one of the first steps in making use of data, rather than a ritual signifying the end of the job.

The second alternative emphasizes, instead, the theory-model side of the triangle. If pushed to a logical extreme, this alternative could produce models of such complexity that they would be difficult to handle mathematically and to relate to empirical evidence. Most general theories are so complex that how they work as a whole is not at all evident. Clearly, the point of constructing theories is to be able to understand and predict, and the use of more formal approaches to theory simply furthers the clarity of understanding and predicting. The model, then, must be kept within reasonable bounds by simplification and abstraction.

Seeking an ideal posture which avoids the difficulties of either of the above alternatives suggests a compromise between pure data-description and pure theory-representation. The model should be a go-between which is readily related to either of the other two points of the theory-model-data triangle. Such a compromise requires keeping in mind the theoretical interpretation of the equations, the analytical simplicity of the overall model, and the type of data likely to be analyzed.

It should be evident from what has just been said that mathematical models, as discussed in this book, are not simply something to do with numbers. Data description in the statistical sense may be a useful approach to working inductively from data to model, but statistical procedures are not our focus. Throughout, the emphasis will be on models as a tool for developing theory.

It is not uncommon for someone developing a mathematical model to conclude that equations necessary for reflecting the theory or data are too complex to admit solution. Rather than giving up the task, he should consider the possibility of using computer simulation to ascertain the consequences of his model. Direct solution should not be the absolute criterion of whether a model is useful. Of course, it is easier to determine the consequences of a model if it can be directly solved mathematically, but long-range convergence of patterns or stabilization of trends may be just as evident in computer runs as in direct solution. In fact, it is reasonable to suggest that the more interesting sociological models are going to be sufficiently complex that direct solution will be virtually impossible.

The empirical adequacy of a model is assessed in terms of the degree to which it fits some set of data. This is what is usually meant by "testing" a model. Attempting to test a model will often result in new research designed for that purpose, although data banks and archives offer increasing opportunity for direct test without the necessity of new research. It is likely that the job of testing models will be made easier even for the noncomputer-oriented researcher by ever simpler programming languages and interactive devices for working with computers. With these procedures and extensive computerized data banks it should be possible eventually to test a mathematical model with a variety of data sets at one "sitting."

We evaluate the theoretical adequacy of a model by asking whether it deals with problems that interest sociologists, generates new or surprising conclusions, integrates previously unrelated theories, and/or clears up ambiguities of definition or logic. Theoretical adequacy is probably the most difficult aspect of a model to assess, since there is disagreement among sociologists about what is theoretically interesting and important, and what a new or surprising conclusion might be. In this respect, mathematical models do not differ from other approaches to theory, and many objections to mathematical approaches are really objections to the substantive problem to which mathematics is applied rather than to the mathematics itself.

Ideally, a model will be adequate on all three criteria: however, most will be particularly strong on one or two and somewhat weak elsewhere. Finding the weak points of a model helps provide information about where to start more work if one wishes to continue developing the model. For example, if a model fits some interesting data well but has little theoretical meaning, the next step might be to proceed inductively from model to theory, trying to attach a more general theoretical meaning to the model's assumptions.

Four Types of Models. With the exception of the final chapter, the balance of this book will be devoted to examining and evaluating a variety of mathematical models. For convenience, those models are grouped into four fairly distinct types. There is a common distinction between structure and process models, and we shall use it here. Chapters 2 through 6 concern structural models; Chapters 7 through 11, process models. The distinction should not be too rigid, however, because of the implicit process behind any structure.

Within the structure and the process sections of the book it will be helpful to distinguish between models which use primarily variables that have only a few discrete states (male or female; white, Spanish-speaking, or black) from those models which are concerned primarily with continuous variables or reasonable approximations of continua (for example, number of years of education is a discrete variable but may be considered continuous). The term "scale" will be used to refer to a variable which is more or less continuous and will be treated as a continuum.

From the income-education example it should be evident that some models may involve both states and scales. The primary equation of that example, though, involved two scales, income and education, and a power function linking those scales. The sex and race-ethnicity variables only defined different populations. The distinction is useful primarily for emphasizing the fact that rather different types of mathematics are commonly employed for models using states than for models using scales. These differences should become evident as the different models are encountered. At least one model of each of the four types (structure-state, structure-scale, process-state, process-scale) will be presented in considerable detail, so that the reasons for the mathematical form can be discussed and the appropriateness of the model examined. Various other models will be presented more briefly to give greater breadth of substantive and mathematical content.

Although the particular applications represented by these models are substantively interesting, it is important that each model be carefully evaluated on all three bases.

some comments
on the uses of mathematics in sociology

Benefits of Mathematical Sociology, or Why Bother? The benefits of mathematical sociology are of three major types. First, mathematical formulations provide greater precision and power than do less rigorous forms of discourse. Most of this book will be devoted to demonstrating the wealth and variety of such contributions. At the simplest level, mathematical statements can provide more accurate descriptions of phenomena. This accuracy, coupled with the wide variety of procedures available for mathematical reasoning, allows far greater scope and accuracy of conclusions based on any piece of research, or any attempt to integrate different research efforts.

Not all types of research are amenable to formalization. It is by no means possible or desirable to have every sociological project wrapped in equations. To the extent that data and theoretical forms are appropriate to formalized treatment, however, the following comments appear warranted. Any formalized logic is more subject to scrutiny for error of reasoning than is "armchair philosophizing." As noted above, the more complex the logic form, and the more subtle its potential treatment of the subject of discourse, the more its conclusions can match the subtlety and complexity of reality. Mathematics has developed as such a subtle and complex reasoning tool.

An acquaintance with only classical mathematical analysis may lead to the conclusion that traditional algebra or calculus forms do not do justice to many types of sociological subject matter. Precisely that sort of limitation in existing mathematics has led to branching into diverse and sometimes rather bizarre mathematical areas. Differential calculus, for example, has been of little use in analyzing structures, but the relatively new field of graph theory offers considerable power in that type of analysis. For most types of research and theory-development in sociology, there are mathematical forms that will extend the reasoning power of the theorist and the analytic power of the researcher beyond what he can accomplish without using mathematics.

The second type of benefit for sociology provided by mathematics is that it provides connections between diverse pieces of research or of theory. It is necessary, when formalizing any piece of work, to abstract and simplify it so that the basic ideas and processes are selected out of the variety of minor patterns and individual eccentricities. Some disadvantages of such abstraction and simplification will be discussed shortly. The desirable consequences of abstracting and simplifying are that they permit more ready comparison and integration across different projects. Particularly in mathematical form it is easy to detect similar types of processes by the fact that similar sets of equations apply. Special conditions can be more easily examined as particular cases in more general formulations. Apparently different kinds of process can be shown to be parts of a single overall process, though perhaps from different points in time or under different conditions.

Because of this ease of comparison and integration when using mathematical formulations, it is reasonable to suggest that mathematics can provide one important basis for unification of the field of sociology. Other disciplines have shown their most rapid advancement in unification as a consequence of mathematical efforts. What is clearly needed in any discipline is a way by which patterns can be discerned out of the richness of reality, and the consequences of those patterns can be deduced, generalized, and interrelated. In one form or another, mathematics provides just that capability.

The easy transferability of a particular mathematical formulation from one field of inquiry to another, which enables unification through mathematical treatment, also makes it easy to borrow successful ideas from one area and try them in a possibly comparable area. Models of growth, for example, may be derived from biological sciences and found applicable to areas such as innovation and diffusion. Models of force or gravitation derived from physical sciences may be applicable to population movement or interpersonal attraction. Staying within social science, models developed in experiments on choice behavior have been applied to leadership selection. Sociometric models, borrowed originally from economics, can be applied to questions of general status and structure. The completely abstract character of mathematics makes wide application of any particular model worth attempting, reducing the work needed to develop new models while demonstrating interrelationships of diverse subject matters.

The final type of benefit to be derived from working with mathematical models is also a consequence of their abstract character. Unfortunately, much theoretical endeavor in sociology is linked to "schools of thought," each with its own defenders and viewpoints. The trouble with such schools is that they develop preconceptions which make it difficult to obtain a fresh view of a problem or to avoid built-in biases. Terms like "functional," "symbolic," "operant," or "dialectic" either act as automatic inducement to look only for particular patterns or as a red flag to those who do not accept the tenets of the particular approach. Mathematical formulation has the desirable property of being relatively free of such dogma.[2] It is, in fact,

[2] Not entirely, of course; some of the problems of this sort that appear in mathematical sociology are discussed in Chapter 12.

possible to use mathematical models to demonstrate the similarity of ideas which diverse schools have propounded, even though terminology and the allegiance of the various proponents has obscured those similarities.

To work in mathematical form, then, is to free oneself from some of the mental roadblocks in theoretical development. It is, of course, necessary to relate the mathematical form back to the theoretical level eventually, which may mean translating back into the more traditional terminologies. To the extent that a relationship can be established for diverse terminologies, the mathematical endeavor will have served another integrative purpose.

Costs of Mathematical Sociology: Is It Really Worth It? It would be inappropriate to give the impression that mathematical work in sociology is all benefit and no cost. One of the obvious costs is that the user must be trained sufficiently to work and, perhaps more difficult, to think creatively in mathematical form. A considerable range of mathematics may be desirable, depending upon the nature of the theory or body of data that has initiated the formalization. Ordinarily, though, no one individual need be expert in all types of mathematics that might be useful. That would be a bit too much even for a professional mathematician. Instead it is desirable to be acquainted with a variety of approaches, with some idea of their application in sociology, so that better choice among alternatives is possible when a particular problem arises. Probably anyone working on mathematical development of his research or theoretical interests will find that one or two approaches will be best suited to those interests. Obviously, a degree of expertise in those areas may be well worth the investment, while other areas of mathematics would be less so. Only involvement in mathematization of theory or research can provide a basis for determining which types of emphasis in mathematical skill will be most profitable.

The following types of mathematics are most commonly used in formalization in sociology, and will be used in this volume: linear algebra, particularly matrix algebra; differential calculus, particularly working with differential equations; and probability theory. Less common, but increasingly useful, is graph theory, particularly well suited to the study of structural form.

The extent of sophistication which this book requires is not great, but it would be incorrect to suggest that persons with no mathematical training would find it easy to read. Typically, the reader will need only an introductory knowledge of each of the above types of mathematics to follow the development of specific models. To an extent, basic ideas will be discussed in the text as part of illustrative material. Basic sociological statistics is also an essential tool; this book assumes approximately an intermediate level statistics course, including linear regression and analysis of variance.

A second cost involved in using mathematics is a forced concern for compatible details in the model being developed. Initial attempts to employ mathematical rigor for theoretical or empirical work are apt to be accompanied by a feeling of undue restriction in handling nuances of the subject. Before useful results can be obtained it is necessary to work out rules of correspondence between the empirical or theoretical area and the model being developed. It is not uncommon for these rules to seem simple initially, but for difficulties to develop as the work progresses. Variables which were thought of as quite independent at a substantive level may well prove to be interrelated mathematically in such a way that their definitions in mathematical form become confused. Relationships which intuitively are not complex may prove to be mathematically very difficult to state. Consequently, the feeling of restriction is joined by an uncertainty as to how to determine the appropriate mathematical form to fit intuitive or discursive forms.

These problems of concern for compatible mathematical details should not suggest that the endeavor is either impossible or not worth the effort. As mentioned earlier, mathematical modeling involves simplification. One reason for the simplification is to enable us to use the logical power of the mathematics without becoming bogged down in indecision concerning a wealth of minor aspects of the theory or data. To employ mathematics adequately, then, requires a willingness to forego the richness and intuitive feel of the original research. It is usually possible, as initial simplified work is found promising, for models to be elaborated to take care of the more complex form of the real data or substantive theory. Once a general, simple mathematical model is established, it is relatively easy to adapt it to the subtleties of complex reality—certainly easier than it is to begin trying to build initial models with all the subtleties immediately represented.

Related to these problems is a frequent feeling that the more highly formalized and mathematized work is increasingly removed from the substantive frontiers of the discipline. For someone who has entered a field out of a genuine interest in a particular area of social behavior, such a removal from the realities "out there" is difficult to accept. Mathematical models are highly abstract and highly simplified, and this suggests to many people that they are also highly dehumanized. But the contribution that can be made to the understanding of the substantive area via mathematical endeavor may outweigh the temporary feeling of intellectual anomie which their employment might produce. In the extreme case, a reader of mathematical sociology, if not someone working in that area, might conclude that most mathematical work is exceedingly tedious and sociologically trivial. The tedium, of course, derives from the necessity of careful concern with rules of operation which any precise logic must have. Trivial indeed are some of the uninteresting examples to be found in the literature. The potential value of mathematical work in sociology is great enough, however, that the field ought to be willing to overlook occasional bad examples.

We might inquire whether there is a field which can be properly called mathematical sociology. The first consideration here is that mathematical work is relevant to theoretical and to empirical work. Therefore, if there is such a field as mathematical sociology, it is neither a theoretical nor an empirical field but overlaps both. Second, the very abstractness of mathematical formulation means that model building is applicable to many substantive areas in sociology. Therefore, no bounded subject matter is represented by the term mathematical sociology. Finally, it should be evident from the preceding discussion that mathematics represents an integrating tool. Just as statistical procedures are applicable to any data analysis question, provided the assumptions of the statistical model can be met by the data, mathematical model building can be applicable to any substantive theoretical or empirical endeavor in sociology, provided that the correspondence between the theory or data can be established. We conclude that there can be no subfield within sociology called mathematical sociology in the sense that there is a political sociology or a small-group sociology. There can, however, be use of mathematics throughout sociology as a way of furthering all the concerns of the discipline.

This chapter has indicated the place and purpose of mathematical models in sociology, including some of their advantages and disadvantages. One reason for working with models has not yet been mentioned: modeling can be fun! To the novice, that assertion may be laughable. Given sufficient command of techniques and understanding of their theoretical and empirical translations, however, modeling can be as enjoyable as doing puzzles, playing chess, or creating works of art. It is not a bad thing that such useful tools also provide intriguing ways to spend time.

CHAPTER 2

a power-function model of status

With this chapter we begin the presentation of a series of mathematical models drawn from sociological literature. The model presented in this chapter describes a structure and uses variables that are scales. It involves a power curve, which is the type of equation that provided a good fit for the education-income example in Chapter 1. For someone not used to mathematical forms, it may seem mysterious at best when the "right" type of equation is apparently drawn out of thin air. How did a power curve get selected in the first place? Is it purely trial and error?

To the contrary, we borrowed the power curve from work by Robert L. Hamblin and his associates, a portion of which we will examine in this chapter. Hamblin, in turn, had acquired the general model from another scientific field altogether. In this borrowing, the type of problem being analyzed seemed comparable to a type already well analyzed by an existing model. If mapping from one theoretical area to the other can be satisfactorily carried out, then borrowing the accompanying mathematical form is a "good bet." It provides a ready-made model with known empirical applicability and, usually, with its problems of parameter estimation already solved.

Borrowing a model may seem too simple, but in fact it is a good way to begin a discussion of the use of mathematics in sociology, because applying a model developed elsewhere makes the actual mathematics less of a problem than in a model developed from scratch. This allows us to concentrate on some of the other problems of building mathematical models, such as translating into sociological variables, testing for empirical adequacy, and understanding theoretical meaning.

The model is one that has been successfully applied to a number of sociological and social-psychological problems by Robert L. Hamblin and his associates.[1] In particular, we will refer to part of an article published in 1971.[2] The model is called Stevens' Law, after the psychologist S. S. Stevens, who developed it from work in psychophysics. In a typical psychophysical study, an experimenter presents a subject with a stimulus of measured intensity such as a sound of so many decibels. He instructs the subject to use that intensity as a standard with which to compare other sounds, and presents a series of stimuli of varying intensity, which the subject rates in comparison with the standard. For example, if the stimulus sound is assigned the value ten, and the next sound is heard as half as loud, the subject rates it as five. For an extremely wide variety of sensory phenomena including loudness of sounds, intensity of lights, length of lines, and so on, the relationship between objectively measured intensity of a stimulus and subjects' reports of subjectively experienced intensity is described by the function:

$$\psi = c\phi^n \qquad (2\text{-}1)$$

where ψ is the magnitude of the sensory response, ϕ is the magnitude of the related physical stimulus, and c and n are parameters which can be estimated and which vary from situation to situation. Such a function, as noted in Chapter 1, is called a power function. This highly regular relationship between stimulus and response is apparently related to neural processes; the intensity of neural response to physical stimulus follows the same function.

---

[1] Robert L. Hamblin, "Mathematical experimentation and sociological theory: A critical analysis," *Sociometry*, vol. 34 (1971), pp. 423–452; Robert L. Hamblin, David A. Budger, Robert C. Day, and William L. Yancey, "Interference-aggression law?," *Sociometry*, vol. 26 (1963), pp. 190–216; Robert L. Hamblin, David Buckholdt, Daniel Ferrotor, Martin Kozloff, and Lois Blackwell, *The Humanization Processes* (New York: John Wiley & Sons, 1971); Robert L. Hamblin and Carole R. Smith, "Values, status, and professors," *Sociometry*, vol. 29 (1966), pp. 183–196.

[2] Hamblin, in *Sociometry*, 1971.

22   Mathematical Sociology

translation into mathematics

What Hamblin has done is to take the power function, which seems to describe a regular and highly general human response process, and apply it to sociological questions. This procedure makes two demands of the sociologist: (1) he must be able to find a pair of sociological variables that can be thought of as a stimulus and a response to that stimulus, and (2) he must be able to produce continuous, ratio-scale measurements of both variables. The first is a theoretical question, the second a question of research methods. Hamblin asserts that it makes sense to think of status evaluations as a response, subjectively experienced, to the stimulus presented by characteristics such as years in school or dollars of income. The fact that perceptions of status increase when income and education of the person being evaluated increase has long been known, but the exact shape of the relationship has not been known, nor is there general agreement about how people combine more than one dimension to yield a single general status evaluation.

To collect data that meet the demands of the model, Hamblin used a procedure similar to the psychophysical experiments. He asked a set of people to assign a value of 100 to the amount of respect or esteem people in their home towns assign to a college graduate, and then to rate the status of a high-school graduate, a person who has finished fourth grade, a person with an annual income of $8,000, and a number of other education and income levels, relative to the status of the college graduate. Both education and income are ratio-scale variables, and this procedure of asking about perceptions of status produces a set of ratio-scale measurements. We will describe Hamblin's reported results and the nature of the measurements after discussing the general form of the model as it is related to this kind of data.

Questions About the Choice of the Model. One of the most crucial parts of mathematical work in sociology is the translation between the terms and assumptions of the model and the variables and relationships in theory or data. To make the points of correspondence explicit, we find the accompanying translation diagram (2-1) very useful. As one goes through the process of constructing a diagram like this, the appropriate questions to ask about the model come up naturally.

As this diagram indicates, the source is a preexisting model and the initial mapping is from model to data. When we work deductively from model to data, the important concern is that the variables and relationships represent appropriate specifications of the mathematical forms. Then the deductions in the mathematical model can be translated directly to theoretical or empirical deduction without difficulty.

Note that c and n are the parameters of the model, although there will

Translation Diagram 2-1

PSYCHOPHYSICAL MODEL	SOCIOLOGICAL DATA		SOCIOLOGICAL MODEL

Variables

Stimulus $\begin{cases} 1.\ \text{Years of education} & \longrightarrow E \\ 2.\ \text{Dollars of income} & \longrightarrow I \end{cases}$

Response $\begin{cases} 1.\ \text{Perceived status based on education} & \longrightarrow S_e \\ 2.\ \text{Perceived status based on income} & \longrightarrow S_i \end{cases}$

Relationships

Stevens' Law, $\quad \begin{cases} \text{Status is a function of} \\ \text{education or of income} \end{cases} \longrightarrow \begin{cases} 1.\ S_e = cE^n & (2\text{-}2) \\ 2.\ S_i = cI^n & (2\text{-}3) \end{cases}$
$\psi = c\phi^n$

be different values of each of these parameters for the equation involving education versus the equation involving income. We will be concerned not only with how well these equations fit Hamblin's data, but also with the interpretation of the parameters for each of the equations. In the present case, this means that the data had to be collected specifically to test the model, according to a research procedure not commonly used by sociologists. The numbers that go into an equation such as (2-2) or (2-3) must be continuous (implying that they are scales rather than states, since something has to have values to be continuous) and nonrandom.

The variables Hamblin uses are summary; that is, each data point represents a mean of responses of a sample of individuals. Hamblin reports that he used the geometric mean of his subjects' responses to define his variables. The geometric mean of a set of numbers $x_1, x_2, \ldots, x_n$ is defined as $\sqrt[n]{x_1 \cdot x_2 \cdot \ldots \cdot x_n}$. This measure of central tendency is less sensitive to extreme values than is the arithmetic mean, the measure usually used in sociological statistics. In other words, if one subject gives a response that is quite different from the others, his response affects the value of the geometric mean less than it affects the value of the arithmetic mean. Using the geometric mean is one way of handling the problem of being required to have variables that are nonrandom when the data actually are random. If we were developing a model that assumed a random variable, the arithmetic mean would be more appropriate, since it is a better estimate of the mean of the normal distribution.

Finally, we can note that time does not appear either as a variable or in the form of the relationship in this model, and that it is thus a structural model. Similarly, there are no feedback loops which link the dependent variable, perceived status, as an input to the independent variables, education or income.

The proposed relationship between status and the other variables is asymmetric; we assume that years of education and dollars of income cause perceived status to vary rather than the other way around. If we were working with a theory of status consistency, we might hypothesize that perceived status affects income, by thinking of a process which allows someone who has high status to get a better-paying job. The model we would need to describe the effects of status on income would not necessarily look like the one we have to describe how status depends on income, however, and the data we have would not be adequate to test such a model.

The relationship proposed by the model is deterministic; for each possible value of education, there is a single predicted value of status. A stochastic relationship might be one that predicted a range of values as a possible response to the stimulus of education, or one that predicted one of two possible responses, with a probability attached to each, and so on. The relationship expressed by a power function is continuous; it is represented by a smooth curve. A model that proposed a discontinuous relationship might be one that pictured a jump in status on completion of a diploma—for example, hypothesizing that a high-school graduate has not only more status than a nongraduate but considerably more than someone who has almost but not quite graduated from high school.

development and tests of the model

When a model has been stated in the sense that its variables and relationships have been defined and translated into something sociologically meaningful, the process of building it is only partly finished—a fact that novices often fail to understand. Having put out the creative effort to transform a sociological question into mathematical form, they feel they ought to be able to take a well-deserved rest. But two activities remain: testing the model and using it. These are related, in that a model that is not tested is of doubtful usefulness, and also in that one has to derive consequences from a model in order to test it. It may help to remember that a mathematical model is a link to a theory; like a theory, its contribution depends upon its being tested and used.

There are a number of fairly standard techniques for testing models, which are comparable to the standard statistical techniques of hypothesis testing. Where these are appropriate, we suggest that they be used, but we also suggest that the researcher try to exercise some ingenuity in developing tests for his model. Assuming that the mathematical adequacy of the model has been established, all procedures for testing a model require that one use the relationships in the model to derive predictions and then see if the predictions make sense either by comparison with data or in terms of some theory, or both. The analyses in Hamblin's work illustrate several approaches to testing a model.

1. *Graphing the data.* The data from two samples of subjects who were asked the kind of question described earlier appear in Figure 2-1. In the case of education, status seems to be an accelerating function of the stimulus, and in the case of income, a decelerating function. The general shape of both curves is consistent with the hypothesized power function. A more informative test is to graph the data onto paper which shows both coordinates in logarithms (log-log graph paper). On logarithmic coordinates, a power function appears as a straight line, because when the variables are transformed to logarithms, the equation becomes linear. More will be said about this later.

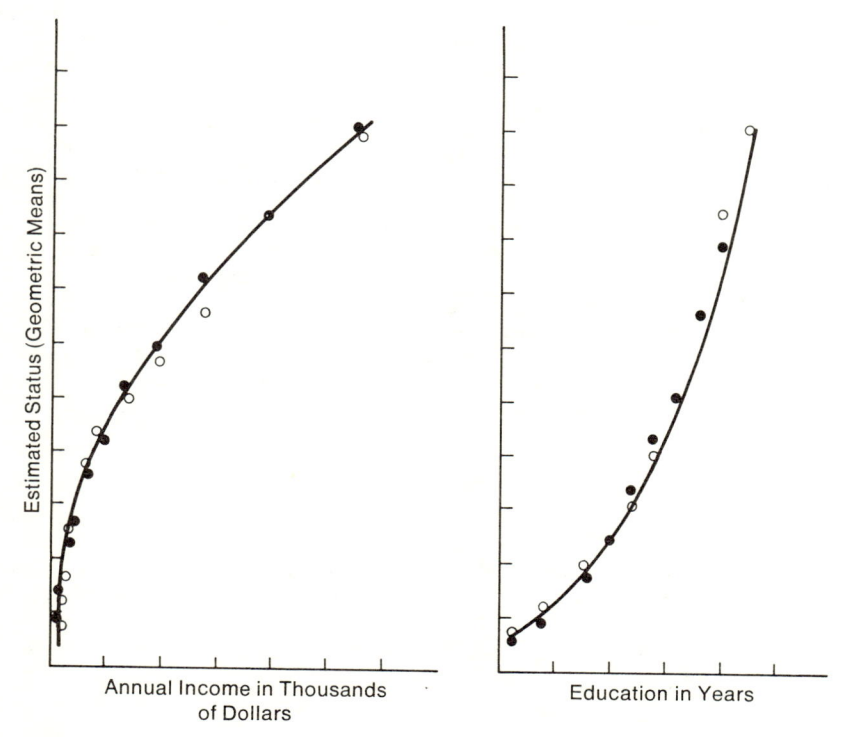

Figure 2-1

Estimates of status based on income and education of a hypothetical stimulus person. Filled dots are from a sample of 30 navy men and unfilled dots from a sample of 22 college students

Source: Robert L. Hamblin, "Mathematical experimentation and sociological theory," *Sociometry*, vol. 34 (1971), p. 431. By permission of the author and the American Sociological Association.

Figure 2-2 shows what happens when the data in Figure 2-1 are plotted on log-log paper. To begin with, the lines are not quite straight but are slightly curved at the bottom. Hamblin suggests that this could be due to a misplacement of the origin. He had assumed that a person with no education or no income would have a status of zero and had placed the origin of his scales accordingly. If in fact a person with no education has some status, this means the origin for status should be placed below zero on the education scale. Since the model requires ratio-level data, a mistake in deciding where zero is could lead to the model's not predicting accurately what the relationship between the two variables is. It is reasonable to think of education as beginning before the first grade (learning in the home, and preschooling), so Hamblin moves the origin, resulting in the second set of curves in Figure 2-2. These are indeed straight lines, as expected.

The results of the first test are to force a modification of the model, although the modification is simple and appears successful. The modification is of substantive interest, as it suggests that people think of formal education as a continuation of preschool experiences (a notion that is supported by sociological data, by the way), and that even a person with no education has some measurable status in our society.

2. *Estimating the parameters.* The most basic step in testing any model that involves equations is to estimate the parameters of the equations. Occasionally this can be done using theoretical considerations, but usually we substitute some real data for the variables of the equations and solve for the parameters as unknowns. Depending on what the equations look like, it may be very difficult or quite easy to find a way of estimating parameters. The power-function equations are easy, because there are standard techniques for handling these equations. The process is as follows.

a) Transform the equations into linear equations. The task of estimating the parameters can be made much easier by using the properties of logarithms to rewrite the equations as linear rather than nonlinear functions. Note that moving the origin has changed the basic equations (2-2) and (2-3) into the following:

$$S_e = c_e(E + E_0)^{n_e}, \qquad (2\text{-}4)$$
$$S_i = c_i(I + I_0)^{n_i}, \qquad (2\text{-}5)$$

where E_0 and I_0 are additional parameters, representing corrections of the origin. The analysis in Figure 2-2 results in values for these parameters: $E_0 = 4$ and $I_0 = -1,000$.

If we transform both sides of (2-4) and (2-5) into logarithms, we get

$$\log S_e = \log c_e + n_e \log (E + 4) \qquad (2\text{-}6)$$
$$\log S_i = \log c_i + n_i \log (I - 1000) \qquad (2\text{-}7)$$

b) Use a least-squares procedure to find the line that best fits the data. To take equation (2-6) as an example; what we have now is a simple linear equation, in which we can think of c_e and n_e as unknowns. If we had two values each for S_e and E, we could find c_e and n_e by solving the two equations simultaneously. Actually, of course, more than two values of S_e are provided by the data. There are several standard techniques for finding the straight line that best

Figure 2-2

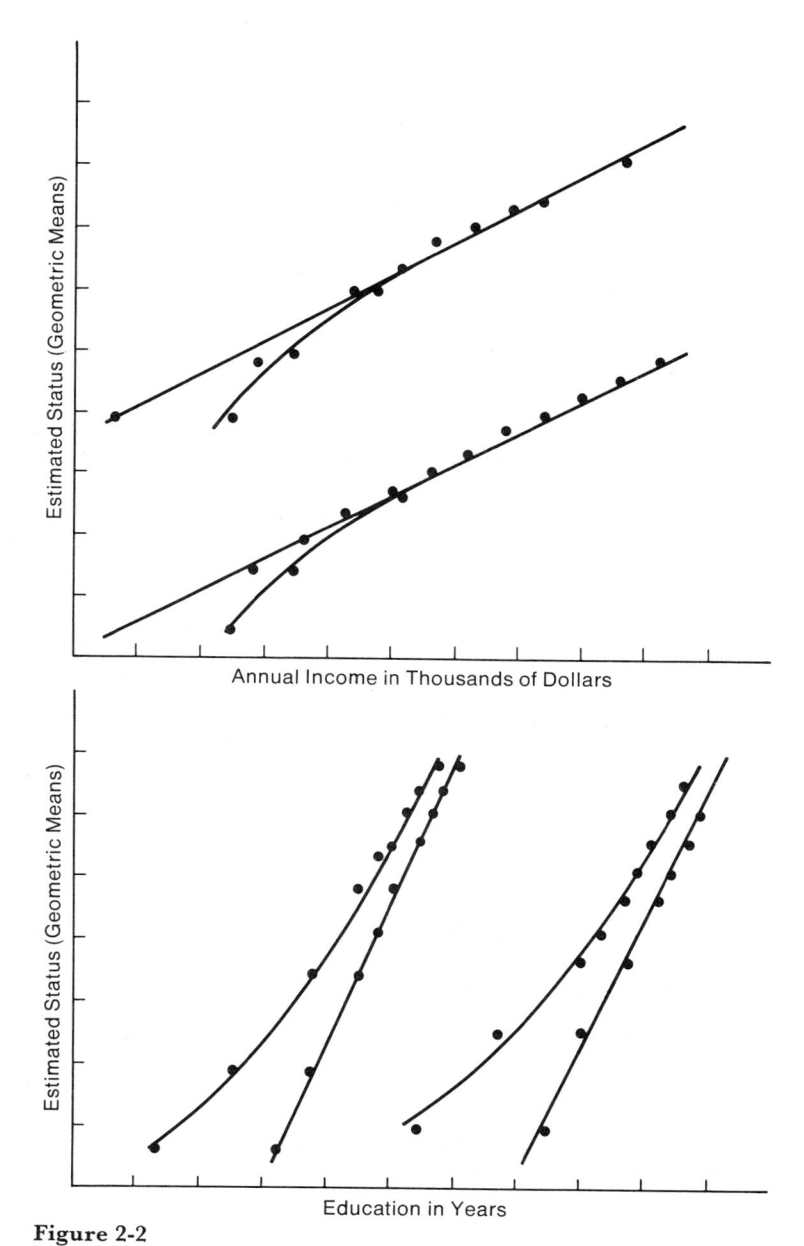

Estimated status as a function of education and income of a hypothetical stimulus person, plotted on logarithmic coordinates. Curves with origin set at zero, straight lines with origin corrected

Source: Robert L. Hamblin, "Mathematical experimentation and sociological theory," *Sociometry*, vol. 34 (1971), p. 431. By permission of the author and the American Sociological Association.

fits a set of points; Hamblin uses a least-squares procedure.[3] For his two samples combined, the parameters that result are:

$$c_e = .22, \quad n_e = 2.1,$$
$$c_i = .45, \quad n_i = .53.$$

If we did not already know from looking at Figures 2-1 and 2-2, the values of the parameters would tell us that status is an accelerating function of education (since n_e is greater than 1) and a decelerating function of income (since n_i is less than 1).

3. *Comparing predicted with actual values of status.* Now that we know what the parameters of the model are, we can develop more specific predictions than that the relationship between two variables should form a straight line when graphed on log-log coordinates. For each value of education that was used as a stimulus, we can find a predicted value of status by substituting the amount of education for E in equation (2-4), using the value for c_e and n_e noted above, and solving for S_e. This value can then be compared with the actual value of S_e that appears in Figure 2-1 for that amount of education. Hamblin compares the actual with the predicted values of status by using a linear regression. The values of r^2 obtained from the regression of predicted S_e on actual S_e and of predicted S_i on actual S_i are both .99, which indicates that the fit of the model to the data is excellent.

4. *Applying the model to other populations.* Another standard way of testing a model is to apply it to data collected from a population other than the one originally used to develop it. This is a particularly useful test if the model has been developed by some sort of curve-fitting process, as this one has. Applying this model to a different population constitutes an indpendent test of both the general shape of the relationship and the specific parameters. Hamblin's article reports results from similar status studies by two other investigators who used different and larger samples of subjects. For these samples, the power function relationship between perceived status and each of the two variables of income and education holds; the explained variance is smaller than in the first study, but still impressive. The values of the parameters c, n, E_0, and I_0 vary from one population to another, which Hamblin interprets as an indication of differences in subcultures. Comparing the parameters for different populations can thus provide some information about differences between populations in the way status is determined.

5. *Applying the model to other variables.* The confidence with which we regard a model, and its usefulness are augmented if it can be shown to predict relationships between variables that are not exactly those it was originally designed for. Hamblin reports that the power function fits well data from experiments on the relationships between several other social-psychological variables that can be thought of as stimulus and response—for example, teaching ability, number of publications, and professional activities as determinants of the status of professors in the eyes of graduate students,[4] or amount of interference and subsequent aggression.[5]

6. *Comparing the model with alternative models.* The least-squares procedure has guaranteed that the correlation coefficient between predicted and actual status will be as high as it can possibly be for the power function model; it does not guarantee,

---
[3]A description of the least-squares procedure can be found in Chapter 7.
[4]Hamblin and Smith, in *Sociometry*, 1966.
[5]Hamblin, Budger, Day, and Yancey, in *Sociometry*, 1963.

however, that some other equation might not fit the data as well or better. One of the usual ways of testing a model is to compare how well it fits a set of data with how well some reasonable alternatives fit. This is equivalent to testing several alternative hypotheses. Although rejection of alternative hypotheses does not conclusively establish the truth of the nonrejected one, it increases our confidence in it.

In the case of the power-function model, we might reasonably ask whether some other monotonic, nonlinear equation might not describe the data as well. Hamblin presents two alternatives. One is an exponential function,[6]

$$\log S_e = a + bE, \qquad (2\text{-}8)$$

and the other is a log function,

$$S_e = a + b \log E. \qquad (2\text{-}9)$$

The parameters a and b in each of these equations can be estimated with a least-squares procedure, using the same data the power function was developed for, and the fit of the resulting line evaluated by finding the correlation between predicted and actual status. The correlation coefficients are reported in Table 2-1.

Table 2-1

Results of Comparing Three Alternative Models for Goodness of Fit; Entries Are r^2, for Regression of Predicted on Actual Value of Status

VARIABLE	FUNCTION	COLLEGE SAMPLE	NAVY SAMPLE
Education	exponential	.965	.910
	log	.789	.921
	power	.986	.996
Income	exponential	.641	.667
	log	.986	.888
	power	.994	.995

Source: Robert L. Hamblin, "Mathematical Experimentation and Sociological Theory," *Sociometry*, vol. 34 (1971), p. 434. By permission of the author and the American Sociological Association.

extensions of the model

A good strategy in building models is to start with the simplest possible form of the model and make it more complicated as either (1) the simple form leads to problems when compared with data or (2) the simple form passes

[6] In a power function, the dependent variable is raised to a power; in an exponential function, the dependent variable is e raised to a power; and in a log function the dependent variable is a logarithm (each of these being when the independent variable is expressed as a number rather than a log).

enough tests to be accepted with some confidence, and then is applied to more complicated theoretical problems. Hamblin extends his model by taking up the problem of describing the way people combine several status dimensions to get a perception of general status. This question can be attacked by a straightforward extension of the model to a multivariate power function. The data were collected in the same way as previously, and from the same subjects, except that each subject was given three items of information about the hypothetical stimulus person; his years of education, dollars of annual income, and occupation. (Occupation turned out not to be correlated significantly with the dependent variable and was subsequently dropped from the analysis.) The hypothesis for the extended model was that the relationships between perceived status and the two independent variables would be:

$$S_g = c_g \cdot S_e^{n_e} \cdot S_i^{n_i}, \tag{2-10}$$

where S_g is perceived general status, S_e and S_i are estimates of status based upon years of education and dollars of annual income, respectively, according to the previous work, and c_g, n_i, and n_e are parameters. In logarithms, equation (2-10) becomes:

$$\log S_g = \log c_g + n_e \log S_e + n_i \log S_i. \tag{2-11}$$

For this set of data, too, the parameters can be estimated with a least-squares procedure and the goodness of fit assessed with a linear (multiple) regression analysis. The equation after estimating the parameters is:

$$S_g = 6.90 S_e^{.34} \cdot S_i^{.43}. \tag{2-12}$$

Once again, the apparent fit of the model to the data is quite good; $r^2 = .984$.

Let us return to the income-education example from Chapter 1. Referring to Table 1-2, note that the value of the power, n, for white males is 3.68, and the multiple, b (c in Hamblin's equations) is .29. The whole equation for the income-education relationship for white males is

$$I = .29 E^{3.68}. \tag{2-13}$$

Combining that result with Hamblin's solution for status dependent upon income gives

$$\begin{aligned} S_i &= .45 I^{.53} \\ &= .45(.29 E^{3.68})^{.53} \\ &= .23 E^{1.96}. \end{aligned} \tag{2-14}$$

Thus status based on income has been translated into status based on education via the income-education relationship. The parameters in equation (2-14) agree quite well with Hamblin's solution for status based on education alone. Those parameters were .22 and 2.1, compared with .23 and 1.95 above, for the multiple and power, respectively. Notice, though, that the values were derived in part from the earlier examination of 1970 census data and in part from Hamblin's technique involving response to written stimuli (for example, "a person with a high-school education.") The close agreement gives further confidence in the model.

A second point of interest is that the parameters from the census data were for white males, and those parameters differ noticeably from the other sex and racial-ethnic categories. If parameters for other groups were used, the agreement with the Hamblin solution would have been poor. We can conclude, then, that Hamblin's respondents had in mind the white male status structure when they answered his questions. Had they been thinking of, for example, black women, their responses and the resulting parameters would have been quite different, but the form of the curve would still be a power curve.

To carry the work one step further, Equation (2-14) can be used in conjunction with Equation (2-12) for general status, and Hamblin's S_e solution.

$$S_g = 6.9(.22E^{2.1})^{.34}(.23E^{1.95})^{.48}$$
$$= 2.44E^{1.65}. \qquad (2\text{-}15)$$

Remember that equation (2-15) is solving for the general status of a white male based on his education and the average income that his educational level would provide him. If the parameters for the other sex and racial-ethnic groups are substituted into the S_i equation and then the results used in the S_g equation, the values of the parameter n (the power of the curve) would be as shown in Table 2-2. Note that, even if the general status input of one's educational attainment is not dependent upon sex or racial-ethnic status, the differential earning power of a given level of education, across sex and race-ethnicity categories, will result in overall status advantages for

Table 2-2

Estimated Powers of E for S_g by Sex and Race-Ethnicity

	MALE	FEMALE
White	1.65	1.53
Spanish-speaking	1.37	1.29
Black	1.35	1.40

white males. Without further research it is not possible to know whether the S_e portion of Hamblin's equation would remain the same over the sex and race-ethnicity groups.

evaluating the model

Most models can be subjected to a number of tests, and will perform well on some, less well on others. In addition to running through a variety of tests, therefore, one should also pay some attention to assessing the overall value of a model, taking into account the specific tests and other criteria. As a framework for evaluating a model, we have suggested returning to the theory-data-model triangle and paying attention to the model's performance in each of these areas. By performance, we mean two things: (1) does the model pass any tests of its validity or adequacy? and (2) is it useful?

Testing and using a model can be seen as different activities; a model is useful if it tells us something we didn't know before. In the course of testing the power-function model, we discovered several new things. One is that the origin of the status scale must be treated as a parameter, and the value assigned to it provides information about the minimum level of a stimulus characteristic necessary to be in the status system at all. On the education scale, for example, it appears that even an illiterate can have some measurable status, while a person with an income of less than $1,000 per year is not part of the system; below that level the relationship between income and education takes a different form. Another discovery is that the parameters differ from one population to another, telling us that we have a new technique for comparing populations.

We will now proceed to a more systematic analysis of the adequacy and usefulness of the model. For the data point of the triangle, the criterion to be assessed is empirical adequacy; for the theory point, theoretical meaningfulness; and for the model point, the mathematical and logical consistency of the model.

1. *Mathematical consistency.* This model is quite simple mathematically; it uses a type of equation that is well known and whose properties are well worked out. With this sort of model, assessing the mathematical consistency is mostly a matter of checking to see that the equations are set up correctly, that the use of logarithms is proper, that the procedures for estimating the parameters and finding the goodness of fit are correct, and that the alternative models are properly stated mathematically and tested using the same procedures. In mathematical models, as contrasted with other types of theories, by the time one has finished developing the model one is usually fairly sure the logic is proper and consistent, since it is easy to check.

2. *Empirical adequacy.* Most of the tests we have just described are assessments of the empirical adequacy of the model. On the basis of several kinds of tests, it seems to fit data well.

   Probably the strongest criticism of empirical adequacy could be made on the grounds of representativeness of samples. The model should be applied to a variety of populations and possibly other variables before any generality is claimed for it.

3. *Theoretical value.* A model is theoretically valuable if it tells us something new or surprising, explains something better than previously available models, allows us to develop new questions for research, provides a way of incorporating previously distinct theories, and/or talks about theoretical issues of interest to sociologists. We have mentioned some of the ways in which this model does the first three things; the last two deserve more discussion.

Hamblin and his associates suggest in several other places[7] that the stimulus-response power function is applicable to social exchange theory. Taking an exchange approach to social behavior means thinking of people's actions as having rewards and/or costs to themselves and to others, and viewing social phenomena such as status as the result of exchanges of rewards and costs between people. In very general terms, this approach assumes that the amount a person performs for another person of some valued act is directly proportional to the amount of valued acts he receives from the other person. The exact form of the relationship, however, has seldom been specified. The stimulus-response power-function model can be translated into exchange theory by defining the "stimulus" as the behavior or characteristics of the other person and the "response" as the evaluation of that behavior by the subject.

One of the troublesome aspects of exchange theory has been the question of how to distinguish values from behavior; in theory, the elements of an exchange are (1) act by one person, (2) evaluation of that act by a second person, (3) act by second person in response to evaluation, and (4) evaluation of the response by both persons. In practice it has proved very difficult to conceptualize and measure evaluations separately from responses. Since the theory postulates that behavior is a function of value received, this has tended to make the exchange analysis tautological. Hamblin's model provides a possible solution to this problem by having us conceptualize a value as a nonvoluntary conditioned response to a stimulus, just as the perceived intensity of a sound is a nonvoluntary conditioned response to the actual decibel level of the sound. In the case of status, for example, the "esteem" with which a person is viewed can be seen as a nonvoluntary internal response to the stimulus presented by that person's behavior (such as finishing a certain number of years of school or earning a certain income). "Behav-

---

[7]See especially Hamblin and Smith, in *Sociometry*, 1966.

ior" can then be seen as a choice made by the person doing the evaluating, following his evaluation; for example, a person may or may not choose to behave deferentially toward someone for whom he has high respect. Conceptually, values and behavior are now distinct; furthermore, values can be measured as a response to a stimulus using the method of the psychophysical experiment. Also, several dimensions can be combined to make a single evaluation. The model also provides a prediction about how the magnitude of evaluation will be related to the magnitude of behavior.

In Translation Diagram 2-2 we show how these ideas can be expressed as a process of translating from the model to a theory, by mapping the variables of the model into concepts in a theory. Once this mapping has been done, a relationship in the model can be used to provide a statement in the theory. In this case, we are using the model as a source, and mapping from it to theory, primarily deductively, since we are assuming the concepts in the theory are special cases of the variables of the model and deducing from that what the relationship between concepts in the theory must be.

From the point of view of a sociologist primarily interested in social exchange theory, the biggest problem with this model is one it shares with many mathematical models. This problem is that it deals with only a small portion of the process or situation in which we are interested. The evaluation a person attaches to the behavior or characteristics of another person is one step in a social exchange; we would also like to be able to predict his voluntary response, and how that is related to his evaluations, also how the other person's evaluations and behavior are related to the evaluations and behavior of the subject. The model and its results must be integrated with other aspects of exchange theory before questions like these can be answered. Although this is in some respects a limitation on the usefulness of the model, it is also a benefit because it points to some specific areas in which theoretical and empirical questions can be asked.

Translation Diagram 2-2

MODEL THEORY

Variables

$\phi \longrightarrow$ Behavior by person 2
$\psi \longrightarrow$ Person 1's evaluation of the behavior of person 2 ("esteem")

Relationships

$\psi = c\phi^n \longrightarrow$ Esteem increases as a power function of behavior

conclusions: benefits and costs of mathematics

In the first chapter we mentioned several benefits and some costs of mathematics to the sociologist. Since this is the first chapter that discusses an actual mathematical model, we can refer back to that discussion and use this chapter's material as an illustration. The model can be compared to verbal theoretical statements, on the one hand, and to standard statistical analysis on the other. We suggested that mathematics has an advantage in power and precision over both.

The general verbal statement in the theory behind the model was that education and income act as stimuli to which status is a response. The equations of the model are more precise: they say the same thing the verbal statement does and also more, because they tell us what the exact shape of the relationship should be. The model also has an advantage in predictive power; if we know the equations and parameters, we can predict exactly how high the status of a person with any given education or income will be. With the verbal statements, we would be able to predict only that it would be higher or lower than some other person's. We can also predict exactly how much education or income a person must have in order to achieve a given status level. Another increase in precision over the verbal statements occurs when we use the model to compare populations; we can say not only that the populations differ in the way status is determined, but exactly how they differ, and what the differences in status will be for individuals with the same education or income.

In comparison with standard statistical analysis, there is also a gain in precision. The standard analysis implies a linear model, according to which

$$S_e = a + bE + \text{error}.$$

Since the data are obviously nonlinear, the model will result in our concluding that there is a lot of error. We would probably attribute the unexplained variance to measurement error or to the presence of other variables affecting status which we had not measured, or possibly to heterogeneity of the population being sampled. The better fit of the power-function model indicates that these sources of error are not as important as we would think them if we used a linear model.

Another benefit we suggested for mathematics is that it allows us to connect diverse pieces of research and theory. This model draws on psychophysics for the form of the equations, and the fit of the equations to this set of data suggests that something similar to the processing of information about physical stimuli may operate in the processing of information about social stimuli. This is of interest theoretically, not only for the parallel it points to between physical and social perception but because it raises the more general question of how information is processed in the human mind, a problem sociologists do not always consider relevant. The research described here cannot provide a definitive answer, but use of the model has forced us to consider the question.

In Chapter 1 we also mentioned some costs of mathematics, and it seems only fair to return to them here. One we mentioned was the extra investment in time and training required to use and understand the mathematics. Although this model does use some kinds of mathematics sociologists do not ordinarily employ, it is probably no worse than many techniques of statistical analysis we frequently employ. Some of the other models we will discuss are more costly than this one regarding mathematical sophistication. We have pointed out how this model does have some costs in forced attention to detail. The model pays attention only to a small part of a process of status development or social exchange, and it may omit the aspects some sociologists would think most interesting.

The third cost we mentioned is a sort of dehumanization that some people feel comes from mathematical approaches. Hamblin pays some attention to this problem, apparently in response to criticisms of his work on the grounds that it reduces human social behavior to a mechanical, predetermined response to a stimulus. He points out that his model does not imply a lack of "freedom"—for two reasons: (1) the model does not predict behavior, which can be assumed to be a voluntary response to the nonvoluntary evaluation, (2) people are good at managing stimuli, for example through selective perception, thereby exercising control over their own and others' responses. The model does not deal with this aspect of behavior either, although it could conceivably be made to do so. This might be done, for example, by including a feedback loop, through which the individual compares the status he assigns to another person with some ideal status (perhaps using a criterion of status consistency), and if they do not match, revises the stimuli to which he pays attention to bring his response closer to the ideal state. Of course, developing and testing such a model would require much more information about how people view their own and others' statuses, and how the management of stimuli is accomplished, than was required for development of the simple form of the model. The model would probably have to become a process model, as it would include changes over time, and the mathematics would become much more complex.

problems

1. Many theoretical hypotheses in sociology are stated, as Zetterberg did, in the form "The greater the A, the greater the B." For convenience of data analysis these monotonic hypotheses are often interpreted as linear func-

tions. Are they at least as likely to be power curves? Can you identify examples of such hypotheses from the sociological literature that are so stated and probably (or at least plausibly) involve power relationships? What about Zetterberg's formalization of Durkheim's work (see Hans L. Zetterberg, *On Theory* and *Verification in Sociology* (Totowa, N.J.: The Bedminster Press, 1965).

2. Draw a graph of $Y = \ln_{10} X$ and another graph of $Y = \frac{1}{2}(X^{1/2} - 1)$ for $1 \leq X \leq 10$. Compare the curves and decide whether you could tell a logarithmic function from a power function by inspection of data. How might theoretical considerations guide your choice?

3. Is physical aggression a power function? Murray A. Straus has presented a graph of physical aggression between spouses as a consequence of verbal aggression ["Leveling, civility and violence in the family," *Journal of Marriage and the Family* 36 (February, 1974), 13–29]. Although the actual values of the variables are not given, use the graph scales to estimate the coordinates of the points, then determine how well they are described by a power function. Interpret your results theoretically with regard to marital behavior or aggression in general.

CHAPTER 3

the distribution of acts in small groups

At first glance it may seem that the shift from status, as a function of variables like level of education, to examination of how often people talk to each other in small-group discussions is a rather large substantive jump. Two aspects of small-group behavior make that jump less difficult. First, there are status structures in small groups just as there are in larger social systems. Second, those structures are the consequence, presumably, of the responses of the group members to the interpersonal behaviors and the group problem-solving contributions of the others in the group. It is reasonable to view the resulting distribution of acts as indicative of a social stimulus-response type of phenomenon which reflects status distinctions in the group.

The preceding remarks suggest a model which develops out of assumptions about status structures or stimulus-response sequences. Rather than work from a theoretical discussion to a model to empirical evidence, however, we will begin at the data point of the theory-model-data triangle.

Small-group research initially had a strong observational emphasis, such that data regularities were encountered for which theoretical interpretation was lacking. To illustrate the process of beginning with data and developing first a mathematical representation of regularities, then a theoretical interpretation of them, we will start with specific research findings.

Early work on the observation of small discussion groups by Bales[1] and various associates led to a variety of informally stated conclusions about such groups. One project by Borgatta and Bales[2] concluded that the rate at which individuals interact in a group will be an inverse function of the average characteristic interaction rate of that individual's co-participants. However, the idea of a characteristic interaction rate was not clearly formulated, and the expression "inverse function" was only an informal representation of the trend of the data. A second paper by Borgatta, Couch, and Bales[3] demonstrated that individuals who were particularly active participators in first experimental sessions showed a considerable tendency to maintain high interaction rates through three subsequent sessions involving different other participants. These data clearly suggest that individual behavioral constants (possibly personality factors) were operating in the experimental discussions. It may therefore be hypothesized that each individual has a constant tendency to initiate behavior in a discussion group.

Because of the task-oriented, discussion-group focus of Bales' research and that of his associates and followers, we assume that only that type of situation is under consideration. It remains to ask later whether such limitations are necessary for the model which will be developed. Often it is preferable to develop a model which has limited generality but good empirical fit, then explore ways of broadening the applicability of the model once it is well formulated.

The observation by Borgatta and Bales that rates of interaction will be inverse functions of the average characteristic rates of coparticipants suggests a normalization of the hypothesized initiation constants. That normalization would consist of dividing each individual constant by the average constant for coparticipants. If, instead, the sum of the constants for the whole group is used in the normalization, the result will have desirable probability properties. That is, the sum of the normalized constants will always be unity for any group. In fact, these normalized constants will become reasonable

[1]Much of this tradition of research appears in A. Paul Hare, et al., eds., *Small Groups*, rev. ed. (New York: Alfred A. Knopf, 1965). Two papers of particular relevance are Robert F. Bales et al., "Channels of communication in small groups," *American Sociological Review*, vol. 16, no. 4 (1951), pp. 461–468; and Robert F. Bales, "The equilibrium problem in small groups," in Hare et al., *Small Groups*, 444–476.

[2]Edgar F. Borgatta and Robert F. Bales, "Interaction of individuals in reconstituted groups," *Sociometry*, vol. 16 (1953), pp. 302–320.

[3]Edgar F. Borgatta et al., "Some findings relevant to the great man theory of leadership," *American Sociological Review*, vol. 19, no. 6 (1954), 755–759.

estimates of the probabilities that individuals will initiate acts in the particular group under discussion. Those probabilities should operate over time in the process of group interaction such that they will be reflected in the observed proportions of all behavior which each of the individuals initiated.

From the preceding comments, two major variables can be defined. First is an initiation tendency (individual degree of talkativeness) associated with each member of the group. That tendency is assumed to be constant for the individual across the various groups in which he may participate. Second is an observed proportion of acts initiated by that group member. Both of these variables will be considered to be continuous. As with the Hamblin model, there is no concern at this stage of model development with underlying processes which produce the structure. Only description of the fully developed structure is intended. We therefore will be working with a structure model using scales. A translation diagram, thus far, would be as follows (working from data to model).

Translation Diagram 3-1

DATA   MODEL

Variable

Proportion of all acts ⟶ p_i: individual probability
which each member initiates   of initiating acts in a
    given group

Observed Regularity

Stability of individual ⟶ c_i: constant individual
rates across groups   initiation tendency,
    regardless of group

Observed Relationship

Apparent inverse function ⟶ Normalization of each c_i by
for initiation rates   other (or all) c_i for each
    group

Translation into Mathematics. The statement that tendencies should be normalized by the sum of tendencies present provides the first relationship of the model:

$$p_i = \frac{c_i}{\sum_{n} c_i}. \tag{3-1}$$

Assuming that there are n actors in the group under analysis, then equation (3-1) says that the individual's probability of initiating acts (p_i) is simply his tendency (c_i) divided by the sum of the tendencies of the group members. In order to test such an equation empirically, it is necessary to find some way to determine the values of the c_i. Following the lead of the studies mentioned earlier, it is possible to create a variety of groups such that each person encounters different coparticipants in his interaction history. Equations can then be worked out which solve for the best estimates of the c_i to satisfy all groups and all individuals simultaneously. An adaptation of equation (3-1) would be needed to keep track of group as well as individual. Because the estimation of the c_i is somewhat peripheral to this discussion, we will not follow that digression.

Another of the early observations about small-group-act distributions was that a matrix showing each actor's frequency of addressing each other actor in the group provides a surprisingly consistent pattern. That pattern can be represented more or less as a function of the product of the initiator's tendency to initiate acts and the recipient's tendency to receive acts. Because there are no observations of an actor talking to himself, however, a simple independent function such as that just described will not quite fit. It has been shown[4] that if each probability of initiating acts is augmented by a constant multiple unique to that actor, and the same is done for the probability of receiving acts, then the product of these individually augmented probabilities will reproduce the interaction matrix with a high degree of accuracy. If the probability that Actor i addresses i' is designated as $p_{ii'}$, and $p_{i.}$ indicates Actor i's total probability of initiation while $p_{.i'}$ indicates Actor i''s probability of receipt, then equation (3-2) (below) expresses the relationship just indicated. The parentheses in that equation are for convenience in keeping track of the initiation-versus-receipt aspects of the relationship.

It should be evident that adding Actor i's probabilities of initiating acts across the various i' others in the group will produce his overall initiation probability. Therefore, summing equation (3-2) (both sides) over all i' not equal to i will produce $p_{i.}$ on both sides. The necessary value of a_i can then be deduced and fed back into equation (3-2) to get equation (3-3). The distribution of acts is now expressed as a function of initiating and receiving probabilities and an as yet unidentified parameter b.

$$p_{ii'} = (a_i p_{i.})(b_{i'} p_{.i'}) \tag{3-2}$$

so that

$$a_i = \frac{1}{\sum_{i' \neq i} b_{i'} p_{.i'}}$$

---

[4]Robert K. Leik, "Type of group and the probability of initiating acts," *Sociometry*, vol. 28, no. 1 (1965), pp. 57–65; and "The distribution of acts in small groups," *Sociometry*, vol. 30 no. 3 (1967), pp. 280–299.

and

$$p_{ii'} = p_{i.} \frac{b_{i'} p_{.i'}}{\sum_{i' \neq i} b_{i'} p_{.i'}}. \qquad (3\text{-}3)$$

Equations (3-1) and (3-3) are basically descriptive equations which derive from observations of group discussions. Can they be interrelated in a theoretically useful manner? Also, are there other bases for writing equations about initiation and distribution of acts? The latter question will be approached first, since it will lead to an answer to the former.

Developing the Model. The implication of equation (3-1) is that individuals will act as often as their individual tendencies dictate, subject to competitive limitations. A plausible alternative would be that an individual will act in response to others who have acted. This is more of a social-reciprocity, or stimulus-response, approach rather than a built-in drive type of approach. Are the two compatible?

Suppose that each actor directed his acts to others in proportion to the extent to which they provided stimuli by their own acts. The equation would look like

$$p_{ii'} = p_{i.}(\alpha_i p_{i'.}) \qquad (3\text{-}4)$$

Such an equation has been shown to fit observed data very well.[5] Assuming that all acts are directed to individuals (not true, but temporarily convenient) allows the deduction that α_i must equal $1/\sum_{i' \neq i} p_{i'.}$. Now equation (3-4) provides an alternative to equation (3-2). If both are valid, then the right side of (3-2) must equal the right side of (3-4).

$$(a_i p_{i.})(b_{i'} p_{.i'}) = p_{i.} \frac{p_{i'.}}{\sum_{i' \neq i} p_{i'.}}$$

or

$$a_i \sum_{i' \neq i} p_{i'.}(b_{i'} p_{.i'}) = p_{i'.}. \qquad (3\text{-}5)$$

Since the sum over all actors of their initiation probabilities must equal unity, it can be deduced that

$$a_i \sum_{i' \neq i} p_{i'.} = \frac{1}{\sum_{i'} b_{i'} p_{.i'}},$$

---

[5]Gray tested a simpler version of equation (3-4) which does not require that each actor have a unique value of α. Although the laws of probability require that such an equation be somewhat in error, the data fitted the simpler equation surprisingly well (average correlation between observed and predicted values exceeded .8). See Louis N. Gray, "Variation in attitude and structure over time through group interaction," unpublished M. A. thesis, University of Washington, 1965.

so that, restating equation (3-5),

$$p_{i'} = \frac{b_{i'} p_{.i'}}{\sum_{i'} b_{i'} p_{.i'}},$$

or, more generally,

$$p_{i.} = \frac{b_i p_{.i}}{\sum_i b_i p_{.i}}. \quad (3\text{-}6)$$

Note that equation (3-6) is essentially the same as equation (3-1), with $b_i p_{.i}$ substituted for c_i. Using a reciprocity basis for act distribution in conjunction with a form which is known to be descriptively valid [equation (3-2)] has led to a new interpretation of the first equation of the model. One's tendency to act is statable as a response to the behaviors of the others in the group. The parameter b_i is no longer just a convenient term for fitting data, but an indication of the degree of reciprocation in verbal interaction. Aside from their purely mathematical use, can equally theoretical interpretations be found for the parameters a_i and α_i?

First, it has been noted that $\alpha_i = 1/\sum_{i' \neq i} p_{i'.}$. But that denominator is the sum of all initiation probabilities less $p_{i.}$, or more simply $1 - p_{i.}$. Therefore equation (3-4) reduces to

$$p_{ii'} = \frac{p_{i.}}{1 - p_{i.}} p_{i'.}. \quad (3\text{-}7)$$

The effect of α_i is simply to adjust the amount of response to Actor i' in accordance with how active Actor i is. Note that increments in $p_{i.}$ are reflected in both the numerator and denominator of equation (3-7), meaning that i' gets disproportionately greater return from active others than from inactive ones. Such a pattern will tend to create an apparent leadership situation by establishing relatively high frequencies of acts flowing from and to the highest initiators. If both $p_{i.}$ and $p_{i'.}$ are low, there will be very few acts flowing between actors i and i'.

The interpretation of α_i, then, appears to be more in the nature of a hierarchy effect than a basic interaction principle such as reciprocity. However, that effect is caused by the demands of reciprocity in a system where each actor's rates of initiating and directing acts are dependent upon the rates of the others in the system. Is a_i to be similarly interpreted?

It can be readily shown that a_i is simply α_i divided by $\sum_i b_i p_{.i}$. A look at equation (3-2) indicates that, by writing the foregoing denominator under the righthand term and replacing a_i by α_i, the relationship allows the equivalence of equations (3-2) and (3-4). Therefore a_i incorporates both the hierarchy effect and the normalizing (denominator) portion of equation (3-6). We can conclude, then, that two empirically determined equations

(3-1) and (3-2) can be explained and interpreted in terms of the response demands (reciprocation) and hierarchical characteristics of small-group discussions.

Because of the laws of probability, α_i and b_i must be related. It is possible to show that

$$b_i = \frac{1}{\sum_{i' \neq i} \alpha_{i\cdot'} - (n - 1)}. \qquad (3\text{-}8)$$

This result indicates that even the reciprocal aspect of interaction is subject to the competition implied in the augmenting effect ($\alpha_{i'}$) of the other actors' rates of initiation and the sheer size of the group.

One aspect of equation (3-6) suggests that reciprocity might not be quite an appropriate interpretation of the parameter b_i. Since there is no direction involved in the equation, that parameter may be more indicative of a perceived right to speak, or at least of an invitation to do so. In this sense it is difficult to determine whether the parameter would be more appropriately indicative of opportunity or of obligation. As will be discussed shortly, it may be useful to separate so-called "proacts" from "reacts" in the model. Doing so could help solve the current problem, in that reaction is of the nature of socially expected response whereas proaction seems more a seizing of opportunity.

Evaluating and Extending the Model. The model which has just been developed involves fairly simple equations which have theoretical interpretations, and which have been shown in previous research to provide quite accurate descriptions of observed discussions. However, there are difficulties inherent in the model. The most obvious difficulty, for one who is familiar with small-group observational studies, is that many acts are directed to the group as a whole rather than to individual members. It would be possible to take this factor into account in various ways. Most simply, it can be assumed that a constant proportion of each actor's acts are directed to the group as a whole. Thus a parameter K can be inserted into equation (3-2) [or equation (3-6)] which would reduce the amount of behavior initiated to particular others in proportion to that amount which is initiated to the group as a whole. Such a parameter will have no serious consequences for the rest of the model, but does have one drawback. It is simply not the case that individuals are constant in their tendency to initiate acts to the group as a whole. In fact, at least two factors seem to increase the extent to which acts are directed to the group. The first is leadership, which seems to require a more general kind of group-oriented statement, and the second is the sort of undirected remarks which a person is likely to make when no particular other people are paying attention to him yet he feels impelled to speak. The latter, in fact, seems to occur when someone would like to exert leadership but can induce no followership.

A second obvious difficulty with the model is that it pertains to a particular kind of interaction situation. Clearly, one's likelihood of being stimulated by the remarks of others in the group will vary depending upon the topic of conversation. Also, as suggested earlier, there is no provision for being more reactive to particular others' comments as would be the case if some members were close friends while others were strangers. More complex models have been developed to take these limitations into account. Rather than discuss them in detail at this time, it will be sufficient to indicate the changes in the first model which would be required.

In order to get around the limitation to a particular kind of activity, it would be possible to keep track of different kinds of behaviors in the model. For example, a convenient distinction might be task behavior versus general social behavior in a task-oriented group. This is a very common distinction in small-group research. At this point the reactive versus reciprocal tendencies in the model can be separated. It would be possible to reexpress equation (3-5):

$$p_{i..} = \frac{d_{ij} + b_i p_{.i.}}{\sum_i (d_{ij} + b_i p_{.i.})}. \qquad (3\text{-}9)$$

There are now three subscripts in order to keep track of: the speaker, the person spoken to, and the type of act. The parameter d indicates the individual's tendency to initiate behavior of a particular type without regard to the behavior of others. This would represent essentially his interest in that kind of behavior, and would be the basis for what has been called proaction in small group research. The $b_i p_{.i.}$ is exactly the same as used in equation (3-5). Thus, behavior has been divided into proaction and reaction to the behavior of others, and can be specified by the kind of behavior such as task versus social acts. It would be necessary to adapt equation (3-2) or equation (3-6) appropriately.

To take care of the problems of differential act initiation toward the group as a whole and of possible interpersonal links which induce or retard acts directed to specific others, it is possible to incorporate a new parameter for each actor-object pair. Equation (3-10) shows such an adaptation.

$$p_{ii'j} = \begin{cases} e_{ii'} a_i p_{i.j} p_{i'..} & \text{for } i' \neq \text{group} \\ p_{i.j} \dfrac{(e_{ii'})}{\sum\limits_{i' \neq i} e_{ii'}} & \text{for } i' = \text{group} \end{cases} \qquad (3\text{-}10)$$

The range of the index i in equation (3-10) would still be 1 through n (the members of the group), but the range of i' now includes G, or the group, as a potential object of acts. The parameter K which was suggested as a possible way of treating acts to the group for the earlier model is no longer necessary, because each actor has his own specific link with the group as a whole. Parameters a and b would now have somewhat more complicated forms, and estimation equations would be more difficult. However, the model would now be extremely subtle. By appropriate values of the parameters b and d for each actor it would be possible to represent a considerable range of actor types. By appropriate choice of the $e_{ii'}$ values, it would be possible to represent specific leadership roles, friendship cliques, interpersonal antipathies, or other facts which could structure the distribution of acts in the group. Of course, the number of parameters is now rather large. For n actors and m types of acts under consideration, there will be $n(n + 2m)$ facts needed. The model could describe $2n^2m$ aspects of the behavior of such a group.

For a four-person group with only two act types, this means only about two outputs per input in the model. That is not particularly efficient model building. The number of required parameters could be reduced, for example, by determining whether the proactive tendencies and the reactive or reciprocating tendencies of individuals are related. If so, only half as many parameters would be needed. Although the initial equation of the first model has been proven quite accurate for interaction among strangers, there is no way at this time to know how accurate the more complex model would be. Unfortunately, as the number of parameters required approaches the number of variables which are produced by the model, the easier it is to obtain a "good" fit of the model to any kind of data. The value must then be in terms of theoretical interpretability and the extent to which it generates further research or further theoretical inquiry. It should be evident that as one moves from highly accurate but highly limited models to more general models it is likely that either accuracy will be lost or testing of the models will become extremely difficult.

Thus far the evaluation of the model has concerned its generality. We have attempted to provide theoretical interpretation as development proceeded, so that the model should by relatively acceptable at the theoretical level. Also, concern with the probability requirements and the mutual implications of the equations should have guaranteed mathematical adequacy. Because the original equations (3-1) and (3-3) were based on empirical regularities and have considerable accuracy, it is tempting to conclude that the entire model is empirically sound. Unfortunately, a check against data does not substantiate that faith.

Table 3-1 shows a who-to-whom matrix for a four-person discussion which was part of a large study of three-, four- and five-person groups. It is not necessarily an "ideal" matrix, but seems to represent fairly well the way data for such groups appear after about an hour's problem-solving effort. Minor irregularities are to be expected, but the model should come fairly close if it is a good model.

Table 3-1

A Four-Person Who-to-Whom Matrix

SPEAKER (WHO)	\multicolumn{4}{c}{OBJECT (TO WHOM)}	TOTAL TO INDIVIDUALS
	A	B	C	D	
A		71	57	28	156
B	64		15	1	80
C	50	24		1	75
D	32	9	2		43
Total Received	146	104	74	30	354

Acts to the group as a whole are omitted. In this particular group they were exactly proportional to the acts initiated to individuals.

Table 3-2 presents the estimates of Table 3-1 entries using equation (3-7) and multiplying the estimated $p_{ii'}$ by the total number of acts to individuals, 354. Because there is only one matrix involved, and consequently no way of estimating the c_i except by examining the entire set of data from the study, the values of $p_{i.}$ were taken directly from the table rather than estimated by equation (3-1). Thus the question at hand is whether equation (3-7) will suffice for describing the interior of the matrix once the row totals (or probabilities) are known.

Note that all entries in the first column of the matrix are too low, as are the estimates for the number of acts persons A and C directed to person B. All other entries are too high. The impression is that, the higher the value of $p_{i'.}$, the greater the underestimation of $p_{ii'}$ which equation (3-7) provides. That pattern should seem familiar. If we were to take seriously the argument

Table 3-2

Initial Estimation of Table 3-1

SPEAKER (WHO)	A	B	C	D	TOTAL TO INDIVIDUALS
A		63.9	59.6	32.5	156
B	45.9		22.1	12.0	80
C	42.2	21.7		11.1	75
D	21.6	11.1	10.3		43
Total Received	109.7	96.7	92.0	55.6	354

48   Mathematical Sociology

behind equation (3-4), that acts to others are in response to the stimulus provided by their rate of action, then we should ask whether Stevens' Law, as described in Chapter 2, should apply. That type of function says that response is a power function of stimulus strength, whereas equation (3-4) expresses a linear function, as is evident by rewriting equation (3-4) as a conditional probability.

$$\frac{p_{ii'}}{p_{i.}} = \alpha_i p_{i'.} \qquad (3\text{-}11)$$

What happens if a power function is used? Equation (3-12) provides the power-function version of equation (3-11), recognizing that the value of α_i will not have the same solution that it had previously:

$$\frac{p_{ii'}}{p_{i.}} = \alpha_i p_{i'.}^n. \qquad (3\text{-}12)$$

If n is greater than 1.0, the result will be that $p_{ii'}$ will be increased for larger $p_{i'.}$ relative to smaller $p_{i'.}$. That sounds like what is needed. First, it is necessary to check on the mathematical implications of a power function.

Rewriting equation (3-12) to be in the same form as equation (3-4), and solving for α_i, gives

$$p_{ii'} = \alpha_i p_{i.} p_{i'.}^n.$$

which, summed over all $i' \neq i$, requires that

$$p_{i.} = \alpha_i p_{i.} \sum_{i' \neq i} p_{i'.}^n,$$

or

$$\alpha_i = \frac{1}{\sum_{i' \neq i} p_{i'.}^n}. \qquad (3\text{-}13)$$

Previously it was convenient to use $1 - p_{i.}$ rather than the expression $\sum_{i' \neq i} p_{i'.}$. Because the powers of $p_{i'.}$ do not sum to unity, that reexpression must be modified. If the sum over all actors of $p_{i.}^n$ is called $S(n)$, a similar expression for α_i is

$$\alpha_i = \frac{1}{S(n) - p_{i.}^n}.$$

Then the power-curve equivalent of equation (3-7) becomes

$$p_{ii'} = \frac{p_{i.}}{S(n) - p_{i.}^n} p_{i'.}^n. \qquad (3\text{-}14)$$

It is not easy to solve for n in the above expression. An iterative procedure seems to be easiest, setting n at some value for establishing the denominator values, then using logarithms to estimate n in the numerator. This new value can be reentered in denominator calculations and the process repeated until the estimates converge. For some distributions of p_i. this process might oscillate rather than converge, requiring a compromise estimate at each iteration.

How well does equation (3-14) estimate the matrix in Table 3-1? The answer appears in Table 3-3, using a power of $n = 1.8$. Clearly the fit is greatly improved, although some deviations remain. Evidently a power function applies to conversational stimuli as well as other kinds of stimuli.

Table 3-3

Power-Curve Estimation of Table 3-1

SPEAKER (WHO)	\multicolumn{4}{c}{OBJECT (TO WHOM)}	TOTAL TO INDIVIDUALS
	A	B	C	D	
A		71.4	63.2	21.4	156
B	59.0		15.7	5.3	80
C	53.7	16.4		4.9	75
D	27.4	8.3	7.3		43
Total Received	140.1	96.1	86.2	31.6	354

Attempts to apply equation (3-14) to various other who-to-whom matrices have not been systematic, but two apparent trends have emerged. First, for Bales' often-reproduced six-person matrix,[6] the appropriate power is only slightly greater than unity. For the four person matrix of Table 3-1, the power was 1.8. For some three-person matrices the power seems to be even higher, around 2.0 or greater. In other words, the power seems to depend upon the size of the group. If subsequent analyses demonstrate that this informal conclusion is valid, then it follows that differences in amount of speech (or at least, in relative amount of speech) are virtually accurately perceived and acted upon in larger groups, but become increasingly magnified in smaller groups. This fact, in turn, implies that there should be notable changes in the interpersonal relationships for groups of different size simply because of this differential responsiveness.

A second, more subtle trend appears to be that the power is not constant for all members of the group, but varies inversely with p_i. Thus, group members who speak relatively seldom are apt to address highly disproportionate numbers of remarks to high-frequency participants. The latter, on the other hand, are closer to proportional allocation in their addressing

[6] Bales, "The equilibrium problem in small groups," in Hare *et al.*, *Small Groups*, p. 458.

fellow members. This trend, should it stand the test of more systematic inquiry, suggests that lower-status (frequency) participants exaggerate status differences, whereas higher status participants do not, at least not as much. Such an observation appears entirely plausible, but cannot at this time be considered more than an interesting possibility for further research.

Another aspect of evaluating a structure model concerns whether it can reasonably be incorporated into or predicted by an appropriate process model. For example, one might ask whether any reasonable process could produce the differences in the observed p_i by internal dynamics of the group rather than by assuming that individual tendencies to act, c_i, are imported to the group by the members.

Various theoretical attempts have been made to provide such a process model. The most notable are by Bales[7] (a nonmathematical programmatic statement of how such a model might work), Coleman[8] (basically concerned with statistical aggregation rather than group process), Horvath[9] (a status based right-to-speak model), and most recently by Fisek.[10] The Fisek model builds on both the Horvath approach and a considerable body of research and theory on status structures and interpersonal expectations which are relevant to task performance (hence task-oriented discussions).[11] It is not appropriate to explore these process models here, but they represent a surprisingly extensive development of mathematical, theoretical, and empirical work.

In a parallel vein, an earlier, very simple, empirically derived model of the distribution of the p_i for a group was formulated by Stephan and Mishler[12] as an exponential function, based on group rank. For example, the third most talkative member was expected to initiate some proportion, r, of the second-rank participant's amount of initiation. Similarly, person 4 was presumed to initiate rp_3 which amounts to $r^2 p_2$, and so forth. Owing to unusually large rates of initiation by task leaders, the leader's p value was excluded from the model. For all others, though, it was hypothesized that

$$p_i = ar^{i-1}. \qquad (3\text{-}15)$$

[7]Bales, "The equilibrium problem in small groups," in Hare et al., *Small Groups*, pp. 461–67.

[8]James S. Coleman, "The mathematical study of small groups" in H. Solomon, ed., *Mathematical Thinking in the Measurement of Behavior* (New York: The Free Press, 1960).

[9]W. J. Horvath, "A mathematical model of participation in small groups," *Behavioral Science*, vol. 10 (1964), pp. 164–66.

[10]M. H. Fisek, "A model for the evolution of status structures in task-oriented discussion groups," in Joseph Berger, Thomas L. Conner, and M. Hamit Fisek, *Expectation States Theory: A Theoretical Research Program* (Cambridge, Mass.: Winthrop Publishers, 1974).

[11]See other discussions in Berger et al., op. cit.

[12]F. Stephan and E. G. Mishler, "The distribution of participation in small groups: an exponential approximation," *American Sociological Review*, vol. 17 (1952), pp. 598–608.

The Stephan-Mishler equation has been more of an empirical than a theoretical curve, although Horvath suggested his process model in an attempt to generate the Stephan-Mishler distribution. Kadane and Lewis,[13] after extensive work with theoretical probability distributions, have concluded that none of the proposed models for accounting for the $p_{i.}$ distributions can generate exactly an exponential function such as (3-15). They suggest, therefore, that perhaps the exponential function is not theoretically correct, even though it has considerable empirical justification. Again, this variety of research and theory demonstrates both the creative potential and the rigor of work in mathematical model building.

problems

1. Ideas which were discussed in this chapter included
   a) internal "talkativeness,"
   b) responsiveness to social stimuli,
   c) social reciprocity,
   d) right to speak as a function of status
   as possible ways of accounting for differential rates of initiating behavior. Do these imply similar or different types of mathematical representation? What facts would you need to know about each person, or at least would need to represent in equations, for these different approaches? To what extent do they depend on other persons in the group?
2. Following are two different distributions of $p_{i.}$. For each distribution, compute $p_{i.}^n$ for n equal to 1.0, 1.5, and 2.0. Then, for each of these powers, for each of the distributions, compute $\Sigma_i p_{i.}^n$ and divide that sum into each value of $p_{i.}^n$ to get relative magnitudes of the powers of the $p_{i.}$. Compare the changes in relative dominance implied by these relative magnitudes when different powers of $p_{i.}$ are used as the stimulus in the small-group equations. How does group size seem to affect these changes?

GROUP A		GROUP B	
Person	$p_{i.}$	Person	$p_{i.}$
1	.47	1	.36
2	.30	2	.19
3	.23	3	.15
		4	.12
		5	.10
		6	.08

[13] J. B. Kadane and G. Lewis, "The distribution of participation in group discussions: An empirical and theoretical reappraisal" *American Sociological Review*, vol. 34 (1969), pp. 710–722, and J. B. Kadane, G. Lewis, and J. Ramage, "Horvath's theory of participation in group discussions," *Sociometry*, vol. 33 (1969), pp. 348–361.

3. The study of small-group discussions that produced the four-person matrix used in this chapter also had persons A, B, and D from that group engage in a triadic discussion of a different problem. Their matrix is as follows.

ACTS DIRECTED TO

		Individuals A	B	D	The Group as a Whole	Total
Actor	A		71	60	43	174
	B	68		10	21	99
	D	54	22		8	84
Total		122	93	70	72	357

Let $p_{i.}$ stand for the number of acts which person i directs to individuals divided by the total number of acts directed to individuals by the entire group (for example, $p_{A.} = 131/285 = .460$). Let $P_{i.}$ designate the total number of acts by person i (including those to the group as a whole) divided by the matrix total (for example, $P_{A.} = 174/357 = .487$).

a) Estimate the entries in the matrix above using

(i) $\quad p_{ii'} = \dfrac{p_{i.}}{1 - p_{i.}} p_{i'.}$

and also using

(ii) $\quad p_{ii'} = \dfrac{p_{i.}}{1 - P_{i.}} P_{i'.}$

b) Which stimulus value seems more appropriate theoretically, $p_{i'.}$ or $P_{i'.}$?
c) Prove that the term $1 - P_{i.}$ in the denominator of (ii) is a necessary consequence of using $P_{i'.}$ in the numerator.
d) Try using a power of $P_{i'.}$ (or $p_{i'.}$ if you prefer) which is greater than unity. Comment on the extent to which it improves or reduces accuracy of prediction.

CHAPTER 4

graphs, matrices, and structural balance

Chapter 2 presented a model of response to social stimuli, and Chapter 3 incorporated that model into representation of the structure of small discussion groups. Many structures of interest in sociology, derivative of such interaction episodes, develop emotional ties between the people involved so that the structure has a permanence not implied in most small groups. Two aspects of these interpersonal structures are of immediate interest. First, is there an appropriate type of model for describing the emotional or affective structure of interpersonal relations? Second, is there a mathematical way of describing who belongs to what grouping?

Two types of mathematics are particularly well suited to this kind of analysis: matrix algebra and a branch of topology known as graph theory. Since we do not expect our readers to have been introduced to graph theory, we will discuss some of the basics of this kind of mathematical language and also spend some time showing how it can be used in conjunction with matrix algebra.

The first application we will discuss is the representation of balance theory in graph notation. This model contrasts with the models we have presented so far in several ways. The variables are relationships of liking or disliking between people, which are difficult to represent as numbers but easy to represent in other mathematical notations. In other words, there are mathematical models that do not use numbers as a basic variable. This model is also a good illustration of the process of revising and elaborating a model once its basic form is established; the first authors presented a model that later authors felt did not describe actual sociometric structures adequately. The later authors examined the assumptions of the model, changing one at a time and retesting until a revised and more satisfactory version was developed. In the process, they encountered one of the problems of testing models—the development of ways of estimating parameters that will allow a statistical test of the goodness of fit of the model and also allow comparison of different populations by using the model.

The first structural model we will discuss is D. Cartwright and F. Harary's graph theoretical representation of F. Heider's theory of structural balance.[1] Heider's theory is a type of cognitive consistency theory, derived from general assumptions about the psychology of interpersonal behavior.[2] The part of the theory that sociologists have found most useful is based on the assumption that the relationship between two people may be influenced by the relationship of each to a third person. Heider recognized two kinds of relationships—evaluative (like or dislike) and association (for example, having made an object, working with a person)—and he hypothesized that evaluations are transitive. For example, if I have a friend (someone I like) and that friend likes a third person, then I should also like the third person because that is consistent with my evaluation of my friend and his evaluation of the third person. Heider predicted that people who found their evaluations contradicting this principle would feel uncomfortable and would try to change. Thus, if I find that I don't like someone my friend likes, I may change my mind about the third person (he's not really so bad after all), about my friend (maybe he's not so great after all), or try not to see both of them together and avoid discussing the third person with my friend.

---

[1] Dorwin Cartwright and Frank Harary, "Structural balance: A generalization of Heider's theory," *Psychological Review*, vol. 63 (September, 1956), pp. 277–293.

[2] Fritz Heider, "Social perception and phenomenal causality," *Psychological Review*, vol. 51 (November, 1944), pp. 358–374; Fritz Heider, "Attitudes and cognitive organization," *Journal of Psychology*, vol. 21 (January, 1946), pp. 107–112; and Fritz Heider, *The Psychology of Interpersonal Relations* (New York: John Wiley & Sons, 1958). There is a large body of literature on cognitive consistency; for an introduction to some of the research and theory in this area, see R. P. Abelson, E. Aronson, W. J. McGuire, T. M. Newcomb, M. J. Rosenberg, and O. H. Tannenbaum, eds., *Theories of Cognitive Consistency* (Chicago: Rand McNally, 1968).

There are other situations in which, according to Heider, I should feel uncomfortable; if my enemy and I turn out to have similar tastes or a mutual friend, I will have difficulty thinking of him as an enemy or I may change my mind about liking the thing he does. On the other hand, if my friend and I both dislike the same person, I should not feel uncomfortable because we agree.

translation into mathematics

Formalization of the Theory. To put the theory into more formal terms, begin by considering a set of three persons. Following standard terminology, we will refer to them as P, O, and O'. P is the person whose point of view we take in making statements of evaluation, unless otherwise specified. The theory also talks about two kinds of attitudes: positive and negative. For three people, there are thus eight possible combinations of relationships (see Table 4-1). The theory says that for P to feel comfortable and the situation to be stable, if P likes O, P and O should agree on their evaluation of O', either both liking O' or both disliking him. If P dislikes O, then P and O should disagree in their evaluation of him. When other combinations occur, the situation is unstable, because P will feel uncomfortable and tend to change his evaluations. The stable, comfortable situations Hieder calls *balanced* and the unstable, uncomfortable ones *imbalanced*. In Table 4-1 the eight possible combinations are displayed and labeled balanced and imbalanced according to the basic assumption of the theory.

These assumptions are substantively interesting because they provide a set of simple principles from which a large number of predictions about the structure of interpersonal relations can be derived. They also provide a way of integrating individual psychological processes with social structure.

Table 4-1

RELATIONSHIP BETWEEN:

P and O	O and O'	P and O'	STRUCTURE IS:	
+	+	+	balanced	*P* and *O* like each
+	−	−	balanced	other and agree,
−	+	−	balanced	or dislike each
−	−	+	balanced	other and disagree
+	+	−	imbalanced	*P* and *O* like each
+	−	+	imbalanced	other and disagree,
−	+	+	imbalanced	or dislike each
−	−	−	imbalanced	other and agree

56 Mathematical Sociology

Basic Concepts of Graph Theory. Cartwright and Harary translated Heider's concepts and assumptions into graph theory.[3] A *linear graph* is defined as a finite collection of *points* $(X_1, X_2, \ldots)$ together with a prescribed subset of the set of all unordered pairs of distinct points. Each of these unordered pairs of points is a *line*. Figure 4-1 shows an example of a linear graph; this graph has 4 points and 4 lines. The subset of pairs of points included in this graph is: *AC, AD, CD*, and *BC*.

Graphs can also be represented as matrices, with the rows and columns representing the points; an entry of 1 in a cell indicates that the points of that row and column are joined by a line, 0 indicates that they are not. The matrix corresponding to a graph is called the *adjacency matrix* of the graph. Figure 4-2 shows a matrix representation of the graph in Figure 4-1.

A *completely connected graph* has a line between every pair of points. In addition to simple linear graphs, there are two other types of graphs it is useful to think about. A *directed graph*, also called a *digraph*, in which the pairs of points are ordered, is the equivalent to a set of asymmetric relationships (see Figure 4-3). A *signed graph* has lines that are either positive or negative in value (see Figure 4-4). We can also have a signed digraph, in which there are both one-way lines and positive and negative values (see Figure 4-5).

A *path* is a set of pairs of points such that the second point of one pair is the first point of the following pair; in Figure 4-1 the set *AC, CD, DB* is a path.

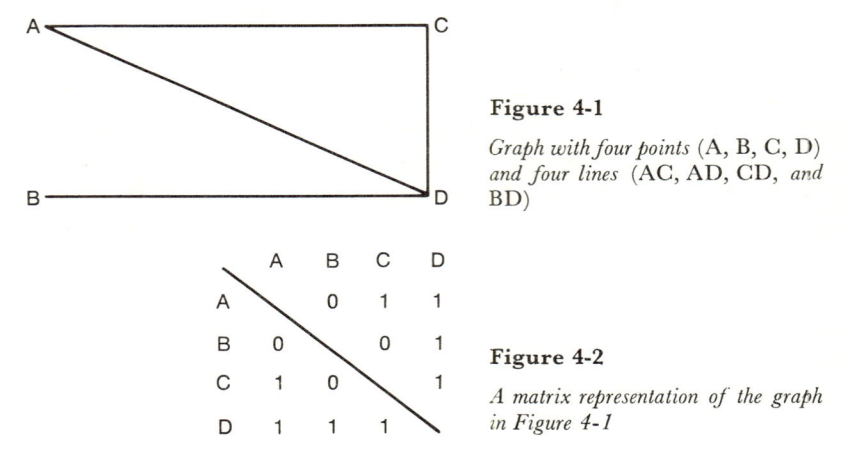

Figure 4-1

Graph with four points (A, B, C, D) *and four lines* (AC, AD, CD, *and* BD)

	A	B	C	D
A		0	1	1
B	0		0	1
C	1	0		1
D	1	1	1	

Figure 4-2

A matrix representation of the graph in Figure 4-1

---

[3]An introduction to the mathematics of graph theory can be found in: Frank Harary, Robert Z. Norman, and Dorwin Cartwright, *Structural Models: An Introduction to the Theory of Directed Graphs* (New York: John Wiley & Sons, 1965); Claude Flament, *Applications of Graph Theory to Group Structure* (Englewood Cliffs, N.J.: Prentice-Hall, 1963); and Claude Berge, *The Theory of Graphs and Its Applications* (New York: John Wiley & Sons, 1962).

graphs, matrices, and structural balance 57

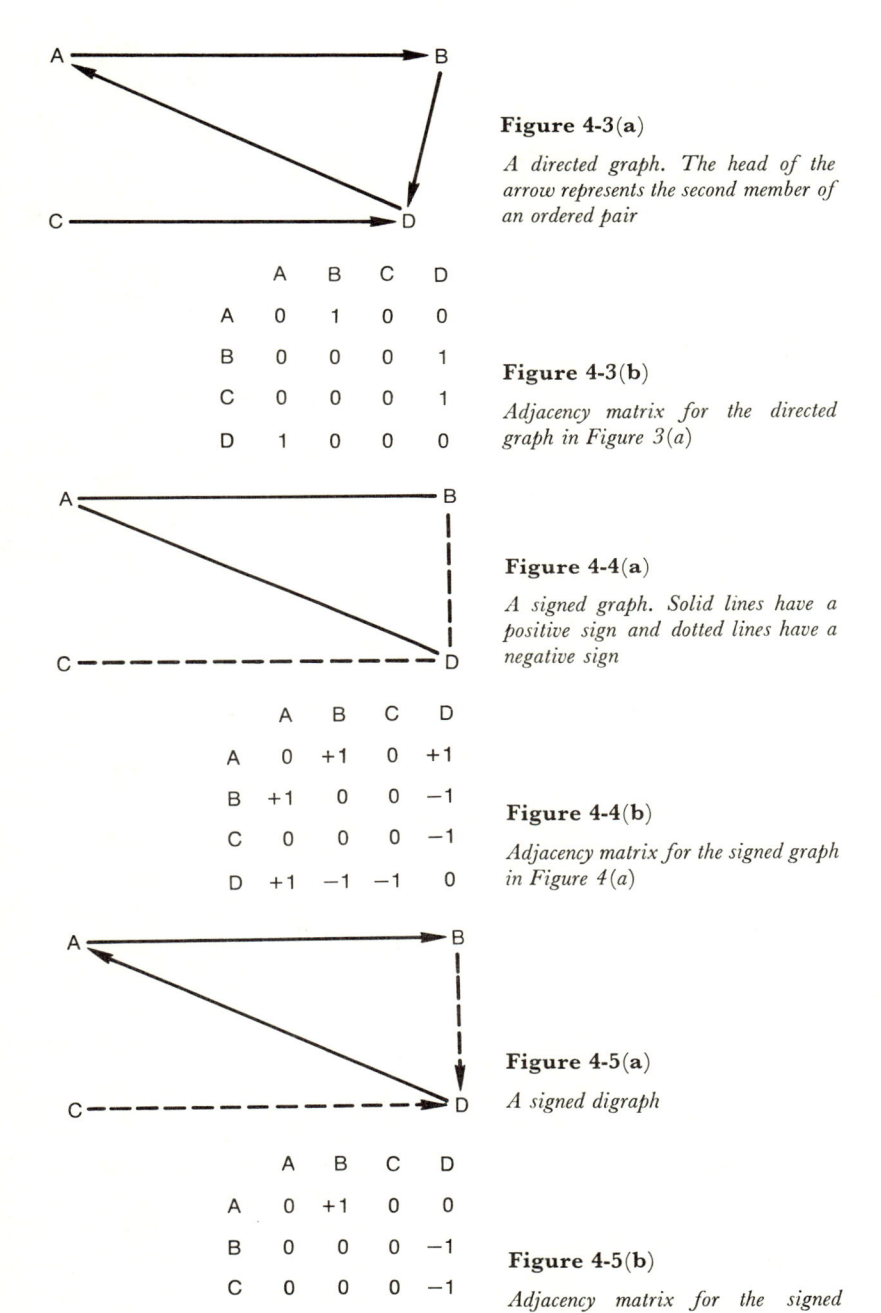

Figure 4-3(a)

A directed graph. The head of the arrow represents the second member of an ordered pair

	A	B	C	D
A	0	1	0	0
B	0	0	0	1
C	0	0	0	1
D	1	0	0	0

Figure 4-3(b)

Adjacency matrix for the directed graph in Figure 3(a)

Figure 4-4(a)

A signed graph. Solid lines have a positive sign and dotted lines have a negative sign

	A	B	C	D
A	0	+1	0	+1
B	+1	0	0	−1
C	0	0	0	−1
D	+1	−1	−1	0

Figure 4-4(b)

Adjacency matrix for the signed graph in Figure 4(a)

Figure 4-5(a)

A signed digraph

	A	B	C	D
A	0	+1	0	0
B	0	0	0	−1
C	0	0	0	−1
D	+1	0	0	0

Figure 4-5(b)

Adjacency matrix for the signed digraph in Figure 5(a)

A *cycle* is a path that is closed—that is, the second point of the last pair is the first point of the first pair; in Figure 4-1 *AC, CD, DA* is a cycle.

In a signed graph, the *sign of a cycle* may be defined; it is the product of the signs of its lines. If there are an even number of negative lines in a cycle, the sign of that cycle will be positive; an odd number of negative lines will yield a negative sign. In Figure 4-4 the sign of the cycle *AB, BD, DA* is negative.

Translating from Theory to Model. In applying this model to Heider's theory, Cartwright and Harary use points to represent persons or things and lines to represent evaluations. Positive and negative evaluations can be represented by positive and negative lines in a signed graph; directed lines represent evaluation *by* the first member *of* the second member of a pair. In Figure 4-5, *A* likes *B* and *D* likes *A*; *B* and *C* both dislike *D*. *Balance* can then be defined as present in a cycle when the sign of the cycle is positive. If the sign of a cycle is negative, the cycle is *imbalanced*. Cartwright and Harary extend the discussion to sets of more than three people, by defining a *balanced graph* as one in which all of the cycles are positive.

Translation Diagram 4-1 applies to this model.

Translation Diagram 4-1

THEORY   MODEL

Variables

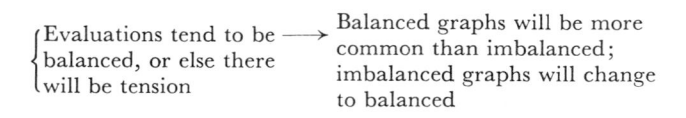

People	⟶	Points
Evaluations	⟶	Directed signed lines
Balance	⟶	Cycle with a positive sign
Imbalance	⟶	Cycle with a negative sign
Balanced system	⟶	Graph of four or more points, all of the cycles of which are positive

Relationships

| Evaluations tend to be balanced, or else there will be tension | ⟶ | Balanced graphs will be more common than imbalanced; imbalanced graphs will change to balanced |

Development of the Model. One use of the model becomes apparent during the process of translation, as questions appear about the precise meaning of some of the concepts in the theory. For example, the definition of balance in the model applies only to cycles; what about paths—

are they balanced or not? If P likes O and O likes O', but P does not know O', is P going to feel uncomfortable or not? In one sense he ought to because he and O do not share a relationship with O'; in fact, Heider suggested that a negative association could lead to imbalance just as a negative evaluation could in the same situation. However, he never entirely clarified the nature of such a situation.

Cartwright and Harary suggest that this problem can be solved by defining a graph as *vacuously balanced* if it has no cycles. A vacuously balanced graph should be neutral—neither pleasant nor unpleasant. Cartwright and Harary use this addition to resolve a puzzling question that arose out of an early attempt to test Heider's theory empirically. Jordan[4] had performed an experiment in which he asked subjects to rate the pleasantness or unpleasantness of hypothetical situations which he classified as balanced or imbalanced. Jordan was testing the proposition that lack of balance causes tension; he found, as he had predicted, that the mean pleasantness of the balanced states was higher than the mean pleasantness of the imbalanced states. However, within each category there was great variability, and some of the "imbalanced" situations were rated about the same as some of the "balanced" situations. This left investigators wondering why the theory worked for some cases but not for others. Cartwright and Harary reanalyzed Jordan's data with the idea of vacuous balance in mind. They found that the anomalous cases were vacuously balanced; that is, they contained a "non" relationship rather than a negative relationship. The vacuously balanced cases turned out to be midway between the balanced and imbalanced cases, and when they were made into a third category the difference between balanced and imbalanced increased. This case very neatly illustrates how a mathematical model can be used as an aid to thinking by helping to explicate the concepts and assumptions of a theory.

Another use for the model is to extend the range of the theory. Heider defined balance only for sets of three persons or two persons and one object. With the graph representation of balance, it is possible to apply the same definition of balance to sets of four persons or more. Cartwright and Harary also use the model to provide a way of defining balance that encompasses asymmetric relations (for example, P likes O but O does not like P); they point out that the model can be used to describe not only evaluations but social structures or any other structure in which relations and their opposites must be specified.

---

[4]Nehemiah Jordan, "Behavioral forces that are a function of attitudes and of cognitive organization," *Human Relations*, vol. 6 (1953), pp. 273–287. A more detailed description of this and other explicational uses of the Cartwright and Harary formalization of Heider's theory appears in Joseph Berger, Bernard P. Cohen, J. Laurie Snell, and Morris Zelditch, Jr., *Types of Formalization in Small-Group Research* (Boston: Houghton-Mifflin, 1962), pp. 9–36.

60 Mathematical Sociology

One problem with talking about balance in large systems is the difficulty one has counting up all the relations and checking to see if each cycle is positive or negative. As an easier way of finding out whether a structure is balanced, Cartwright and Harary propose and prove the following:

> **Structure Theorem.** A signed graph is balanced if and only if its points can be separated into two mutually exclusive subsets such that each positive line joins two points of the same subset and each negative line joins points from different subsets.[5]

In sociological terms, this theorem states that a structure is balanced if it is divided into two cliques, with only positive relations between members of the same clique and only negative relations between members of different cliques. In a structure in which all relations are positive one of the cliques is empty.

Figure 4-6 presents some examples of balanced and imbalanced structures arranged to illustrate this principle.

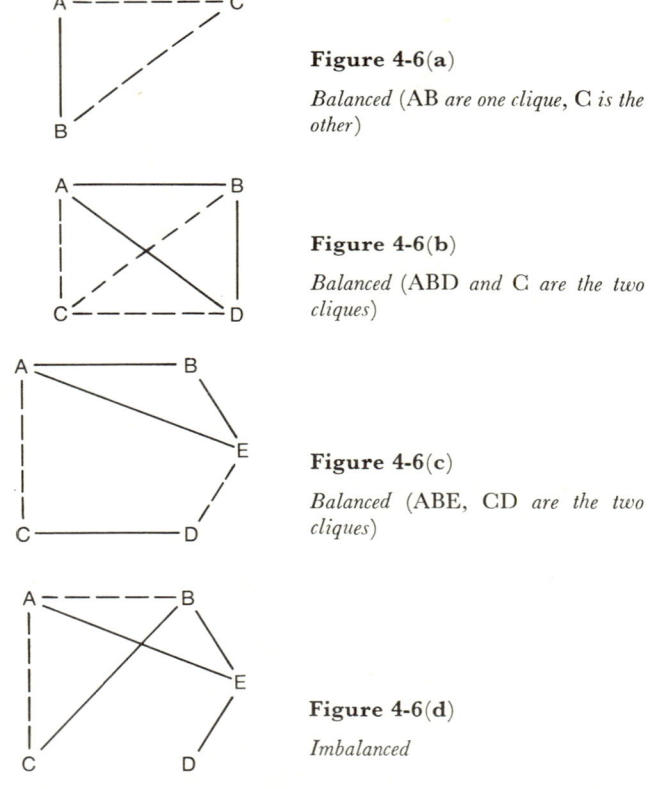

Figure 4-6(a)

Balanced (AB *are one clique,* C *is the other*)

Figure 4-6(b)

Balanced (ABD *and* C *are the two cliques*)

Figure 4-6(c)

Balanced (ABE, CD *are the two cliques*)

Figure 4-6(d)

Imbalanced

[5]D. Cartwright and F. Harary, in *Psychological Review*, 1956.

This theorem, when translated back into the theory, has some interesting consequences. Since the theory states that structures tend to become balanced, the structure theorem causes us to predict that social systems will (if there are any negative evaluations) tend to develop two cliques, with positive evaluations being confined to members of the same cliques and negative evaluations running between cliques. If a social system does not have this kind of structure, it is imbalanced, and the theory makes us predict that members of the system will experience tension. This is a somewhat surprising conclusion, and one that can be tested. It means that perfect balance is divisive for the whole system in that it produces two totally distinct cliques with nothing in common. Consequently, system integration is low when individual comfort is high, and vice versa.

Cartwright and Harary also extended their model to include a definition of degrees of balance. The *degree of balance* of a signed graph is the ratio of the number of positive cycles to the total number of cycles.

$$b(G) = \frac{C+(G)}{C(G)},$$

where $b(G)$ is the degree of balance of a graph G,
$C+(G)$ is the number of positive cycles of G, and
$C(G)$ is the total number of cycles of G.

The measure $b(G)$ will range between 0 and 1 and will equal 1 when G is balanced. The theory would lead us to predict that amount of tension in a system will be proportional to the degree of imbalance, and perhaps that the instability of a system will also.

Another concept Cartwright and Harary develop is local balance; a graph is *locally balanced at point P* if all cycles through P are positive. In substantive terms, this means that one member of a group may be in a state of balance while others are in a state of imbalance.

other mathematical representations of balanced structures

In this section we discuss two alternative mathematical notations for balance theory. We hope by doing this to show the formal equivalance of several different notations, and to illustrate the process of translating from one formal system into another, in addition to introducing matrix and set-theoretical representations of social structures.

Matrix Representation. We pointed out earlier that the information contained in a graph can be put into a matrix, as illustrated in Figures

4-1 and 4-2.[6] In small graphs we can easily see important features such as paths, cycles, and balanced relationships by simply examining the graph; in larger graphs this is much more difficult. The larger the graph, the more useful the alternative matrix notation is, especially since computers can be used to perform the necessary operations on large matrices. The translation from graph to matrix notation looks like this:

GRAPH	MATRIX
Points	Rows and columns of a square matrix
Line from point x to point y	Entry of 1 in cell xy of the matrix

Digraphs and signed graphs also have matrix representations, as shown in Figures 4-3, 4-4, and 4-5. In a digraph (Figure 4-3), an entry in cell ij indicates a line from point i to point j. Since there is not necessarily a line from point j back to point i, the adjacency matrix of a digraph will not usually be symmetrical.

In the adjacency matrix representing a signed graph, entries of $+1$ and -1 indicate the sign of the line between i and j [see Figure 4-4(b)]. A signed digraph may be represented by combining the two [see Figure 4-5(b)].

In an adjacency matrix M, a *path* from i to k to j will be indicated by an entry in the ikth cell of M^2. This is because the entry in the ikth cell of M^2 is equal to

$$c_{ik} = c_{ij}c_{jk},$$ where c_{ij} is the entry in the ijth cell of M.

If there is no line from i to j, or no line from j to k, for at least one j, the value of c_{ik} will be zero. In other words, $c_{ik} = 0$ if and only if there is a two-step path from i to k. Similarly, the existence of at least one three-step path from i to k is indicated by an entry in the ikth cell of M^3.

Since in a matrix with p points there are at most $p - 1$ steps from any one point to any other, the longest possible path is $p - 1$ steps in length. Therefore, if any path exists between two points in a graph of p points, it must be indicated by a nonzero entry in one of the matrices $M^2, M^3, \ldots, M^{p-1}$.

The matrix

$$R = (I + M + M^2 + \cdots + M^{p-1})$$

[6]Harary, Norman, and Cartwright, *Structural Models*, chap. 5, presents an extensive discussion of matrix representation of graphs.

graphs, matrices, and structural balance 63

is called the *reachability matrix* for the graph whose adjacency matrix is M. An entry in cell ij of R indicates that there is at least one path from i to j. The identity matrix I is included because by definition any point is reachable from itself.

A cycle in a graph is a path that begins and ends on the same point. In matrix notation, the existence of a cycle of two steps beginning and ending on point i is indicated by an entry of the diagonal of M^2. The existence of an entry in the iith cell on the diagonal of $R - I$ (subtracting the identity matrix which only indicates cycles of one step) will indicate the existence of at least one cycle through point i.[7]

Next we need to know how to translate "balance" into matrix notation. One thing we know about balance is that, according to the structure theorem, if a graph is balanced its points can be divided into two discrete sets, within each of which are only positive relations (or no relations) and between which are only negative relations (or no relations). Take the balance structure in Figure 4-6(c), for example. In matrix form this is Figure 4-7.

The two cliques in Figure 4-6 are *ABC* and *D*. By using elementary matrix operations of transposing rows and columns we can segregate the cliques in the matrix, producing Figure 4-8.

In a balanced structure, the structure theorem tells us that the adja-

	A	B	C	D	E
A	0	+1	−1	0	+1
B	+1	0	0	0	+1
C	−1	0	0	+1	0
D	0	0	+1	0	−1
E	+1	+1	0	−1	0

Figure 4-7
Adjacency matrix for a balanced graph

	A	B	E	C	D
A	0	+1	+1	−1	0
B	+1	0	+1	0	0
E	+1	+1	0	0	−1
C	−1	0	0	0	+1
D	0	0	−1	+1	0

Figure 4-8
Matrix in Figure 4-7, rearranged to show the cliques

[7]The number on the diagonal will indicate the number of cycles, but will include cycles that pass through the same point more than once; for example, a cycle that goes from i to j, back to i, then to k, back to i again will be counted as a three-step cycle from i. Finding the number of cycles that pass through each point only once is more complicated. Techniques for doing it are presented in Harary, Norman, and Cartwright, *Structural Models*, pp. 141–157.

cency matrix can be divided into four submatrices—two square ones with entries of $+1$ or 0, and two nonsquare ones with entries of -1 or 0. The two square submatrices represent the relations within cliques, the two others represent relations between cliques. It can be proved that a matrix that satisfies this condition represents a structure in which all the cycles are positive (this proof is left as an exercise).

Set-Theory Representation of Balanced Structures. Graphs can also be represented in the notation used for set theory.[8] To do this, we define a *graph*, G, as

$G = (X, V)$, where X is a set of points $x_1, x_2, \ldots, x_n$, and V is a set of pairs of points. That is, V is the set of lines between points.

In a *digraph*, each element of V is an ordered pair of points. The pair $x_i x_j$ means a line from x_i to x_j.

A graph is *symmetric* if for any pair (x_i, x_j) in X, $(x_i x_j)$ is in V if and only if $(x_j x_i)$ is in V. A *signed graph* can be represented as a set

$G = (X, P, N)$, where X is the set of points x_i, P is the set of positive relations, and N is the set of negative relations.

To represent the principle of balance, we can use a signed graph $G = (X, P, N)$ in which the following statements are true:

1. If (x_i, x_j) is in P and (x_j, x_k) is in P, then (x_i, x_k) is in P.
2. If (x_i, x_j) is in P and (x_j, x_k) is in N, then (x_i, x_k) is in N.
3. If (x_i, x_j) is in N and (x_j, x_k) is in P, then (x_i, x_k) is in N.
4. If (x_i, x_j) is in N and (x_j, x_k) is in N, then (x_i, x_k) is in P.

Statement 1 is equivalent to saying the relationships in set P are transitive. This representation reveals that the positive relationships are the only ones assumed to be transitive; any triad containing a negative line is *not* balanced if it is transitive.

Although the set representation can help clarify the nature of the logical assumptions being made about relationships—for example, that negative relationships are not transitive—it has difficulty representing any

---

[8] A discussion of set-theory representations of graphs and their matrices can be found in Flament, *Applications of Graph Theory to Group Structure*, Chap. 1. Chapter 3 of Flament's book discusses balancing processes in particular.

specific structure, particularly if the structure is incomplete or has some imbalanced cycles. In general, the more abstract set representation is more useful in describing abstract principles, while the less abstract graph or matrix representations are more useful in application to real sociometric data or other problems dealing with sets of arbitrary relations.[9]

tests and extensions of the model

Application to Sociometric Data.[10] The Cartwright and Harary formalization of Heider's theory leads to predictions about patterns of interpersonal choice—namely, that the imbalanced structures should be less common than the balanced structures, especially where interpersonal choices are not constrained by external requirements. Sociometric data from relatively small groups would seem suitable to test these predictions. Data of this kind, however, pose some problems, both theoretical and practical, which have led to modifications of the model. The problems and modifications illustrate some of the ways one can move from model to data and then from data back to model as part of testing a model.

The first major problem encountered in testing the model is a statistical question: how do we assess the degree to which actual research results confirm or contradict predictions? Do the balanced structures occur often enough to be attributed to something other than chance, and do imbalanced structures occur significantly less often than chance would predict? Since there are a large number of possible structures even for small numbers of people, deciding how often any given structure might occur by chance is not simple. Holland and Leinhardt[11] have presented a statistical model which estimates the frequency with which any given configuration of positive, negative, and asymmetric choices among subsets of three persons in a group will occur, given the number of positive choices each person makes. There is also a computer program[12] that will count the number of configurations of various kinds of choices for all subsets of three persons in an actual sociogram. The actual occurrence of balanced and imbalanced triads can then be compared with the expected frequency if chance rather than struc-

---

[9]Flament, *Applications of Graph Theory to Group Structure*, p. 19, suggests this.

[10]There have been many other research studies based on empirical predictions derived from the balance principle. We have chosen one sequence of research that is consciously concerned with the mathematical model as well as the substantive predictions.

[11]Paul Holland and Samuel Leinhardt, "A method for detecting structure in sociometric data," *American Journal of Sociology*, vol. 76 (November, 1970), pp. 492–513.

[12]Samuel Leinhardt, "SOCPAC I: A FORTRAN IV Program for Structural Analysis of Sociometric Data," *Behavioral Science*, vol. 5 (1971), pp. 515–516.

tural balance is arranging relationships. This procedure operates on triads both for reasons of simplicity and for theoretical reasons derived from the modified balance model it was designed to test (described below). Note that the statistical test provides not only a way of testing the goodness of fit of the model, but also a parameter by which different sociograms can be compared with each other.

Davis and Leinhardt[13] subsequently used this statistical model to test the balance model using a secondary analysis of data from 742 sociograms collected by other researchers for a variety of purposes. Most of the sociograms were collected by asking each member of a group such as a classroom, military unit, or club to name one or more other people in the group he likes, is friends with, would choose as a co-worker on a task, would choose as a leisure-time companion, and so on. The groups ranged in size from 8 to 80. The researchers' conclusion was that imbalanced sets of choices do appear with significant frequency, and that the groups do not seem to split up into exactly two cliques as the structure theorem would predict. There are often distinguishable subgroups, but there may be three, four, or more of them in one group. In particular, the imbalanced structures involving three or more negative relations do not occur less frequently than would be predicted by chance. This and similar conclusions by other researchers lead to the second major problem: how to modify the model to fit reality better.

The third problem in applying the model to sociometric data is defining the meaning of rejections and nonchoices. In the signed graph model, three kinds of lines are defined: positive, negative, and absent. In a group small enough to use for a sociometric study, however, people usually know everybody else. In this situation a lack of positive choice could be defined as rejection. On the other hand, in many small groups the members are generally positively disposed toward each other, and failure to choose someone as a "friend" or person in some special category may not indicate dislike but only lack of any special positive feeling. Since the model does not allow for a distinction between lack of any evaluation and feelings that exist but are neutral, a decision must be made whether to count nonchoices as present and negative or as absent.

Modifications of the Model. Davis[14] proposed as a modification of the balance model a version that can be called the clusters model. In answer to the question of what to call nonchoices in a sociogram, this model assigns a nonchoice a negative value. In addition to the arguments in favor

---

[13]James A. Davis and Samuel Leinhardt, "The structure of positive interpersonal relations in small groups," in *Sociological Theories in Progress*, ed. Joseph Berger, Morris Zelditch, Jr., and Bo Anderson, vol. 2 (Boston: Houghton-Mifflin, 1972).

[14]James A. Davis, "Clustering and structural balance in graphs," *Human Relations*, vol. 20 (1967), pp. 181–187.

of such a solution already mentioned, this has the mathematical advantage of providing a completely connected graph to work with, since there are no pairs of points between which a line does not exist. Having a completely connected graph simplifies the analysis of the structure; how it does this will be explained later.

Noting that the biggest empirical problem with the balance model is its inability to predict the occurrence of structures with several negative relations, Davis retains the assumption that people like to agree with their friends but abandons the assumption that people like to disagree with people they dislike. Instead, he assumes that the basic principle of structure is that people avoid getting themselves into a situation in which there is a set of three people with exactly one negative relationship. A triad with three negative relationships, which is assumed to be unstable under the balance principle, is stable under this principle. The only unstable triad is one with one negative and two positive relationships.

This assumption can be represented by a signed graph, in which a *clustering* exists.

> **Definition.** A clustering is a partition of the points in a graph into subsets ... such that each positive line joins two points in the same subset and each negative line joins two points from different subsets.[15]

Davis proves the following major theorem about clusterings:

> **Theorem.** Let S be any signed graph. Then S has a clustering if and only if S contains no cycle having exactly one negative line.[16]

And, as a consequence of the major theorem, Davis proves that the following statements are equivalent for a completely connected graph:

1. S has a clustering.
2. S has a unique clustering.
3. S has no cycle with exactly one negative line.
4. S has no three-cycle (triad) with exactly one negative line.[17]

Statement 4 says that in a completely connected graph we can acquire complete information about the structure by examining all the triads, thus being relieved of the necessity of examining all cycles.

In completely connected graphs the clustering principle divides a graph into several cliques, not just two as the balance principle does. This is more consistent with the way groups actually do seem to be arranged. Statement

---

[15]Davis, *Human Relations*, vol. 20, p. 181.
[16]Davis, *Human Relations*, vol. 20, p. 181.
[17]Davis, *Human Relations*, vol. 20, p. 183.

68 Mathematical Sociology

4 also has the theoretical advantage of enabling us to simplify the kinds of assumptions we have to make about human social psychology; we are required only to hypothesize how people will arrange relationships among three people and are not required to assume that ordinary people are constantly making evaluations of complex social structures that sociologists must resort to computers to analyze.

Table 4-2 shows the difference between balance and clustering principles in triads.

When Davis tested the clustering model using the statistical technique developed by Holland and Leinhardt, and the data from the secondary analysis of sociograms, the clustering principle seemed in general to be well supported.[18] The triad which clustering and balance agree is imbalanced, the $++-$ triad, occurs with frequency less than chance expectation in 90 percent of the sociomatrices, and the one triad both models agree is balanced, the $+++$ triad, occurs with less than chance frequency in only 1 percent of the sociomatrices. The triad $+--$, which is defined as balanced by both models, occurs with frequency less than chance expectation in 37 percent of the sociomatrices, and the critical triad $---$, on which the models disagree, occurs with frequency less than chance in 41 percent of the sociomatrices. Since the clustering model predicts that $+--$ and $---$ are similar, while the balance model predicts they are different, the clustering model seems to work better. Neither model had predicted that $+--$ would be different from $+++$.

Table 4-2

Comparison of Balance and Clustering Principles

Triad	Fits Balance Model	Fits Cluster Model
△	Yes	Yes
△	No	No
△	Yes	Yes
△	No	Yes

[18]James A. Davis, "Clustering and hierarchy in interpersonal relations: Testing two graph theoretical models on 742 sociomatrices," *American Sociological Review*, vol. 35 (October, 1970), pp. 343–852. The data cited are abstracted from Table 1, p. 845.

There is yet another problem in applying graph theory to sociometric data. This is how to treat asymmetric relationships, such as: A chooses B but B does not choose A. Both the balance and the clustering model, as we have described them, assume choices are mutual. In fact, there will be some asymmetric choices in any real sociogram. One approach to asymmetric choices is to treat them as a kind of measurement error. The questions that generate sociometric data usually allow only two alternatives: choice or nonchoice. When feelings are intermediate, neither highly positive nor highly negative, one would expect asymmetric choices to appear even when the neutrality is mutual. If asymmetric choices do indeed indicate intermediate feelings, the triads containing them should be intermediate in frequency between the clustered and the unclustered triads, because they are neither clustered nor unclustered. Davis, in the study already mentioned, tested this hypothesis and found some support for it in his sample of sociograms.[19]

Another approach to asymmetric relationships is to treat them as representing a genuinely different kind of social relationship. To handle this approach we need to use digraphs. In a digraph there are three possible kinds of relationships between any pair of points: positive (mutual choice), negative (mutual rejection), and asymmetric. Adding one more relationship to the possibilities greatly increases the number of possible configurations of relationships in each triad. There are now 16 possible types of triads, as illustrated in Table 4-3.[20]

Since neither the balance model nor the clustering model makes allowances for asymmetric relationships, the model must be extended. Assumptions are needed about which of the triads containing asymmetric relationships should be expected with frequency less than chance. Davis and Leinhardt[21] propose a model that combines the clustering hypothesis with an assumption that asymmetric choices tend to flow upward, yielding a model that has clusters arranged in hierarchies. Within each cluster are only positive mutual choices; if two clusters are on the same level of a hierarchy, there are only negative mutual choices between them, and if two clusters are on different levels of a hierarchy, there are only asymmetric positive choices between them. Furthermore, asymmetric choices all flow in the same direction, upward in the hierarchy.

Davis and Leinhardt prove that a necessary and sufficient condition for a structure to fit this model is the absence of seven of the triads in Table 4-3: triads 2, 11, 12, 13, 14, 15, and 16.

This translates into an empirical prediction that these triads will occur

---

[19]Davis, *American Sociological Review*, vol. 35, pp. 846–849.
[20]Harary, Norman, and Cartwright, *Structural Models*, p. 20, show all the possible structurally distinct triads in a signed digraph.
[21]Davis and Leinhardt, in Berger, Zelditch, and Anderson, *Sociological Theories in Progress*.

Table 4-3

Possible Triads in a Signed Digraph, and Whether the Occurrence of Each Fits Two Different Models

Triad	Fits Clusters-and-Hierarchy Model	Fits Transitivity Model
1.	Yes	Yes
2.	No	Yes
3.	Yes	Yes
4.	Yes	Yes
5.	Yes	Yes
6.	Yes	Yes
7.	Yes	Yes
8.	Yes	Yes
9.	Yes	Yes
10.	No	No
11.	No	No
12.	No	No
13.	No	No
14.	No	No
15.	No	No
16.	No	No

Note that triad 2 is the critical triad in distinguishing the two models.

less often than chance expectation, and the others will occur more often. In an empirical test employing the same set of data used to test the clusters model, Davis and Leinhardt find that the clustering-and-hierarchy model does quite well but that several triads fare poorly. In particular, triads 2 and 16 do not seem to occur less often than we would expect on the basis of chance.

The partial failure of the clustering-and-hierarchy model generated still another modification of the theory, this one proposed by Holland and Leinhardt.[22] In their model, the fundamental principle is transitivity of positive relations. For any two points x_i and x_j, the statement $x_i \, c \, x_j$ means that x_i chooses x_j. In order for positive choices to be transitive, cycles must be so arranged that:

$$\text{If } x_i \, c \, x_j \text{ and } x_j \, c \, x_k, \quad \text{then } x_i \, c \, x_k.$$

If either of the first two parts of this statement is not true—that is, if $x_i \, c \, x_j$ or $x_j \, c \, x_k$ is not true—then the cycle is vacuously transitive; it cannot contradict the criterion of transitivity because the initial conditions of transitivity are not met. If a transitive graph has no asymmetric lines, the graph is clusterable as Davis defines the term; clusterability is a special case of transitivity. The transitivity principle differs from the clustering-and-hierarchy principle in its predictions of frequency for triad 2 in Table 4-3, one of the problem triads for the latter. This triad is vacuously transitive and therefore not one of the triads that should seldom occur.

Although at first glance the transitivity model seems to be a simplification of the previous models, it really isn't, because transitivity is a property of cycles and every complete triad has six cycles, one in each direction from each of the three points. To figure out whether any given triad is transitive or not we must look at every cycle in the triad, and a triad may have some transitive and some intransitive cycles. For example, the triad labeled number 10 in Table 4-3 is analyzed by cycles in Table 4-4. It has one intransitive and five vacuously transitive cycles.

Holland and Leinhardt tested the hypothesis that triads with more intransitivities relative to transitivities would be less frequent, by ranking the triads in order of number of transitivities minus number of intransitivities. As they predicted, this corresponds (with one exception) to the rank order of triads in frequency relative to chance. In other words, the more intransitive a triad, the less frequently it occurs. The critical triad that differentiates this model from the cluster-and-hierarchies model, number 2, appears in the order predicted by the transitivity model.

[22]Paul W. Holland and Samuel Leinhardt, "Transitivity in structural models of small groups," *Comparative Group Studies*, vol. 2 (May, 1971), pp. 107–124.

Table 4-4

Cycles in One Triad (Number 10 in Table 4-3)

Cycle	Values	Transitive?
XYZ	++−	No
XZY	−−−	Yes (vacuous)
YZX	+−+	Yes (vacuous)
YXZ	−−−	Yes (vacuous)
ZXY	−++	Yes (vacuous)
ZYX	−−−	Yes (vacuous)

evaluating the model

This model presents examples of problems with adequacy on all three of the general criteria, and of attempts to solve these problems. In terms of empirical validity, the major problems were, first, that data did not support the balance principle in all of its predictions—in particular, the derivative principle that groups should divide into exactly two cliques; second, when only mutual relationships are allowed, data cannot easily be found to test the model; most groups have some one-way choices. Each variation of the structural model fits the data better than the previous one in one or both of these areas. Testing the model has also led to new techniques for statistical analysis of the kind of data needed to test it.

In considering this model's performance on the criterion of mathematical consistency, we come across a problem. Since there are several versions of the structure model, the mathematical consistency of the different versions needs to be assessed before they can be compared. On the one hand, the search for new structural principles that include the old ones as special cases is an example of how a model can be revised to be consistent with earlier versions. The transitivity and the clusters-and-hierarchy models, which deal with mutual and asymmetric relations, incorporate the structural models that deal with mutual relationships only. The process of trying to achieve greater generality results in greater abstractness of the mathematics; the later models come closer to being expressed in terms of set theory than the earlier ones.

On the other hand, there is at least one point at which the various versions seem to be inconsistent. In the earlier versions a distinction is made between negative relations and no relations, while in the later versions there are only negative relations. That makes the later versions somewhat different mathematically; all the graphs are completely connected. Questions such as how "distant" one point is from another are not suitable for these versions, while they are for the versions in which absent relations are allowed. The two forms of models also have different variables; in the earlier versions lines can have three values, in the later only two. Since the variables as well as the assumptions are slightly different, it is hard to compare the two general kinds of models—to analyze reasons for differences in performance in empirical tests, for example.

In evaluating the theoretical adequacy of the models, we can point out several contributions that the development of the different versions have made to theory. One is a reconceptualization of the effects of positive and negative interpersonal relations. The structural balance principle says that people want to agree with their friends and disagree with their enemies; the clustering principle says that people want to agree with their friends but what their enemies think does not affect relationships with third parties; and the transitivity principle says that people want to agree with their friends on the things they like but neither their friends' dislikes nor their enemies' feelings affect other relationships. It appears that while negative feelings affect the structure of a group by leading to mutual avoidance, they do not affect the structure indirectly through relationships with third persons as positive feelings do. Another contribution to theory is the model of social structure that comes out of the cluster-and-hierarchy version.

This model pictures groups as consisting of several levels, on each of which is one or more equal-status but distinct subgroup. This is probably a better aid to thinking about social structure than more simplistic models that assume that there is a single hierarchy with everyone above or below each other person, or even the more complex model that assumes ranked groups but supposes everyone on the same level is in the same subgroup. All of the models provide alternatives to the notion that the best group is one in which everyone is on the same level and there is only one clique, coincident with the whole group.

Finally, the models make a contribution to theory by showing how a fairly complex social structure can be derived from a few simple social-psychological assumptions, using only three kinds of pair relations (positive, negative, and asymmetric) and analyzing only triads.

problems

1. Find the adjacency and reachability matrices for the graphs in Figures 4-6(a) and 4-6(d).
2. Find the degree of imbalance in the graphs in Figures 4-6(c) and 4-6(d). For each point in these graphs find whether there is local balance.
3. For the graphs in Figures 4-6(a) through 4-6(d) find the triads. For each triad, decide whether it is balanced, clustered, and transitive. (To find transitivity, you will have to analyze the cycles in each triad.)
4. For the following digraphs find all the triads and decide whether each is balanced, clustered, transitive, or none of these.

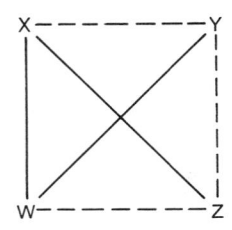

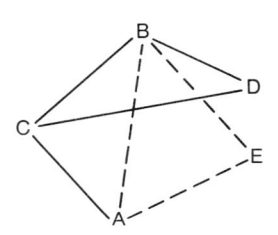

5. State the clustering principle in matrix representation.
6. State the clustering principle in set-theory representation.
7. Prove the structure theorem in matrix representation. [*Hint:* This means proving that the adjacency matrix for a balanced graph as defined in the chapter also represents a graph in which all cycles are positive.]
8. Compare the concept of vacuous balance in the Cartwright and Harary model with the concept of vacuous transitivity in the Holland and Leinhardt model, with regard to their possible theoretical and empirical meaning.
9. The problem set for Chapter 5 includes some examples of real sociomatrices. Try finding balances and clustered triads in these data.

CHAPTER 5

kinship and clique structures

Chapter 4 focused on balance theory as represented in digraph form. Central to that representation is the linkage of people (points in the graph) by evaluation (signed, directed lines in the graph). If the idea of people linkage is broadened to include a variety of other interpersonal relationships, we may generate a number of rather different models to describe and analyze the structures defined by those relationships. The basic question for any pair of points will remain whether a relation exists between the members (a line in a graph, an entry of $+1$ or -1 in the adjacency matrix) or does not exist (no line in the graph; an entry of zero in the matrix). Initially, at least, these are the only states which will exist between members of a pair.

Two quite different models will be explored in this chapter. They both begin with the types of pair states just mentioned but involve diverse substantive problems and mathematical treatments. Both employ matrix representation, however, and both require manipulation of those matrices.

The first model is concerned with analysis of kinship structures, as developed by White.[1] Second, we will examine Hubbell's use of an input-output model from economics to analyze sociometric cliques and status structures.[2]

kinship structure models

The Substantive Problem. Kinship relationships are an example of a kind of social structure that can be easily represented as a graph. In fact, a "family tree" is a graph showing kinship relationships among a set of people. Since structures that are representable by a graph can also be represented as matrices, there are also models of kinship systems that use matrix algebra. In the next section of this chapter we will describe one of these models.

If we look at a family tree as a graph, we see that there are two kinds of lines, representing marriage and parenthood. By convention, anthropologists and sociologists indicate males by a triangle, △, and females by a circle, ○ (see Figure 5-1). The marriage relationship is represented by =, and the parent-child relationship by a line. Also by convention, the parents' generation is written above the child's generation, so that the "tree" grows downward. Usually the relationship is described from the point of view of an

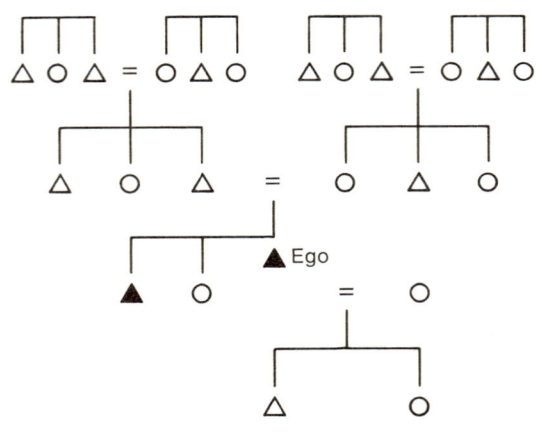

Figure 5-1

A tree diagram showing three generations of relatives

[1] Harrison C. White, *An Anatomy of Kinship* (Englewood Cliffs, N.J.: Prentice-Hall, Inc., 1963).
[2] Charles H. Hubbell, "An input-output approach to clique identification," *Sociometry*, vol. 28, no. 4 (December, 1965), pp. 377–399.

arbitrarily selected person referred to as "ego." From the two kinds of points and two kinds of lines, any relationship can be drawn; for example, ego's brother is male offspring of the same parents, and ego's grandmother is either his mother's mother or father's mother.

A kinship system is both a set of biological relationships and a set of social relationships, the social relationships being role relationships between persons who also have a certain biological relationship. Transformation of a set of biological relationships into a set of role relationships poses two general problems. First, the number of distinct biological relationships proliferates rapidly; ego has two parents, each with brothers and with sisters (six different relations), four grandparents each with brothers and sisters (twelve different relations), and so on. All kinship systems impose some sort of simplification by collapsing different biological relationships into a single social relationship. In our system, for example, if we say "aunt" we may mean mother's sister, father's sister, mother's brother's wife, or father's brother's wife. The second problem is that any pair of people may be related in more than one way. This would result in conflicting role expectations, unless the role categories are set up so that when there is more than one relationship, the roles implied are consistent.

Actual kinship systems solve these problems by placing restrictions on the establishment of the two basic relationships of marriage and parenthood. All kinship systems known have some version of an incest taboo, which prohibits persons who already have one kind of biological relationship from forming a marriage relationship. However, the kinds of biological relationships that are defined as inconsistent with the marriage relationship vary from one kinship system to another. Likewise, there are descent rules that ally a child primarily with one parent or the other or, as in our system, approximately equally with both sides of the family.

Matrix representation of marriage and kinship rules is particularly useful for societies with preferential marriage systems. In a preferential marriage system there are a limited number of kinship groups, and a person in a given group is required to choose a spouse from only one particular group and forbidden to marry persons in all the other groups.[3] The logical nature of the constraints these systems impose has intrigued a number of mathematically minded anthropologists and sociologists. The model we describe here is taken from work by H. C. White.[4]

[3]This is somewhat as if a town had four family names: Smith, Brown, Jones, and Gray. Then, if men named Jones had to marry women named Brown, men named Brown had to marry women named Smith, men named Smith had to marry women named Gray, and men named Gray had to marry women named Jones, the example would be comparable.

[4]Harrison C. White, *An Anatomy of Kinship*. Another useful reference is J. Kemeny, J. Snell, and G. Thompson, *Introduction to Finite Mathematics* (Englewood Cliffs, N.J.: Prentice-Hall, Inc., 1957), chap. 5, secs. 10 and 11.

Although the actual kinship systems White's model applies to are found among Australian aborigines, he points out that some of the logical problems these systems solve will be encountered in any formal organization; for example, in any formal organization, relationships may proliferate rapidly and two persons may be related in more than one way. In other words, a formal organization, like a kinship system, is a structure of cumulated roles. White suggests that "formal explication of principles and ideal structures underlying the aborigines' kinship systems should lead to many other insights and tools for penetrating beneath the everyday perceptions of our social structure, which too often blind social scientists."[5]

The kinship systems White's models are built for can, he says, be described by the following eight statements, which he also calls axioms.[6]

1. For a given society, there are n mutually exclusive kinship groups, which will be referred to as clans.
2. There is a rule fixing one and only one clan among whose women the men of a given clan must find their wives.
3. Men from different clans must marry women from different clans.
4. All children of a couple are assigned to one and only one clan.
5. Children whose parents are in different clans must be in different clans.
6. A man can never marry a woman of his own clan.
7. Every person has some relative by marriage and descent in each other clan.
8. Whether two people who are related by marriage and descent are in the same clan depends only on the kind of relationship and not on the clan either one belongs to.

Statement 6 is the incest taboo; all relatives in the same clan are prohibited as spouses. This will automatically include siblings, and will also include more distant relatives. It will not necessarily automatically include parents. Statements 7 and 8 ensure that role relationships will be consistent throughout the system by making sure that the rules apply in the same way to all members of the society, regardless of what clan they are in.

These statements are based on descriptions of actual kinship systems. They are thus a kind of data, and the problem in building a model at this point is to translate them into mathematical form. Much of the work has been done by the way the empirical statements are set up, and White has set them up in this way so he can use them as axioms on which to build his model.

Translating from Data to Model. The axioms concern two kinds of relationships: marriage and parenthood. For individuals from any two

[5]Harrison C. White, *An Anatomy of Kinship*, p. 2.
[6]Harrison C. White, *An Anatomy of Kinship*, p. 34 (paraphrased).

clans these relationships are either permitted or prohibited. This means that a relationship can be represented as having a state of 0 (prohibited) or 1 (permitted). Thus we can define a variable

w_{ij} which is 0 if male i cannot marry female j and 1 if male i can marry female j. (5-1)

c_{ij} which is 0 if a man in clan i does not have children in clan j and 1 if a man in clan i does have children in clan j. (5-2)

Since there are n clans, we can define an $n \times n$ matrix in which the rows are the clans of males and the columns are the clans of females. w_{ij} is the entry for cell ij in this matrix and tells us whether men from clan i can marry women from clan j. An example of a matrix for a system with four clans is shown in Figure 5-2.

This describes a system of four clans, in which men of clan A can marry only women of clan B, men of clan B can marry only women of clan C, and so on. The matrix with entries of variable w_{ij} is referred to as a W matrix.

Similarly, an $n \times n$ matrix can be defined in which the rows are the clans of fathers and the columns are the clans of children. In this matrix, c_{ij} is the entry for cell ij and tells us whether men of clan i have children in clan j or not. This matrix is referred to as a C matrix. Figure 5-3 shows an example.

The first step of the translation has been taken by defining two $n \times n$ matrices, W and C. The second is the application of the eight general statements to the matrices. They impose the following restrictions on the matrices.

		\multicolumn{4}{c}{Wife's Clan}
		A	B	C	D
	A	0	1	0	0
Husband's	B	0	0	1	0
Clan	C	0	0	0	1
	D	1	0	0	0

Figure 5-2
Example of a W matrix for a four-clan system

		\multicolumn{4}{c}{Child's Clan}
		A	B	C	D
	A	0	0	1	0
Father's	B	0	0	0	1
Clan	C	1	0	0	0
	D	0	1	0	0

Figure 5-3
Example of a C matrix for a four-clan system

Axiom 1 was implicit in the definition of the matrices; n clans means an $n \times n$ matrix.

Axiom 2 means that each row of the W matrix has exactly one entry of 1, and all the rest of the entries are 0. Axiom 3 means that in the W matrix, each column has one and only one entry of 1 (because each row must have its single entry of 1 in a different column).

Axioms 4 and 5 impose the same restrictions on the C matrix.

The kind of matrix defined by Axioms 2–5, in which each row and each column has exactly one entry of 1 and all the rest zeros, is called a *permutation matrix*. The reason is that if a vector is multiplied by a permutation matrix the result will be a vector with exactly the same elements, but in a different order. The identity matrix is a special kind of permutation matrix that perserves the order of the elements.

Axiom 6, which requires exogamy, eliminates any matrix with 1's on the major diagonal from the set of W matrices. A C matrix, on the other hand, could be the identity matrix.

Axiom 8 means that if any diagonal element of C is 1, all diagonal elements must be 1; in other words, the only permissible C matrix with any diagonal entry of 1 is the identity matrix. If any other were allowed, it would mean that men of one clan would have children in their clan while men of another clan would not, in violation of Axiom 8.

The source for this model is data, and the direction is from data to model. The data are statements that describe how the marriage and descent rules of preferential marriage kinship systems work. In addition, the model relies on some assumptions about the psychology of interpersonal relationships, especially that socially defined relationships must be governed by consistent rules. We develop the model by using these statements as axioms (Translation Diagram 5-1).

Translation Diagram 5-1

DATA MODEL

Variables

n mutually exclusive descent groups ⟶ Entries w_{ij} and c_{ij} in the $n \times n$ W and C matrices.

Relationships

Axioms 2 and 3	⟶	W is a permutation matrix.
Axioms 4 and 5	⟶	C is a permutation matrix.
Axiom 6	⟶	The identity matrix cannot be a W matrix.
Axiom 8	⟶	If there is one entry on the diagonal of C, then C must be the identity matrix.

Development of the Model. We will describe only a few of the ways White develops his models. One application of the model is to provide a complete and convenient way of describing kinship relationships. To do this, one combines the W and C matrices, using standard operations for matrix multiplication and inversion, as follows.

Suppose we want to know what the clan is of the son of the sister of a man in clan A. We can find this by figuring that, in the first place, the sister must also be in clan A (by Axiom 4). Her husband's clan can be located in column A of the W matrix; his clan will be the row in which there is a 1. For the example in Figure 5-2, this is row D, meaning that women of clan A marry men of clan D. Next look at the C matrix, in row D. There is an entry of 1 in column B, meaning that men in clan D have children assigned to clan B. Thus, the sister's son of a man in clan A will be in clan B.

The three steps in this reasoning can be used to produce the clan affiliations of the sister's son of any man in this system. The first step, equating the clan of the man and his sister, tells us where to start. This step is equivalent to writing a vector with an entry of 1 in the clan we start with and 0's otherwise. In the example above, this vector is

$$(1, 0, 0, 0).$$

Call this vector A. The second step, looking backward through the W matrix, is equivalent to looking forward through the transpose of the matrix, W^t. The two steps together imply that we have formed a vector-matrix product, AW^t. An interesting fact about permutation matrices, however, will allow a different expression of this product. The transpose, W^t, and the inverse, W^{-1}, of a permutation matrix are identical. The reader may wish to verify for himself that $WW^t = WW^{-1} = I$ for any permutation matrix, W. For reasons of convenience, W^{-1} will be used throughout, even though the tracing may logically have involved transposing rather than inverting the matrix.

Multiplying vector A by W^{-1} produces

$$(AW^{-1}) = (0, 0, 0, 1) \qquad (5\text{-}3)$$

telling us that the husband's clan is D. The third step, looking through the

		Husband's Clan			
		A	B	C	D
Wife's Clan	A	0	0	0	1
	B	1	0	0	0
	C	0	1	0	0
	D	0	0	1	0

Figure 5-4
W^{-1} *matrix for the matrix in Figure 5-2*

C matrix for the clan of the son, is equivalent to multiplying the vector in (5-3) by the C matrix, which gives us

$$(AW^{-1})C = AW^{-1}C = (0, 1, 0, 0), \qquad (5\text{-}4)$$

telling us that the sister's son is in clan B. Since matrix multiplication is associative, this is equivalent to multiplying vector A by $W^{-1}C$. The latter matrix can be considered a "sister's son" matrix; it describes the permutation that transforms a man's clan into his sister's son's clan. This matrix appears in Figure 5-5.

As we have seen, the inverse of the W matrix transforms a woman's clan into her husband's. Similarly, the inverse of the C matrix transforms a child's clan into its father's clan. By multiplying the four matrices W, W^{-1}, C, and C^{-1} by each other in the appropriate order, we may identify the clan of any relative of ego by blood or marriage or combination thereof. For example, ego's grandchildren's clan is C^2 and his great-grandchildren's clan is C^3.

Another way White uses the model is to analyze marriage rules. For example, one type of marriage rule prohibits marriage with some kinds of cousins while encouraging it with others. He shows that marriage with a father's brother's daughter must always be prohibited in a system described by the eight axioms, regardless of what other cousins may be preferred or prohibited by the specific marriage rules of the system. For example, if the preferred marriage for a man is with his mother's brother's daughter, this is indicated in the matrix notation as

$$W = C^{-1}WC. \qquad (5\text{-}5)$$

This means that a man's wife's clan must be the same as the clan of his mother's brother's child, which we derive by the following steps:

Father's clan is found by using C^{-1},
Mother's clan is found by using $C^{-1}W$,
Her brother is also in the clan found by using $C^{-1}W$,
His daughter is in $C^{-1}WC$.

His Sister's Son's Clan

		A	B	C	D
Man's Clan	A	0	1	0	0
	B	0	0	1	0
	C	0	0	0	1
	D	1	0	0	0

Figure 5-5

$(W^{-1}C)$ *for the matrices in Figures 5-2 and 5-3*

If this matrix tells us the man's wife's clan, it must be the same matrix as the W matrix.

The representation for father's brother's daughter is found as follows:

$$\text{father's clan} = C^{-1},$$
$$\text{father's brother's clan} = \text{same as father, } C^{-1},$$
$$\text{father's brother's daughter's clan} = C^{-1}C.$$

From the definition of matrix inverses, however, we know that $C^{-1}C = I$. Axiom 6 prohibits the identity matrix from being a W matrix. In other words, in any system in which the eight axioms hold, marriage with the father's brother's daughter or any woman in her clan should be prohibited.

The same kind of analysis can be applied to other kinds of marriage rules—for example, rules preferring marriage with the mother's mother's brother's son's daughter, and rules which state that clans must exchange wives. Societies whose marriage rules seem to be different may turn out to have the same formal structure, and variations among societies in the ways the clans are related to each other will appear when the kinship systems are compared using these models.

Another way White uses his model is to prove that in any system with n clans there is some power p of C such that $C^p = I$, $1 \leq p \leq n$. This can be proved as follows:

Suppose the C matrix is the identity matrix: $C = I$. In other words, a man's sons are in his clan. Then, by assumption 8, their sons must be in that clan, and $C^2 = I$. Their grandsons are also in the same clan, $C^3 = I$, and so forth.

Suppose the C matrix is not the identity matrix: $C \neq I$. Then it is possible that $C^2 = I$. If this is true, then $C^4 = I$, because $(C^2)^2 = I$ by axiom 8. (In other words, if a man's grandsons are in his clan, their grandsons must be too.) If $C^3 = I$, then $(C^3)^3 = I$ by the same reasoning, and so on for other powers of C. Furthermore, if none of the powers of C, C^2, C^3, ..., C^{n-1} is equal to I, that means no succeeding generation of sons has duplicated the clan of the man we started with. If $C^n \neq I$, there must be more than n clans, which is contrary to axiom 1.

Thus, $C^p = I$ for some p, where $1 \leq p \leq n$. The same conclusion holds for powers of W and for powers of products of C and W.

In substantive terms, this means that the generations cycle so that a person is always in the same clan as some ancestor and some descendant and that the number of generations required to complete a cycle is at most the number of clans. In other words, the very rules that divide the society into mutually exclusive groups in the short run integrate all of these groups into the system in the long run. It is especially interesting to note that axiom 8, which assumes "universalistic" rules (all groups must be treated alike) is necessary to derive this proposition.

Testing the Model. The tests of this model that White presents are restricted to secondary analysis of ethnographic reports. One way to generate testable predictions is to assume that an individual will apply the same kinship term to all of his relatives who are in the same clan; thus, if "mother's brother's daughter" and "mother's mother's brother's son's daughter" are called by the same kinship term, we can predict that they are in the same clan. This equivalence would require that $C^{-1}WC = C^{-1}WC^{-1}WCC$, and we should be able to derive the C and W matrices from a set of descriptions of categories of relatives that are classed together. The matrices should follow the principles stated in the eight axioms. White finds that, in fact, he can develop C and W matrices with the appropriate characteristics from descriptions of the kinship terminology of several societies.

Another possible test is to figure out what the W matrix ought to be, given the kinship terminology, and then see if marriages actually follow the derived pattern. In any society to which these models apply, marriage with the father's brother's daughter should not occur; there will be other restrictions which will vary from one system to another. This sort of hypothesis is more difficult to test because the demographic data are scarce. White presents data from several cases, however, and finds support for his predictions. He also finds exceptions, which could be due to people's failure to follow the rules of the society, to the existence of two or more sets of rules, or to failure of the model to describe the rules accurately.

Evaluation of the Model. Mathematically, this is one of the most elegant and sophisticated of the models in this book. In addition to developing matrix representation of a particular kind of kinship system, White discusses the relationship of graph models to the matrix models and shows how both are examples of the more general mathematical concept of "group." In mathematics, as contrasted with sociology, a group is a clearly defined concept with agreed-upon properties. The term refers to a set of elements and an operation by which pairs of those elements can be combined, and in which (a) the result of combining two elements under the operation is another element of the set, (b) the operation is associative, (c) there is an identity element, and (d) there is an inverse element. Permutation matrices under the operation of matrix multiplication form a group; if you multiply two permutation matrices you get another permutation matrix, matrix multiplication is associative, the identity matrix is the identity element, and inverse matrices are defined. There are many other examples of mathematical groups; one is the integers under the operation of addition (the identity element is 0, and the inverse of integer X is $-X$), and the real numbers under the operation of multiplication. Recognition of the relationship of his specific model to more general mathematical concepts makes available to the researcher all the results of the efforts of mathematicians to describe the characteristics of the more general concept, and White is able to use some of these results in developing his model.

Since the primary aim of White's book is the mathematical development of the model, the empirical side is less well developed. The tests discussed present several interesting problems. One is how to use demographic data, for example the distribution of marriages between different kinds of relatives, to test a structural model. Demographic data usually require some sort of statistical model, assuming an underlying random variable, whereas the structural model assumes no random variation. The same problem appeared in the development of the structural balance models presented in the previous chapter, and it is possible that some of the techniques used for those models would be useful here, too.

Another problem is how to interpret negative results, should they appear. If, for example, the distribution of marriages does not seem to follow the pattern the model predicts, this could be either because the assumptions of the model are incorrect or because the natives are not following the rules they say they have. When the researcher is restricted to secondary analysis of data collected by other people, it may not be possible to settle this issue.

In the area of theory, this model attacks the same kind of question as did the structural models in the previous chapter: how can assumptions about individual and interpersonal psychology be used to develop theories about larger social structures? In this case, for example, the assumption that individuals require clear and consistent rules in order to be able to fulfill role obligations (White's axiom 8) has consequences for the organization of the whole system. These models also can be used to help answer the question of what consequences the incest taboo has for the organization of kinship groups. White also suggests that, while formal organization in our society may not look much like Australian kinship systems, they may have some of the same requirements on the interpersonal and individual level, and that techniques developed for this model may help develop models for them too.

analyzing cliques and status structures

The next example illustrates two potentially useful aspects of mathematical models. First, it involves carrying a particular line of work further by representing it mathematically, then finding a general solution rather than the previously employed arbitrary solutions to certain problems of analysis. Second, finding the general solution was made relatively easy because the mathematical formulation was found to be identical to an existing problem in mathematical economics, as developed by Leontief.[7]

The Substantive Problem. For many years, since the intriguing work of J. L. Moreno,[8] sociologists and social psychologists have been interested in summarizing the implications of sociometric choice data. Typically such data represent the answers of a set of people (such as members of a school class, or inmates of a correctional institution) to questions such as "Who do you like most in this group?" Two kinds of summary information are most often of interest: to what extent do interpersonal choices form interconnected subgroups, or cliques; and to what extent are there "sociometric stars" (highly chosen people) or "isolates" (people not chosen at all) or other distinct types. The latter question generalizes to asking about the status distribution in the group, if one assumes that an individual's status is reflected by the choices he receives. The clique question is usually approached by asserting that individuals should show greater within-clique choice than choice outside or across clique boundaries. In practice, this requirement suggests that all pairs of individuals in a given clique should be linked, for example, by direct reciprocal choice or by mutual linkage to other clique members. Some other approaches to clique identification have emphasized the extent to which clique members show similar patterns of choosing or of being chosen.[9] For present purposes, we shall concentrate on the extent to which there is mutual linkage (direct or indirect via fellow clique members) between all pairs of members of a clique.

Early work with sociometric data tended to focus on the status question. The typical approach was simply to count the number of choices received by each group member. Unfortunately, it is likely that the status of the chooser influences the status of the chosen, so that each chooser's status must be computed before any chosen status can be found. Since choosers and chosen constitute in general the same set of people, each person's status becomes interdependent with everyone else's status, and the problem appears far from simple.

Translation into Mathematics. Work discussed earlier in this chapter, as well as in Chapter 4, should make obvious that we are dealing with a graph containing a directed line for every choice. Because graphs have

---

[7]Wassily W. Leontief, *The Structure of the American Economy, 1919–1929* (Cambridge: Harvard University Press, 1941).

[8]J. L. Moreno, *Who Shall Survive* (Washington, D.C.: Nervous and Mental Disease Publishing Co., 1934).

[9]Such an emphasis is necessary in the use of factor analysis for examining sociometric structures. See, for example, Albert E. Beaton, "An inter-battery factor analytic approach to clique analysis," *Sociometry*, vol. 24, No 2 (June, 1966), pp. 135–145. The identification of cliques is still a current issue in mathematical sociology.

adjacency matrices, it will be possible to work with the matrix representing the choices made.[10] That matrix will contain a "choose" row and a "chosen" column for every member of the group, and entries of 1 or 0 for choice or nonchoice respectively. Later we can consider rejection (-1) rather than simple nonchoice, or even degrees of choice (scales rather than states).

Translation Diagram 5-2 shows the transition from the substantive problem to mathematics.

Translation Diagram 5-2

SUBSTANTIVE PROBLEM		MODEL
Variables		
Responses to a sociometric questionnaire	$\longrightarrow$	Entries in a choice matrix
Sociometric status	$\longrightarrow$	Scores based on choices received
Sociometric cliques	$\longrightarrow$	Subsets of persons who choose more strongly within their own subset than they do outside the set
Relationships		
Status input from i to j	$\longrightarrow$	A function giving person j's score in terms of person i's status and his choice of j
Clique connectivity	$\longrightarrow$	A function of mutual linkage across pairs

Let us begin with the following hypothetical results of a sociometric questionnaire for five people:

A likes B best	($AB = 1$; $AC, AD, AE = 0$)
B likes D best	($BD = 1$; $BA, BC, BE = 0$)
C likes E best	($CE = 1$; $CA, CB, CD = 0$)
D likes both C and E	($DC, DE = 1$; $DA, DB = 0$)
E likes A best.	($EA = 1$; $EB, EC, ED = 0$)

Figure 5-6 represents the adjacency matrix for the graph defined by the answers to the questionnaire. Although A chooses only B, thereby contributing directly to B's status only, he actually contributes to D's status as well by virtue of contributing to B who chooses D. Similarly, A contributes even

---

[10]For early matrix treatments of sociometric data, see R. Duncan Luce and Albert D. Perry, "A method of matrix analysis of group structure," *Psychometrica*, vol. 14 (June, 1949), pp. 95–116; and Leon Festinger, "The analysis of sociograms using matrix algebra," *Human Relations*, vol. 2 (April, 1949), pp. 153–158.

Mathematical Sociology

		Chosen			
	A	B	C	D	E
A	0	1	0	0	0
B	0	0	0	1	0
Chooses C	0	0	0	0	1
D	0	0	1	0	1
E	1	0	0	0	0

Figure 5-6
Adjacency matrix, W, *for choice data*

more indirectly to the statuses of C and E because D chooses them, and E in turn chooses A, meaning that A in a sense contributes very indirectly to his own status.

Parallel to the process of determining the clans of successive generations of descendants for the kinship model, we can trace indirect choice patterns by matrix multiplication. To do this, we can elaborate the idea of reachability matrix, as introduced in Chapter 4. If the A-row vector of W (Figure 5-6) is multiplied through W, only the D entry is nonzero. The fact that it equals 1 means that there is exactly one path from A to D which contains a single intermediary person. There are no other paths of length 2 originating with A. When all rows of W are multiplied through W we have formed W^2, which contains exact numbers of paths of length 2 between any pair of persons. Continuing in this vein will provide all paths of length 3 by computing W^3, or more generally, all paths of length p by computing W^p.

To determine the total number of paths from any person to any other person regardless of path length, we need only to add the powers of W. That is, a reachability matrix y can be defined as

$$Y = W + W^2 + W^3 + \cdots, \tag{5-6}$$

and each cell entry Y_{ij} will state the total number of paths from i to j regardless of path length. If Y were to be used in determining status, some serious problems would arise. First, j's status contribution from i will depend upon i's status as well as on the input paths from i to j. Just counting paths is not sufficient. Second, it is reasonable to suggest that indirect choice (any path of length 2 or greater) should not be as powerful a status contribution as direct choice. Indeed, the longer the path (the more intermediaries in the status-conferring chain), the less important will be i's contribution. Finally, it might be rather inconvenient to require all powers of W, since that is an infinite series.

Earlier matrix treatments of sociometric choice involved just such problems; Katz[11] recommended multiplying all elements of W by some

---

[11]Leo Katz, "A new status index derived from sociometric analysis," *Psychometrica*, vol. 18 (March, 1953), pp. 39–43.

number a, $0 < a < 1$, before computing powers of W. Chains of length 2 would become $a^2 W^2$, length 3 would be $a^3 W^3$, and so on; and higher powers of aW would become progressively smaller because $a^n \longrightarrow 0$ as $n \longrightarrow \infty$. Consequently, the contribution of longer chains would be less than that of shorter chains. Parallel to (5-7) we have

$$Y = aW + a^2 W^2 + a^3 W^3 + \cdots. \quad (5\text{-}7)$$

Each cell in Y contains the extent to which i has provided direct and indirect (via one or more intermediary) input to j, with attenuated strength of the indirect inputs. The sum of all elements in column j of Y provides the totality of input to j from all sources, hence was proposed as a status index by Katz.

$$S = YU, \quad (5\text{-}8)$$

where U is a column vector of 1's.

The Katz solution was a distinct advance. By incorporating indirect choices, the procedure accomplished the equivalent of knowing the status scores of direct choosers. Still remaining, however, was the question of how many powers of W were to be included in Y. For convenience, the first three powers were typically considered sufficient. Of course, stopping at three powers was arbitrary, as was whatever value was assigned to the attenuation constant, a.

Developing the Model. Hubbell proposed two changes in procedure which altered the arbitrariness and the interpretation of the derived scores. Rather than use 0 or a as entries in W (0 or 1 multiplied by a), he suggested dividing the total amount of choice each person made into each entry in his row of W. If it is assumed that person i has invested all of his choice in the group represented in W, then each entry in row i would be normalized by the total of that row, T_i. The sum of the new entries becomes unity. If it assumed that some portion, p_i ($0 \leq p_i \leq 1$), of person i's total choice is invested in the group represented in W and the balance is invested outside the group, then each w_{ij} would be multiplied by p_i/T_i, so that their new sum becomes p_i.

All new values of w_{ij} are consequently between 0 and 1, and they represent the relative strength of choice of j by i. For some i who makes many choices, each choice is a relatively small proportion of his total choice investment; for some other i making only one or two choices, each choice is relatively important. The normalizing of elements of W by each chooser's total investment makes good intuitive sense. Note, though, that the dichotomous state variable (0 or 1 entries in W) has been transformed into a virtually continuous scale.

90 Mathematical Sociology

A more important consequence of the transformations of W_{ij} is that as higher powers of W are formed, the now-fractional entries of W are automatically attenuated. That is, the product of two numbers with absolute values less than unity will be smaller than either of those numbers. As r approaches infinity, values of $w_{ij}^{(r)}$ (entries in W^r) approach zero. An arbitrary value of a is no longer needed.

The second change proposed by Hubbell is the use of all powers of W, including the zeroeth.

$$Y = I + W + W^2 + W^3 + \cdots + W^\infty. \tag{5-9}$$

Conveniently, the above series can be expected to converge if the entries in W have been transformed as recommended.[12] Furthermore, the infinite series has a simpler solution:

$$Y = (I - W)^{-1}. \tag{5-10}$$

An arbitrary termination of the series is therefore avoided.

The values of y_{ij} now contain all of the relative strength of choice from i to j through all chains of whatever length, with longer chains automatically attenuated. According to the earlier argument, we should be able to use the entries in Y to construct a reasonable set of status scores. Following Hubbell's argument, let S_i represent person i's status and v_{ij} represent i's contribution to j's status.[13] Then

$$S_j = v_{0j} + (v_{1j} + v_{2j} + \cdots + v_{nj}). \tag{5-11}$$

Equation (5-11) represents a linear input-output model which includes self-input (v_{jj} is included) and also a potential external system input (v_{0j}). The latter indicates that the model assumes an open system, so that one's status outside the group under analysis can influence his status in that group.[14]

---

[12] The criteria of convergence are that the sum of the absolute values of the entries in each row be equal to unity *including* the proportion of investment in the external system, and that that external investment be nonzero for at least one row (person) in each strong component of the group structure. See Hubbell, *op. cit.*, 384. For the meaning of strong components, see Frank Harary, Robert Z. Norman, and Dorwin Cartwright, *Structural Models: An Introduction to the Theory of Directed Graphs* (New York: John Wiley & Sons, 1965), chap. 3.

[13] The subscripts are reversed here compared to Hubbell's notation. He used the transpose of the W matrix, to maintain comparability with Leontief's notation, but for the sake of unification of treatment in this volume we use the notation more common to previous work in matrix analysis of sociometric structures.

[14] A considerable body of experimental evidence underscores the extent to which external status (status not necessarily relevant to or derived from the purposes of the group under analysis) influences status within the group. Structure models which ignore this fact are therefore less general.

Now let v_{ij} consist of two parts: the status of the chooser, S_i, and his strength of choice (direct choice), w_{ij}.

$$v_{ij} = w_{ij}S_i. \tag{5-12}$$

Substituting (5-12) into (5-11) and letting $v_{0j} = e_j$ (j's external status) provides:

$$S_j = e_j + w_{1j}S_1 + w_{2j}S_2 + \cdots + w_{nj}S_n. \tag{5-13}$$

Examination of Equation (5-13) should make evident that a vector-matrix product is involved:

$$S = E + SW, \tag{5-14}$$

where S is a row vector of status scores, E is a row vector of external status inputs, and W is a choice matrix as defined earlier. This matrix equation can be solved in the following manner.

$$\begin{aligned} S - SW &= E, \\ S(I - W) &= E, \\ S &= E(I - W)^{-1}, \\ S &= EY. \end{aligned} \tag{5-15}$$

Thus the status vector is shown by Equation (5-15) to be a product of the external status vector and Y, the matrix defined earlier. From that earlier discussion, we know that the entries in Y represent the strength of choice from i to j both directly (elements of W) and indirectly via all possible paths. If all members of the group had identical external status, then the status scores would simply be obtained by summing columns of Y: $S = UY$, where U again is a vector of 1's. The extent to which E differs from U is the extent to which external status will have consequences for the status structure within the group.

Thus far it has been shown that Hubbell's general solution of the two problems posed by the earlier matrix approaches (how many powers of W and what value of a?) has produced a mathematical form interpretable as a linear input-output model which produces theoretically reasonable status scores. With one further condition, it is possible to address as well the problem of determining cliques and their boundaries. The solution proposed by Hubbell provides what graph theory calls "strongly connected" cliques.

In general, $y_{ij} \neq y_{ji}$, so that precisely reciprocated choice is not typical. It is reasonable to expect that at least a minimal degree of reciprocal linkage ought to be present in defining any dyad as solidary enough to imply co-membership in a clique. The smaller of the values of y_{ij} and y_{ji} will determine the extent to which reciprocal linkage exists. Define

$$m_{ij} = \min\,(y_{ij}, y_{ji}). \tag{5-16}$$

Then any value of m_{ij} above a specifiable threshhold, ϵ, implies mutual choice sufficient to assure common clique membership. Cliques can be identified by starting with the largest observed m_{ij} and listing i and j as members of the same clique. If the next highest value of m involves either i or j, plus some other person, k, include k in the $i-j$ clique. If neither i nor j is involved in the next value of m, start a new clique with the two persons who are involved. In this manner cliques may have pairs of members who do not reciprocate choice above the threshhold, but all pairs in the same clique will have paths to each other through fellow clique members, and all those paths will be at least ϵ strong. Thus the cliques are strongly connected (any member is reachable from any other member).

Evaluating the Model. On empirical grounds, Hubbell's adaptation of an input-output model appears at least as useful as other models. He reanalyzed sociometric choice data which had been treated by factor analysis[15] and found considerable similarity of solutions while demonstrating certain results which seemed to favor the input-output model. To be certain of the validity of such procedures, however, it would be necessary to gather other evidence of clique boundaries and status distributions. Observational data would be most helpful.

Theoretical utility of the model is evident in the discussion of its development. An input-output interpretation makes good sense and provides a general solution for earlier approaches. It is, of course, questionable whether status inputs are linear, and also whether cliques can include pairs of persons who do not directly choose each other. Also, the notions of "total choice" for normalizing w_{ij}, and of external status input are difficult to operationalize even though they may be theoretically useful.

Regarding mathematical structure, the model is elegantly simple. No parameters need be estimated, although the y_{ij} act as regression coefficients for the status scores in the input-output equation. The model in no way implies a dynamic process, but it would be relatively simple to postulate that choice or nonchoice was a consequence of structural balance or of norms of reciprocity, for example, so that successive time periods tended toward balanced or reciprocal systems respectively.

Some structure models using states exist which contain parameters.

[15]Hubbell, *Sociometry* (1965), pp. 386-397.

One example is the variety of models which deal with random versus biased friendship nets (mathematically a net is a special type of graph).[16] A random net might start with the assumptions that each person chooses exactly k other persons (k is a parameter called "choice density") and that choices are randomly distributed among the population. A model could be developed which would determine via probability theory the answers to such structural questions as how many people could be reached, on the average, by starting with one randomly drawn person and tracing through his friends to their friends, to the friends' friends, and so on. The higher the proportion of the population which could be reached, the greater the overall interconnectivity in the friendship patterns.

One problem with random nets is that, empirically, if A chooses B, then there is a greater than random chance that B will reciprocate that choice. A model might be developed which includes a reciprocation bias (another parameter) to account for this nonrandom aspect of choice, and other biases might also be incorporated. Work by Fararo and Sunshine[17] provides interesting results along this line. The work by Davis, Davis, and Leinhardt, and Leinhardt and Holland, which was discussed in Chapter 4 could have taken this tack in determining the biases which preclude or make less probable certain structural patterns. Although random and biased nets will not be explored here, they constitute an interesting area of development worth exploration by the model builder interested in social structure.

summary

The models in this chapter and those of Chapter 4 provide a variety of approaches to the concept of structure, when a large number of elements are involved. The models that we have discussed by no means exhaust the possibilities, however. Particularly important developments in graph theory have been concerned with analysis of such things as communication systems, authority, power and other heirarchy systems, and preference orders. An

[16] See, for example, Thomas J. Fararo and Morris H. Sunshine, *A Study of a Biased Friendship Net* (Syracuse: Youth Development Center, 1964). A great deal of work on random and biased nets has been done by Rapoport, much of which can be found in the *Bulletin of Mathematical Biophysics* during the late 1940s and early 1950s. See, for example, Anatol Rapoport, "Spread of information through a population with socio-structural bias: I. Assumption of transitivity," *Bulletin of Mathematical Biophysics*, vol. 15 (1953), pp. 523–533; the same work continued with part II: "Various models with partial transitivity," pp. 535–546: and part III: "Suggested experimental procedures," vol. 16 (1954), pp. 75–81.

[17] Fararo and Sunshine.

excellent treatment of this work is provided by Harary, Norman, and Cartwright.[18] Another important area of work in structure is the development of scaling models; many of these are designed as data analysis techniques but are also models in the sense of having a variety of theoretical assumptions. One set of scaling models assumes that there is one dimension underlying an array of data and seeks to discover what relation the data have to that dimension.[19] Others assume that there may be several dimensions and seek to discover how many and what those dimensions are as well as how the data relate to the dimensions.[20]

For each of these many models, some basic concept of how a structure might be defined has led to formalization and mathematical treatment. Whether the model is basically theoretical or primarily statistical, it leads to clearer representation of observable structures. Also, as the model is developed, it usually requires clarification or even considerable reconceptualization of the once-foggy notions of structure which gave rise to it.

problems

1. An executive training institute is running a series of three-week human relations training sessions. The institute is divided into n mutually exclusive training groups, each composed of teachers and students. In addition to being a member of his own training group, each student is required to

[18]Harary, Norman, and Cartwright, *Structural Models*.

[19]Some references to different approaches to unidimensional scaling are: Louis Guttman, "The utility of scalogram analysis," in Samuel A. Stouffer, *et al.*, *Measurement and Prediction* (Princeton, N.J.: Princeton University Press, 1950).
Robert K. Leik and Merlyn Matthews, "A scale for developmental processes," *American Sociological Review*, vol. 33, no. 1 (February, 1968), pp. 62–75.
Herbert Menzel, "A new coefficient for scalogram analysis," *Public Opinion Quarterly*, vol. 17 (1953–54), pp. 268–280.
Karl F. Schuessler, "A note on statistical significance of scalogram," *Sociometry*, vol. 24, no. 3 (September, 1961) pp. 312–318.
Roland J. Chilton, "Computer generated data and the statistical significance of scalogram," *Sociometry*, vol. 29, no. 2 (June, 1966), pp. 175–181.
Clyde H. Coombs, *A Theory of Data* (New York: John Wiley & Sons, 1964).
Warren S. Torgerson, *Theory and Methods of Scaling* (New York: John Wiley & Sons, 1958).
Herbert L. Costner, "Criteria for measures of association," *American Sociological Review*, vol. 30, no. 3 (June, 1965), pp. 341–353.

[20]See, for example, Roger N. Shepard, A. Kimball Romney, and Sara Beth Nerlove, *Multidimensional Scaling: Theory and Applications in the Behavioral Sciences*, 2 vols. (New York: Seminar Press, 1972).
Paul F. Lazarsfeld and Neil W. Henry, *Latent Structure Analysis* (Boston: Houghton-Mifflin, 1968).

confer daily with a teacher from another training group. Teachers and students enter and leave the program at staggered intervals, so there are always new members being recruited to the institute. New teachers and students are admitted by teachers, and each new member is assigned to a training group on the basis of the training-group membership of the particular teacher who admitted him. The directors of the institute want the program arranged so that exactly the same rules apply to all members and so that each training group ultimately has some link with each other group. Can they accomplish this by using the principles of a preferential kinship system?

(In this problem we suggest the following translations: training group = kinship group; conference between teacher and student = marriage; admission into training process = parenthood.) If your answer is that they can, describe several possible structures that will work.
2. Below are three adjacency matrices (questions A, B, and C) based on sociograms from an actual group (in this case a graduate seminar).

	1	2	3	4	5	6	7	8	9	10	11	12	13	14	15	16	17	18	19	20
1								1												
2												1								
3																				1
4								1												
5																	1			
6								1												
7	1																			
8				1																
9										1										
10													1							
11							1													
12																	1			
13	1																			
14																	1			
15																1				
16																	1			
17																1				
18							1													
19																				
20											1									

Question A

"If you were assigned to a research project with one other person from this group, whom would you prefer to have as your work partner?"

96 Mathematical Sociology

	1	2	3	4	5	6	7	8	9	10	11	12	13	14	15	16	17	18	19	20
1				1																
2				1																
3																				1
4	1																			
5																1				
6								1												
7				1																
8						1														
9										1										
10	1																			
11																			1	
12																		1		
13																1				
14																	1			
15						1														
16														1						
17																1				
18											1									
19																				
20		1																		

Question B

"*If you were to share an office (e.g., as a teaching assistant or research assistant) with one other person from this group, whom would you prefer to have as your office partner?*"

kinship and clique structures

	1	2	3	4	5	6	7	8	9	10	11	12	13	14	15	16	17	18	19	20
1																				
2			3							1					2					
3		2		1													1			3
4		3			2												1			
5																3				
6				2				3												
7												2					3		1	
8						3						2					1			
9				1						3							2			
10	3						1										2			
11							2	1										3		
12	2						1										3			
13	2			1												3				
14				1							2					3				
15			3														1	2		
16											1		3		2					
17			2								3	1				3				
18	2	1																		
19																				
20		3							1			2								

Question C

"List in rank order the three people you like most in this group."

    a) Apply Hubbell's analysis to these matrices. Since the matrices are large, we suggest that this exercise is appropriate for those with access to computers that can do the matrix inversions.

    b) Draw the sociograms represented by the matrices. Compare your results with the Hubbell solution.

    c) Compare the Katz solution (first three powers of the adjacency matrix) using some value of an attenuating constant, c, such that $0 \leq c \leq 1$, with the Hubbell solution for at least one of the matrices.

CHAPTER 6

identifying causes in structures

In this chapter we will discuss another structural model, then turn our attention to path analysis as a form of structural model. The model to be discussed first has several features different from others in this book, illustrating some different aspects of the use of mathematical models in sociology. First, it is entirely theoretical; there is no attempt to test the model using data, and the direction of modeling is between theory and model only. Although the model could be tested if appropriate data were available, the kinds of data needed are not, at least not readily. In developing a model to represent theory, the authors are using the power of mathematical formulation to make definitions precise and to derive logical conclusions from assumptions in an area of theory where different people use the same term different ways. Although the meaning of the terms when translated into mathematical concepts may turn out to be not what the previous authors thought they meant, the model has at least forced a more precise definition.

The second feature of this model that led us to include it is that it uses differential equations as the primary mathematical form, and it uses the concept of marginal analysis (marginal utility) borrowed from economics. It thus illustrates a double translation—from theory in one discipline to theory in another, and from theory to mathematics. Another way to put this point is that by using the abstract mathematical form to represent two different concrete situations, we are hypothesizing a formal equivalence between the two, thus making both theories more general.

marginal analysis
using partial differential equations

Differential equations allow expression of the rate of change in the relationship between two variables when one of the variables is actually a function of the other and one or more additional variables simultaneously. Since sociologists are so often concerned with means of "controlling" for some variables while looking at relationships between others, they ought to be more familiar with this technique. Unfortunately, the variables must be such that they can be treated as real numbers—that is, continuous, ratio-scale measurements. The equations that express the relationships must be deterministic in form but may include probability parameters as variables, as this model does.

The model is one developed by A. L. Stinchcombe and T. R. Harris.[1] The basic question they asked is whether there is a mathematical way of treating the importance of various social roles so that the Davis-Moore theory of social stratification[2] can be placed on a firmer basis. That theory indicates that the more important a role is, the more recruitment to that role will be oriented toward performance, which emphasizes ability and training. The consequence of such an emphasis is inequality in the system. The particular context chosen by Stinchcombe and Harris is the question of supervision in production systems. Specifically, they set out to demonstrate that in highly interdependent production, there will be greater gain in productivity for each added amount of supervision than will be the case for independent productivity.

Translation into Mathematics. Stinchcombe and Harris are working from a theory to a model, and they have no immediate intention of relating that model to data. In fact, they specifically state that derivation

---

[1] Arthur L. Stinchcombe and T. Robert Harris, "Interdependence and inequality: A specification of the Davis-Moore theory," *Sociometry*, vol. 32, no. 1 (1969), pp. 13-23.

[2] Kingsley Davis and Wilbert E. Moore, "Some principles of stratification," *American Sociological Review*, vol. 10, no. 2 (1945), pp. 242-249.

of results will be purely theoretical. Their approach is to borrow the idea of marginal analysis from economic theory and apply it in the theory of stratification. Beginning with a few assumptions about the nature of production in independent versus interdependent groups, they develop appropriate mathematics reflecting those assumptions which allow further specific deductions about marginal productivity. Because the nature of the theory which gives rise to the model is not specific with regard to properties of variables or relationships, the model can be developed in any way which is convenient. However, the manner in which Stinchcombe and Harris discuss independence versus interdependence suggests that probabilities will be needed in the model, hence the primary variables will be continuous. Also, because there is no concern with development over time (the emphasis is on the implication of supervision at any given time), the model is a structural rather than a process model. As will be seen, relationships which are deterministic are chosen. Furthermore, they are continuous but not necessarily linear. In fact, the nature of the independence-versus-interdependence distinction gives rise to linearity or nonlinearity, respectively.

It will be helpful to review the production example given by Stinchcombe and Harris so that the development of the model follows more clearly. Their example is the processing of steel in a steel mill. There are evidently two kinds of processing: hot and cold. Hot processing shapes the hot steel by a variety of machines before it gets cold. Cold processing, on the other hand, treats the product after it has cooled. Because the hot processing must take place while the steel is still hot, either the entire chain of processing machines must function in quick consecutive order, or some way must be obtained for keeping the steel hot. The latter is extremely expensive, so the former procedure is used. Because cold steel does not require any special treatment from one machine to the next, nor is the speed with which it moves from one machine to another particularly relevant, one machine can operate relatively independently of the others during cold processing. Should one such machine break down, others may simply pile up inventory rather than stopping also. When a hot processing machine breaks down, however, the entire chain of hot processing must necessarily stop.

The authors then demonstrate that a supervisor on the hot processing line could set the entire line in operation by fixing one machine if that machine had broken down, whereas fixing a single machine in the cold processing line has little implication for the other machines. If it took a supervisor one-half hour to fix either a hot machine or a cold machine, and if one of each were to break down, he clearly should choose to fix the hot-line machine first. The consequence would be to resume production for the entire line, compared to resuming production for a single cold-line machine. In similar vein, a general superintendent who has to decide where to assign various supervisors will prefer to have his most capable supervisor on the hot line.

The sooner any difficulties on that line can be corrected, the sooner the entire set of machines will resume operation. A slow repair job in the cold line has far less effect on overall production.

Moving from Theory to Model. Here we use Translation Diagram 6-1.

Translation Diagram 6-1

        THEORY   MODEL

Variables

{ Machine productivity   ⟶ Probability that machine is running
  Supervision   ⟶ Amount of supervisory activity

Relationships

{ System productivity   ⟶ Independent systems are additive;
  depends upon type   interdependent are multiplicative
  of production
  Changes in amount of ⟶ Marginal productivity of supervision
  supervision are more   is greater in interdependent than in
  important in   independent systems
  interdependent systems

Other translations become evident as the model is developed, but the above constitute the basic ideas at the theoretical level and the manner in which they have been specified for the sake of model bulding. As is typically the case, the model is much narrower or simpler than the theory.

Translation into Mathematics. The preceding example sets the stage for formalizing the ideas of independence and productivity. To simplify the development, Stinchcombe and Harris consider the case of a machine either producing or not producing. Clearly, this is an oversimplification for some kinds of equipment, in that they might simply work at reduced rates. However, it is convenient to assume that when a machine is producing, it produces at a constant rate. The production of any particular machine is therefore strictly proportional to the amount of time that machine is operating. Of course, the amount of time a machine operates is simply a function of the probability that the machine will be running at any given time. To begin the model's development, then, assume that each machine has a probability, p_i, of being in operation at any given time.

To discuss total production it is necessary to establish separate equations for the independent machines (the cold processing line) and the interdependent machines (the hot processing line). In the cold line total production is simply the sum of the production of each of the separate machines. Since that production is a linear function of whether the machine is running, all that is needed is a sum of the probabilities for the different machines being in operation, with each probability multiplied by a factor which transforms "running" into productivity. Assuming that the factor relating production to productivity is constant for all machines, the equation for independent productivity will be:

$$T_1 = \sum_{i=1}^{n} bp_i = nb\bar{p} \qquad (6\text{-}1)$$

The terms in equation (6-1) are as follows: T represents total production of the independent machines. The subscript 1 is to distinguish from total production for interdependent machines, which will be shown in equation (6-2). The p_i represent the probabilities of each individual machine's being in operation at a given time, and b indicates the productivity which results from any machine's being in operation. Because b is constant, it can be factored out of the summary expression, which then is the same as the mean value of p except that it has not been divided by the number of machines. Therefore, the number of machines as well as the average probability of the machine's being in operation appears in the righthand version of equation (6-1).

Interdependence, as indicated in the discussion of the hot line, implies that if any machine is stopped, all machines will be stopped. It is convenient to assume that the breakdown of any machine will be statistically independent of the breakdown of any other machines. Then the probability that all machines will be operating is the product of the probabilities that the individual machines will be operating. Since productivity of this interdependent system is no longer a function of the productivity of the separate parts added together, there will be a single term converting the fact that the line of machines is operating into total productivity. Equation (6-2) gives the total productivity for such an interdependent activity:

$$T_2 = K \prod_{i=1}^{n} p_j \qquad (6\text{-}2)$$

Let us now turn to the question of marginal productivity. For the particular example we have here, marginal productivity means the increase in productivity which a specific increase in either quantity or quality of supervision will provide. This idea requires that we express the change in productivity as a function of change in supervision. Typically, the idea of marginal utility of whatever kind is treated in differential equations. It is possible in such equations to express the rate of change of a variable in terms of other variables in the system. In particular, a partial differential equation expresses the rate of change of one variable in terms of change in one particular other variable. Leaving aside temporarily the question of quality of supervision, the amount of supervision provided can be expressed by the letter c. Then the partial derivative of total productivity with respect to c (amount of supervision) will provide the necessary expression for marginal productivity. Equation (6-3) presents marginal productivity for the independent case.

$$\frac{\partial T_1}{\partial c} = nb \frac{\partial \bar{p}}{\partial c} = \frac{T_1}{\bar{p}} \frac{\partial \bar{p}}{\partial c}. \tag{6-3}$$

Because T_1 was a simple expression involving the constant nb and $\bar{p}$ (the average probability that a machine is operating), the partial derivative of T with respect to the variable c is simply those same constants n and b times the partial derivative of $\bar{p}$ with respect to c. For present purposes it is not necessary to ask what the specific relationship of $\bar{p}$ and c is, in that the intent of the authors is simply to compare the independent with the interdependent system. Therefore they are able to find comparable expressions involving the rate of change of $\bar{p}$ with c, leaving aside the specific form of that relationship. Note that the second part of equation (6-3) reexpresses the partial derivative in terms of the original productivity T_1. That second portion follows directly from equation (6-1).

Marginal productivity for the interdependent case is somewhat more complicated. Clearly the rate of change of T_2 with respect to c is dependent upon the rate of change of the product of the probabilities as c changes. That can be expressed as follows:

$$\frac{\partial T_2}{\partial c} = K \frac{\partial}{\partial c} \left(\prod_{j=1}^{n} p_i \right). \tag{6-4}$$

Fortunately, it is possible to reexpress the partial derivative of the product of the p's in a manner more useful for the purpose at hand. The following expressions restate equation (6-4):

$$\frac{\partial T_2}{\partial c} = K \sum_{i=1}^{n} \left[\left(\prod_{\substack{j=1 \\ j \neq i}}^{n} p_j \right) \frac{\partial p_i}{\partial c} \right]$$

$$= K \left(\prod_{j=1}^{n} p_j \right) \sum_{i=1}^{n} \frac{1}{p_i} \frac{\partial p_i}{\partial c}$$

$$= T_2 \sum_{i=1}^{n} \frac{1}{p_i} \frac{\partial p_i}{\partial c}.$$

Because the rate of change of any particular p with respect to c contains the product of all remaining p's, the reexpression of equation (6-4) initially requires a sum of terms involving $(n-1)$ p's in a product times the partial of the remaining p with respect to c. By multiplying those products by the remaining p term (which requires dividing by that term as well), all product portions of the expression are made equal and can be factored out of the summary portion of the expression. Therefore the first part becomes identical with equation (6-2) and can be restated as T_2.

As it now stands, the expression for marginal productivity in the interdependent case is not readily compared with the expression for the independent case. The former has a sum of derivatives of individual p's, whereas the latter has a derivative of a mean p value. However, it is possible to state some inequalities which must hold. Consider the maximum value of p among the set of p's. If that value is substituted for p_i in the terms immediately following the summation sign, then there will be a constant $1/p$ max. This constant can be factored out of the summary part of the expression and treated as a denominator for T_2. The remaining summary portion now contains just the partial derivatives of each p value, and can be reexpressed as the partial derivative of the mean p value if that expression is multiplied by n. This is comparable to saying that the sum of p's equals $\bar{p}$ times n, although the expressions here are partial derivatives. These two considerations allow the following further reexpression of Equation (6-4):

$$\frac{\partial T_2}{\partial c} \geq \frac{nT_2}{p_{max}} \frac{\partial \bar{p}}{\partial c} \qquad (6\text{-}5)$$

Note the greater-than-or-equal-to expression in these two statements rather than simply an equality sign. This inequality is due to the fact that the various p values will be less than or equal to p_{max}, and p_{max} appears in the denominator of the expression. Therefore, the total expression will be greater than or equal to one which involves p_{max}. This reexpression of equation (6-4) shows that the marginal productivity for the interdependent case is greater than or equal to an expression which involves the rate of change of $\bar{p}$ with respect to c. It is now possible to compare this case with marginal productivity for the independent case.

In order to compare equation (6-5) equation (6-3), we must make some further assumptions. Particularly, we must assume that the characteristics of the workers and the jobs which they perform are identically distributed in the two examples, so that $\bar{p}$ and the partial derivative of $\bar{p}$ with respect to c are the same in those two cases. This is perhaps the most crucial assumption, although it is entirely reasonable for purposes at hand. It is crucial because it is not entirely likely that the selection of workers and the characteristics of jobs will be the same in interdependent versus independent systems. Nevertheless, the intent is to demonstrate the implications of supervision for two different kinds of situations with "all other things being equal." Note the convenience with which theoreticians' assumption that other things are equal can be handled in mathematical formulations. Of course that convenience must be used knowingly, or it may lead to conclusions which are inappropriate.

The assumption about identical distributions of workers and jobs allows the derivation of equation (6-6) from equations (6-3) and (6-4).

$$\frac{\partial T_2}{\partial c} \geq n \frac{\bar{p}}{p_{max}} \frac{\partial T_1}{\partial c}. \tag{6-6}$$

Now note that the right side of equation (6-6) contains the expression $\bar{p}/p_{max}$. That term will approach unity as the variation in workers' productivity decreases. In particular, if all workers were equally productive, then p_{max} would equal $\bar{p}$, and the ratio would be unity. Thus the marginal productivity of supervision for the interdependent case will be greater than or equal to n times the marginal productivity of supervision in the independent case. This conclusion also requires the assumption that total productivity in the interdependent case is at least as large as it is in the independent case; that is, $T_2 \geq T_1$.

Substantive Extensions of the Model. Thus far it has been demonstrated that the increase in productivity for a given increase in the amount of supervision will be considerably greater in the interdependent case than it is in the independent case. What about quality of supervision rather than quantity? Stinchcombe and Harris proceed to demonstrate that exactly the same procedure will reach the conclusion that (other things being equal) a small increase in the ability of the supervisor will increase production nearly n times as much for interdependent production as it would for independent production. Consequently it has been demonstrated that both amount and quality of supervision are much more important when there is interdependence than when there is independence. This was the primary goal of creating the model.

However, it is relevant to ask what the sociological implications of such a conclusion would be, and the authors provide a number of suggestions. Those implications clearly rest not only on the conclusions of the model but also upon certain sociological assumptions. Statements 1 and 2 below are the assumptions which Stinchcombe and Harris add, and the lettered substatements are the conclusions which the assumptions plus the model suggest.

1. When the marginal productivity of supervision is higher, more supervision will be used. In particular, the more interdependent the activities of a group:
    a) the higher the ratio of time spent in supervision to time spent in operative work;

b) the more likely is it that full-time supervisory roles will be established, rather than combinations of supervision with operative duties;

c) together *a*) and *b*) imply that the higher will be the ratio of full-time supervisors to subordinates (the span of control will be smaller if all "supervisors" are formal superiors);

d) hence, in an organization of a given size, the greater will be the number of levels in the hierarchy; . . . .

2. When the marginal productivity of supervisory ability is higher, recruitment should tend to be more on the basis of talent, and talent is more likely to be paid a premium. Hence in interdependent processes we should find:

a) more recruitment of supervisors on the basis of qualifications and talent, less seniority or nepotism;

b) more firing, demotion, or transfer of supervisors whose abilities are not adequate to supervisory positions;

c) more differential wages within the group of supervisors of interdependent processes as compared to the variance within the group of supervisors of independent processes;

d) more inequality in the amount of overtime by able versus less able supervisors;

e) more inequality in the informal respect and recognition of ability of supervisors.

3. When rules do not adequately reflect the contingencies of the productive process, we may postulate that informal adaptations to the reality of the situation will take place more rapidly, the more difference they make to group productivity. Informal adaptations to contingencies are a particular social reflection of supervisory ability. Hence we should expect to find in interdependent processes:

a) more communication outside official channels, backed by more urgent emotional force; in particular, we expect more flow upward of communications about problems from subordinates . . . .

b) more departure of informal, ability-based stratification from formal, especially formal ascriptive, stratification; in particular, the informal status of competent older line foremen, relative to ascriptively higher status but practically less effective new engineers, should tend to be higher in interdependent processes;

c) more departure of actual activities of different supervisors from official manning charts and job descriptions;

d) more esteem, comparatively, of instrumental leaders as opposed to expressive leaders of work groups.[3]

It is clear from these statements that an inventive model builder can use relatively simple conclusions in conjunction with relevant sociological assumptions and derive a considerable variety of suggestions for the way sociological data should occur. Again it should be emphasized that the development was entirely theoretical. There has been no attempt to assess the model in terms of actual data, but simply to indicate what facts should be

[3]Reprinted by permission of the author and the American Sociological Society. Arthur L. Stinchcombe and T. Robert Harris, "Interdependence and inequality: A specification of the Davis-Moore theory," *Sociometry*, vol. 32, 1969, pp. 19–20.

observable if the various formal and informal assumptions are valid. Therefore the model is a particularly good example of using mathematical forms to determine the implications of general theoretical statements. One interesting further development in the model, which will not be detailed here, demonstrates that the same kind of conclusion can be derived if concern is with the ability of the workers rather than the supervisors. In fact, the authors show that the fact that supervision is more important in the interdependent case in no way implies that supervisors are relatively more important than workers. Both are considerably more important in the interdependent than the independent situation.

Evaluating the Model. The Stinchcombe-Harris model is particularly convenient for illustrative purposes because it is relatively simple yet theoretically stimulating. It has subsequently been severely criticized by Starbuck[4], however, and we will consider his criticisms in the light of two questions: (1) Are there problems with the particular model under consideration? (2) Are there implicit guidelines or warnings for model building in general? A more detailed study of Starbuck's comments and Stinchcombe's[5] reply to them is useful, but we will consider only certain major points.

After a short resume of the model, Starbuck raises the following problems: (1) There appear to be dimensional confusions. (2) One of the conclusions evidently contradicts an assumption underlying it. (3) The "everything being equal" assumptions (identical worker ability distributions) and the assumption that workers do not differ much within distributions (so that p_{max} is not too different from $\bar{p}$) are unacceptable in light of observable differences in real production systems (independent versus interdependent). (4) Conclusions are drawn about variables which do not appear in the formal model.

Regarding dimensional analysis, Starbuck suggests that the p_i are indicative of productivity of the individual machines. If that productivity has a dimension of, say, tons/day, then the interdependent system will have total productivity, T_2, in terms of (tons/day)^n rather than just tons/day, where n is still the number of machines. Therefore, the presumed constant, K, must be dimensioned in (tons/day)$^{n-1}$. Clearly, this is a ridiculous dimension for a system constant. Stinchcombe's reply, however, is that the p_i were never intended to refer to amount of production. Instead, they refer only to the probability of a given machine's actually operating at a given time. There is nothing strange about K if used in this manner. Stinchcombe asserts that only by imposing an unintended interpretation on a variable of the system has Starbuck been able to claim ridiculous dimensionality.

[4] William H. Starbuck, "Concerning a misspecified specification," *Sociometry*, vol. 34, no. 2 (1971), pp. 214–226.
[5] Arthur L. Stinchcombe, "Reply to Starbuck," *Sociometry*, vol. 34, no. 2 (1971), pp. 227–229.

The argument is not as trivial as Stinchcombe would make it nor as serious as Starbuck suggests. The model was intended to discuss productivity. If the p_i are strictly defined as probabilities, then the conclusions of the mathematical work must be strictly in terms of productivity in the sense of whether machines are operating, not in terms of how much they produce. If all machines on the interdependent production line handled material at the same rate, then any one of those rates could be used to deduce amount of production from probability of operation. Such an assumption would have to be explicit in the model, however. Furthermore, as Starbuck's discussion points out in considerable detail, independent production systems differ from interdependent ones in many ways. It may be reasonable to make an assumption of uniform production rate for an interdependent system, but is the same assumption appropriate for an independent one? If not, how can productivity be compared across systems by the type of equations used? In short, the dimension problem does not exist if one stays strictly within the intentions of the model builders. Those intentions impose restrictions on the useful interpretations which the model can produce, however, and require careful generalization from the formal results. It should be evident that careful thought must go into the creation of a model if it is not to be so restricted that it is primarily an exercise in formalization.

There is one further aspect of the p_i which deserves attention. By the way Stinchcombe and Harris have developed their model, p_i must be the probability that a machine will continue operating *given that all other machines are operating* when an interdependent system is examined. Whenever any machine breaks down, all stop producing. The total proportion of "downtime" for any machine would include, therefore, a large component attributable to the failure of other machines. Consequently, any empirical estimates of p_i could not rest on time running versus time down, as they might for the independent system, but on the probability that machine i continued to operate versus failing when all remaining machines were operating. Such a probability is not a proportion of observed times, and appears to alter the meaning of p_i from that originally intended by the authors. In general, this point suggests that attention to operationalizing variables in a model may lead to problems not evident at the abstract level.

The third criticism mentioned above relates to similar problems. Stinchcombe and Harris wish to examine particular processes under an assumption that things not considered in the model are equal across the systems under comparison. This "everything being equal" capability is one of the chief strengths of mathematical models, but it must be reasonable to assert such equality for remaining aspects of the systems. It is Starbuck's contention, which Stinchcombe later acknowledges, that the real-world examples of the type of systems being considered simply do not operate so as to make an "everything equal" assumption valid. If there are systems of the type described by the model, then the conclusions are warranted for those systems, but hot versus cold steel production contains too many violations of that assumption.

The charge that one of the conclusions contradicts an assumption which leads to it concerns the variable c, which refers to amount of supervision. Setting amount of supervision in the two types of system equal, the authors conclude that the rate of change of productivity with respect to supervision (marginal productivity) will be greater for interdependent than independent systems. Starbuck argues that this inequality will, in turn, require inequality of amounts of supervision during steady states of the systems, contradicting the equality initially assumed.

The problem, as Stinchcombe points out, concerns whether one is asserting steady-state conditions at the time for which c_1 is assumed equal to c_2. If supervision were set at some particular amount, presumably less than optimal, and then an attempt were made to discover whether more supervision was warranted in either system, the model demonstrates greater added productivity for increased supervision in the interdependent case. If the systems were already operating optimally, the different marginal productivities would already have produced differential supervision. In terms of the classification of models, the problem revolves around using a structure model to discuss system change. There is no reason why the equations cannot be used for a process model of production systems, but then the problem shifts to identifying the starting place of the system(s) and the probable paths which the process will follow. Starbuck's criticism asserts that structures at equilibrium cannot satisfy the condition used by Stinchcombe and Harris. They, in turn, state that it is perfectly appropriate to start a system out of equilibrium and watch its development. Both are correct, but they are using the model for different purposes.

The last criticism by Starbuck is that the authors of the model draw a number of conclusions about variables which are in no way incorporated into the equations. In strict interpretation of the model, that is necessarily impossible. An example of the problem occurs in conclusion $1b$): ". . . the more interdependent the activities of a group . . . the more likely it is that full-time supervisory roles will be established, rather than combinations of supervision with operative duties . . . ." The premise involves conclusions legitimately drawn from the model, but the conclusion of the statement requires further assumptions about the efficiency or desirability of role specialization along supervisory or operative lines. Nowhere has there been consideration of these variables in the model.

Presumably, Stinchcombe and Harris are indicating how the results of their model can be profitably combined with what they assume to be reasonable statements derived from other inquiries into production systems. That purpose is entirely laudable. The only point of concern is with the lack of clarity regarding where deductions from the model stop and joint implications of the model plus other knowledge begin. In general, it would help both sociological theory and mathematical model development if authors of models would more often concern themselves, as Stinchcombe and Harris have done, with how their model's implications link with other knowledge or hypotheses to create still futher theoretical leads. To do so, however, requires careful statement of the boundary between what is strictly deducible from the model and what is further assumed from outside the domain of the model. Without such clarification, it will be difficult to know whether subsequent invalidation of propositions via empirical research requires revision or restriction of the model, or revision of the "facts" from outside the model.

some final notes on structure models

As noted in Chapter 1, the organization of this book follows a distinction between structure models and process models. This chapter concludes the presentation of models of structure. Before turning to process models, however, we will take a brief look at a type of model which is neither theoretical nor empirical *per se*, but attempts to provide a statistical procedure for checking the tenability of causal hypotheses in a multivariate system.

It is increasingly common in sociological writing to discuss and attempt to sort out causal relations. The most popular approach employs path analysis, which can be considered a structural model involving linear relationships among a set of variables. If certain criteria are met, then correlational data allow estimation of the parameters of the model, which are interpreted as indicators of the (standardized) amount of change in a dependent variable that is attributable to (standardized) change in a prior, causal variable.

Assume that there are a set of variables which are at least equal interval level of measurement, are assumed to be asymmetrically dependent upon each other in a specified manner, and have linear relationships. It is possible to write a fairly simple set of equations, including error terms, which specify the linear dependencies. If the relationships were written asymmetrically, but there were in fact symmetrical dependencies, then equations such as those shown below would occur. The equations are for a three-variable model, although any number of variables can be included.

$$X_1 = a_{10} + a'_{12}X_2 + a'_{13}X_3 + e_1,$$
$$X_2 = a_{20} + a'_{21}X_1 + a'_{23}X_3 + e_2, \quad (6\text{-}7)$$
$$X_3 = a_{30} + a'_{31}X_1 + a'_{32}X_2 + e_3.$$

If $x_j = X_j - \bar{X}_j$ and $a_{ij} = -a'_{ij}$, then equation (6-7) may be rewritten

$$\begin{aligned} x_1 + a_{12}x_2 + a_{13}x_3 &= e_1, \\ a_{21}x_1 + x_2 + a_{23}x_3 &= e_2, \\ a_{31}x_1 + a_{32}x_2 + x_3 &= e_3. \end{aligned} \qquad (6\text{-}8)$$

These equations can be expressed in matrix form as

$$Ax = e,$$

where A is a matrix of dependence coefficients and x and e are vectors.

The system of equations above does not have a unique solution; in fact, there is an infinite set of possible solutions. Asymmetric dependence, however, eliminates that problem. To change equations (6-8) into asymmetric dependence equations requires that some of the a_{ij} equal zero. The simplest form is a recursive system such as shown below.

$$\begin{aligned} x_i &= e_1, \\ a_{21}x_1 + x_2 &= e_2, \\ a_{31}x_1 + a_{32}x_2 + x_3 &= e_3. \end{aligned} \qquad (6\text{-}9)$$

For a general discussion of recursive systems and of the problem of identifiability (unique solution of the equations) see Blalock[6] and Boudon[7].

Equations (6-9) now state that variable x_1 does not depend on other variables under analysis. It is completely "error" in terms of predictability within this three-variable system. Variable x_2 depends on x_1 and is otherwise unpredictable within the system, and variable x_3 depends on both x_1 and x_2 as well as having some random or error variation. The coefficient matrix A is now

$$A = \begin{pmatrix} 1 & 0 & 0 \\ a_{21} & 1 & 0 \\ a_{31} & a_{32} & 1 \end{pmatrix},$$

which means that a_{ij} is zero when i is less than j, is unity when $i = j$, and is generally nonzero when i is greater than j.

---

[6] Hubert M. Blalock, Jr., "Theory building and causal inferences," chap. 5 in Hubert M. Blalock, Jr., and Ann B. Blalock, eds., *Methodology in Social Research* (New York: McGraw-Hill, 1968); and Hubert M. Blalock, Jr., *Theory Construction* (Englewood Cliffs, N.J.: Prentice-Hall, Inc., 1969).

[7] Raymond Boudon, "A new look at correlation analysis," chap. 6 in Hubert M. Blalock, Jr., and Ann B. Blalock, *Methodology in Social Research*.

To relate this system of equations to observable data relationships it will be helpful to postmultiply both sides of the equation $Ax = e$ by x' (the transpose of the vector x). The result is

$$Axx' = ex',$$

which represents a set of equations of the form

$$a_{i1}x_1x_j + \cdots + x_ix_j + \cdots + a_{ij}x_j^2 + \cdots + a_{im}x_mx_j = e_ix_j \quad (6\text{-}10)$$

Consider the mathematical expectations (statistical mean value for the population) for equation (6-10). For a terms of the form $a_{i1}x_ix_j$ we get

$$E(a_{i1}x_ix_j) = a_{i1}E(x_ix_j) = a_{i1} \operatorname{cov}(i, j).$$

For x_j^2 we get $E(x_j^2) = \operatorname{var}(j)$.

The terms "cov" and "var" represent covariance and variance, respectively. For the error term, $E(e_ix_j)$, we typically get zero whenever $i > j$, which means whenever x_i depends on x_j. Not all a_{ij} need be nonzero for $i > j$, so some $E(e_ix_j)$ may not equal zero. The term will be zero if a nonzero coefficient of x_j appears in the equation showing the x_i cofficient as unity. Expectations for equations (6-10) therefore are of the form

$$a_{i1} \operatorname{cov}(1_j) + \cdots + \operatorname{cov}(ij) + \cdots + a_{ij} \operatorname{var}(j)$$
$$+ \cdots a_{im} \operatorname{cov}(mj) = 0. \quad (6\text{-}11)$$

Because

$$\operatorname{cov}(1_j) = r_{1j}\alpha_1\alpha_j, \quad \operatorname{cov}(ij) = r_{ij}\alpha_i\alpha_j, \quad \operatorname{var}(j) = \alpha_j^2,$$

and we can define

$$b_{i1} = a_{i1}\frac{\alpha_1}{\alpha_i}, \quad b_{ij} = a_{ij}\frac{\alpha_i}{\alpha_j}, \quad \ldots,$$

these equations become

$$b_{i1}r_{1j} + \cdots + r_{ij} + \cdots + b_{ij} + \cdots + b_{im}r_{im} = 0. \quad (6\text{-}12)$$

The b coefficients are standardized regression coefficients, and the other terms are correlation coefficients. Thus a set of equations can be derived from the linear dependence model which allow solving for the b values in terms of observed correlations. Because original equations (6-7) had reversed signs for the a terms, it will be appropriate to solve for the negative of the b's in equations (6-12).

Consider, for illustration, the following three-variable case. It is hypothesized that, within a particular profession (obviously not intellectuals), income is the basis of both prestige and influence. Also, prestige affects influence. The path diagram would therefore be

$$\text{Income} \begin{array}{c} \longrightarrow \text{Prestige} \\ \downarrow \\ \longrightarrow \text{Influence} \end{array}$$

and the equations would be like (6-9) if Income is x_1, Prestige is x_2, and Influence is x_3. From what has been discussed, the first equation of (6-9) cannot be of use because there is no x_j on which x_1 depends. From the second equation, multiplied by x_1, comes

$$-b_{21} + r_{12} = 0.$$

From the last equation, multiplied by x_1 and x_2 in turn, we find

$$-b_{31} - b_{32} r_{12} + r_{13} = 0,$$
$$-b_{31} r_{12} - b_{32} + r_{23} = 0.$$

These three equations are the only ones with zero righthand expectations. They provide the solutions

$$b_{21} = r_{12}$$
$$b_{31} = \frac{r_{13} - r_{12} r_{23}}{1 - r_{12}^2}, \qquad (6\text{-}13)$$
$$b_{32} = \frac{r_{23} - r_{12} r_{13}}{1 - r_{12}^2},$$

the last two of which are precisely the coefficients for multiple regression (see Boudon[8]).

If the three variables in the somewhat facetious example had correlations of $r_{12} = .65$, $r_{13} = .60$, and $r_{23} = .78$, it can be determined how much Influence is influenced by Income versus Prestige. The respective coefficients are $b_{21} = .65$, $b_{31} = .16$, and $b_{32} = .69$. Clearly there is little direct effect of Income upon Influence. The results almost warrant the simpler chain Income $\longrightarrow$ Prestige $\longrightarrow$ Influence.

The question of whether the path analysis just presented is a good model cannot be answered in terms of whether it is solvable, since solutions to the equations can be found in any recursive case. The extent to which the model fits data can be discussed in terms of the proportion of the total variance

---

[8] R. Boudon, in Blalock and Blalock, *Methodology in Social Research*, Chap. 6.

which the model explains. Exactly as with multiple regression, total variation can be divided into explained and unexplained sums of squares, which provide an appropriate F ratio for a statistical significance test. Alternative models could be compared in terms of their explanatory power as represented by the proportion of total variation which is explained by the model. When a more complex model is used, with considerably more than three variables, it often occurs that parameters are overdetermined. This means that there are more equations than are necessary for solving for the parameters. In such a case, it is possible to use a least-squared-error criterion for determining parameters. It should be evident that if various equations which provide alternative solutions for an overdetermined parameter are in considerable disagreement, the model does not fit the data well.

Two other brief comments are appropriate. First, the solution provided above involves standardized coefficients of regression (b) rather than the nonstandardized coefficients (a). Is that necessarily desirable? The primary advantage of the standardized coefficients is the fact that they represent the relative influence of the different variables in the system without contamination from differing variances of those variables. Therefore comparison is made easy. However, standardized coefficients are not as intuitively useful for prediction purposes as are nonstandardized coefficients. Because there is only a ratio of standard deviations which transforms nonstandardized coefficients to standardized ones, the problem is not a crucial one. So long as the person working with the model understands the meaning of standardized versus nonstandardized parameters, either can be used appropriately.

Blalock[9] has presented a useful discussion of the difference between causal laws and relative importance in causing change. The dependence (regression) coefficients may show that one variable is more important proportionately than another in the mathematical relationships in that it has a larger b coefficient. However, that relative importance is valid only if there is sufficient variation in the prior variable that the relationship has an opportunity to be demonstrated. Thus, one variable may appear twice as important as another in influencing a third, but if the first does not vary while the second varies considerably, obviously the second will be responsible for variation in the third. The causal laws represented by the dependence equations indicate something about the nature of the structure, but not necessarily the relative importance of the variables for actual observed variation of the system.

Because causal analysis is explicitly intended in path-analytic work, it may be instructive to consider the implications of "cause" in the dynamic sense. A causal process may be thought of as a relationship in which change in one variable induces change in one (or more) other variable(s). The process is, at least analytically, asymmetric. That means that, even though there

[9]Blalock, in *Methodology and Social Research*, Chap. 5.

may be feedback from the dependent variable, that feedback is expressed in separate equations. The process may operate at varying rates and possible varying forms (mathematically) at different points in time and for different sets or populations of cases. Such variation may itself be considered the consequence of other causal processes.

Any causal process may be considered subject to limitations or restrictions to the extent that it is part of a larger dynamic system. In general it is safe to assume that change of a system variable cannot continue unchecked. Other processes such as feedbacks, or perhaps natural limits of the system, impose maximum and minimum values, or asymptotes (values which variables can approach but never quite reach). Rates of change necessarily are affected by asymptotic or cyclic aspects of a system. Consequently, it will almost never be safe to assume that linear relationships are compatible with dynamic model requirements. At times linearity is "good enough" for capturing aspects of a structural system, but one should always question the implications of that linearity for underlying dynamics.

Path analysis typically assumes linearity for all relationships in the structure. That in itself may pose serious theoretical problems. Even more confusion can arise, however, by considering the rates at which changes flow along the causal paths of such a system. Assuming a dynamic process implies only one of three interpretations regarding rates of change over time when the model contains paths of different length (different numbers of intervening variables) between various pairs of variables without incorporating rate of change explicitly. The possibilities are: (a) all rates are instantaneous, or (b) all paths with two common points operate at identical rates between those points, or (c) somehow enough time has elapsed that any effects operating at different rates have all run their course and the observed correlations among the variables represent a final stable state of the system.

Instantaneous change can only be considered a convenient fiction. Although some changes appear to ramify almost instantly, most social processes are noticeably slower. As to the second possibility, identical-speed paths are mathematically possible but empirically extremely unlikely. We know that some causal influences operate directly and fairly rapidly, while other ramifications of the same change operate indirectly through other variables and only somewhat belatedly affect the same dependent variable that was directly affected earlier.

The third possibility might be reasonable for "one-shot" types of change, such as the genetic effects of cross fertilization from one generation to another, or the eventual changes induced by a single major policy change. It should be apparent, though, that a model which describes the relationships of variables after the system has come to rest is not the same as a model which describes how the changes take place. For example, if X_1 affects X_3 quickly whenever it (X_1) changes, and X_2 affects X_3 much more slowly whenever it

(X_2) changes, and if both X_1 and X_2 change at the same time, then early data will show a strong relationship (e.g., correlation) between X_1 and X_3 but a weak relationship between X_2 and X_3. Later data, however, after the slower process has had time to work, will show a much weaker $X_1 X_3$ relationship and a relatively stronger $X_2 X_3$ relationship. Thus structural models which rely on relationships among variables at a given time and treat those relationships as indicative of causal processes are likely to be misleading. It is simply preferable to develop appropriate dynamic models and determine whether the data are compatible with the implications of the dynamics. It is to such models that we now turn.

problems

1. The data on income and education presented in Chapter 1 indicate that different sex and race-ethnic categories get different rates of marginal return for investment in education. What would you need to apply the type of analysis that Stinchcombe and Harris use to this set of variables? Can you interpret the information in Table 1-2 as similar to the results of marginal analysis? What kind of people are most likely to drop out of school, based on this analysis?
2. If there are only a few cars on a highway, any one car breaking down will have no consequences for movement of the remaining vehicles. On the other hand, heavily traveled highways are such that, if one vehicle stops, the entire traffic pattern may come to a halt. Analyze the parallel between Stinchcombe and Harris' supervision model and a highway patrol's problems of allocation of emergency services. Note that the amount of traffic is continuously variable, making relative interdependence itself variable. What does that imply about marginal productivity of emergency services? Can you construct an appropriate model? Do Starbuck's criticisms apply to this problem?
3. Find a path analysis (in one of the journals) which contains interaction terms. Reinterpret the solution, if possible, as representing some relationships among parameters of a basic relationship.

CHAPTER 7

*time series data
and diffusion*

With this chapter we turn our attention to process models—models that in one way or another explicitly include time as a variable. Time is a rather different theoretical variable from others, because in general we do not hypothesize that time alone has a causal relationship to other variables. Rather, the passage of time is required for causal relationships between other variables to be demonstrated. One of the generally accepted rules of the philosophy of science is that a *minimum* requirement for postulating that A causes B is that changes in A must precede changes in B. Of course, observation of the conditions of A and B over time are necessary to test such a prediction.

In some cases the changes in the causal variable and/or the steps by which a change is created in the dependent variable are unobservable, or at least unobserved in the data at hand. In this case, one can still predict changes in the dependent variable over time, but the model will appear to use time as

117

an independent variable, although it is not, theoretically. Many of the process models we will discuss are designed to handle unobservable processes. This is one of the major uses of mathematics; one can make assumptions about things that are not directly observable and from those assumptions, using mathematical reasoning, derive predictions about things that are observable.

The models in this and the following chapters were chosen to illustrate a variety of ways in which processes can be represented mathematically. One of the most common mathematical representations of processes is not included because we could find no good examples in sociological literature: the use of differential equations in which partial derivatives are taken with respect to time. Apparently sociologists do not have continuous variables across time often enough to make this a useful technique.

In this chapter we will discuss two approaches to models in which changes in a dependent variable are described as a function of time. In Chapter 8 we describe two quite different approaches; one uses a computer to simulate changes hypothesized to take place as a sequence of events; the other is a model that integrates social and biological processes by using the fact that the biological processes take certain known amounts of time to occur. Finally, in Chapters 9, 10, and 11 we present several examples of stochastic processes, which are mathematical models that deal with events occurring randomly over time.

curve fitting with time series data

Time series data result from measurements on some variable taken at a number of equally spaced intervals, which may be days, months, quarters, years, or decades. One common type of time-series data is some measure of business activity such as dollar volume of goods sold in a given time interval, which leads to the analysis of business cycles.[1] Other types come from census data and may describe birth rates or death rates over the course of a number of years. Time series data usually have been collected by someone other than the person doing the analysis, often by a government agency, and the models that have been developed for time series are designed primarily as tools for secondary data analysis. The techniques for applying these models involve fitting several kinds of curves to some time series data. Curve fitting is often regarded by model builders as inelegant. The reason is that it is sometimes difficult to assign a meaning to the curve that results; there is a problem with

[1]The analysis of time series data has been highly developed by economists. For an example in sociology, see T. Mayer and W. R. Arney, "Spectral analysis and the study of social change," in Herbert L. Costner, ed., *Sociological Methodology 1973–1974* (San Francisco: Jossey-Bass, 1974).

translating back into theory from model. There is no reason, however, that curve fitting should not be considered a legitimate part of the activities of mathematical sociology as long as some attention is paid to providing a meaning for the results.

Since the major problems with this sort of model building seem to involve interpretation rather than technique, we will begin with some comments on methods of interpreting various types of curves. There are three very commonly used curves, all of which are easy to fit to data, especially with currently available computer techniques. One is the linear relationship $y = mt + b$; this is the familiar linear equation except that the independent variable is time rather than some social variable. The second is the parabola $y = mt^2 + nt + b$, and the third is the logarithmic relationship $y = m \ln t + b$, which has appeared in previous chapters and will appear again later. Figure 7-1 shows the shapes of these curves. If there is no theory to suggest a

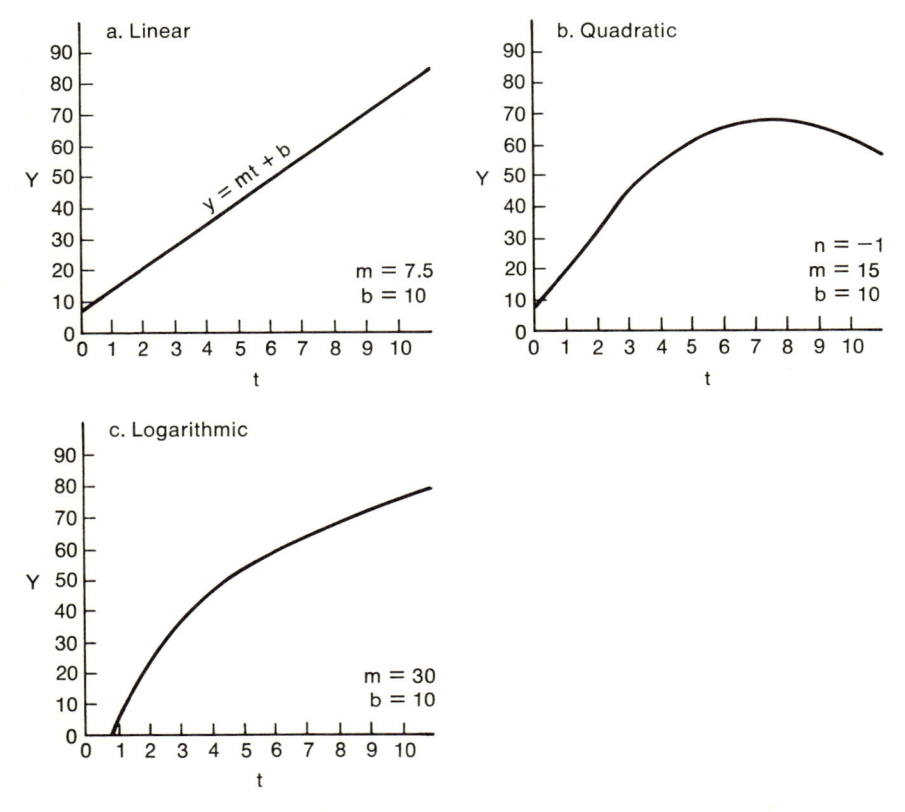

Figure 7-1

Three standard curves for fitting time series data

more complicated relationship, it is most reasonable to begin constructing a model with one or more of these equations.

Most sociologists have at one time or another tried to interpret the meaning of a linear relationship, and most are aware that this involves two kinds of questions: (1) What is the meaning of the values of the parameters m and b (is the slope positive or negative, steep or shallow, greater for one population than another)? (2) How well does the relationship fit the data (how much "error," or unexplained variance, is there)? A third possible question is, what is the meaning of the form of the relationship (that is, why should it be a straight line)? These same questions can be used to interpret the other curves, too. To illustrate, consider what meaning the answers to these questions are given in the case of a linear relationship.

In a linear relationship, values of the parameters are interpreted as the point at which the relationship begins (the intercept, b) and the slope of the curve (m). If the value of m is negative, the relationship is inverse (increase in t causes decrease in y); if it is positive, the relationship is direct; if the value of m is greater for one population than another, the interpretation is that t affects y more in one population than another. The interpretation of the amount of error or unexplained variance is the degree to which the assumptions of the model are not supported by the data. Error is usually attributed to measurement error, the presence of other variables than t, or the existence of a nonlinear relationship. The last possibility can be tested by trying to fit a nonlinear model to the data, which is one of the reasons one may want to engage in curve fitting.

It is less usual to provide an interpretation of the general form of a linear relationship, other than to say it indicates that the variables are related. It is not unreasonable to ask, however, why two variables should be related linearly rather than by some other relationship. One interpretation of a straight line relationship is that it describes a set of individuals who each change over time in a manner independent of all other individuals with no asymptotic limits on the dependent variable (as contrasted with the assumptions of the diffusion models to be presented). A straight line relationship might also be appropriate where each individual is identical to each other in tendency to change; thus one would not expect a lump at one point in time where there are a lot of people changing and a flatter curve at another point where all the easily changed people have been exhausted. A third reason for finding a linear relationship is that one has looked at data from a small part of a process that is actually nonlinear.

If a parabola turns out to fit the data best, the same kinds of questions can be asked. In interpreting the shape of the curve, note that a parabola is a "curvilinear" relationship; it either goes up and then comes down or goes down and then comes up. In either case there is one point at which it changes direction. This can be interpreted as describing a situation in which there is an "optimum" point, after which things start to reverse. A sociological example is the amount of communication addressed to a deviant in a small group;[2] for a while, the other members will try to convert a deviant (that is, as time increases, amount of communication goes up), but after a while they will give up and begin to ignore him (after a point, communication will begin to go down as time increases).

The parameters m, n, and b of a parabola can be interpreted in a way similar to the analysis of a linear relationship, but with slightly more mathematical effort required. A parabola has intercepts just as a straight line does; these are the points at which x equals zero. Perhaps of more theoretical interest is the point at which the first derivative of the curve equals zero, because this tells us the point at which the relationship reverses. The second derivative, which will be a constant, tells us the rate at which the slope changes; it can be used to compare populations just as the slope of a straight line is used. The degree of fit or amount of error can be assessed for a parabola by correlating its predicted values with the actual data, just as the values predicted by a straight line can be correlated with actual data.

The parabola is the second-degree curve of the potential series of curves (the degree of an equation being the number of the largest exponent). Higher-degree potential curves have more change of direction, and so are (in most cases) more difficult to interpret reasonably. A higher-order curve will usually fit a given set of data better than a lower-order one, but the practice of increasing the order of an equation simply to get a better fit is not to be recommended, unless there is some theoretical reason for supposing that the relationship described makes sense. If a set of data exhibit regular fluctuations, probably a cyclic model such as a trigonometric function makes more sense than a higher-order potential curve.

The third type of function typically used for curve fitting is the logarithmic relationship, which describes a variable that increases continually but at a diminishing rate. Several variations on this sort of function and ways of interpreting them will be discussed in the section on diffusion models. They are useful for describing growth processes generally as well as the kind of growth process involved in diffusion.

We will illustrate the process of curve fitting with the data shown in Table 7-1. The data come from census statistics on school enrollments, collected between 1947 and 1965.[3] The table from which we have taken our data presents information about the percent of the U.S. population of a given age that is enrolled in school in a given year. Our interest is in the late teens, when people are deciding to drop out, finish high school, or go on to higher

---

[2]Stanley Schacter, "Deviation, rejection and communication," *Journal of Abnormal and Social Psychology*, vol. 46 (1951), pp. 190–207.

[3]U. S. Office of Education, *Educational Research and Development* (Washington, D.C.: Government Printing Office, 1969).

education. For this reason we will focus on three age groups: 14- and 15-year-olds, 16- and 17-year-olds, and 18- and 19-year-olds. For each of these age groups, we know what percent were enrolled in school in each of ten years. We can look at the percentage as characterizing either the year in which the data were collected (for example, in 1951 94.8 percent of 14- and 15-year-olds were enrolled) or a particular cohort at a given age (for example, of people born in 1936 and 1937, 94.8 percent were enrolled in school in 1951, when they were 15 and 14 years old, respectively). Since the 14- and 15-year-olds in 1951 are the 16- and 17-year-olds in 1953, it seems easier to separate the variables of age and time by thinking in terms of percent of a cohort born in a given year who are enrolled at a given age. Our data are therefore arranged as in Table 7-1.

Table 7-1

Percent of the Population 14–19 Years Old Enrolled in School, by Age and Year of Birth

YEAR OF BIRTH	AGE		
	14 and 15	16 and 17	18 and 19
1932 and 1933	91.6	69.5	26.3
1934 and 1935	93.5	75.1	31.2
1936 and 1937	94.8	74.7	31.5
1938 and 1939	96.5	77.4	34.9
1940 and 1941	95.9	80.5	36.8
1942 and 1943	97.1	82.9	38.0
1944 and 1945	97.5	83.6	40.9
1946 and 1947	97.6	87.1	46.3
1948 and 1949	98.4	87.4	x
1950 and 1951	98.9	x	x

Source: U.S. Census (reprinted in *Educational Research and Development,* U.S. Office of Education, OE-12049, December, 1969)

Note: Data were collected in the period from October, 1947 through October, 1966. The last two age groups had not reached age 18 and 19, and the last one had not reached age 16 and 17, in 1966.

Translation into Mathematics. We are working with three variables; percent school enrollment, age, and year of birth. Since school enrollment is expressed in terms of percentages, it is a continuous variable, ranging from 0 to 100. The age variable is being treated as discrete and ordered, having three values: 14 and 15, 16 and 17, and 18 and 19. Year of birth will be the way of measuring time and will be treated in the models as a continuous variable, ranging from 1 to 10—even though the data are grouped in a way that treats year of birth as a discrete ordered variable ranging from 1932–33 to 1946–47. Time series data are by definition a set of discrete, ordered, equally spaced measurements on an underlying continuous variable, time.

In this case, time is involved in two variables—explicitly in year of birth and implicitly in age, which can be viewed as "time since birth." We will treat the age variable as any other sort of discrete, ordered variable, ignoring the time aspect, and will treat year of birth as time, a continuous variable.

Since year of birth and age in a given year are chronologically prior to school enrollment in that year, we can reasonably call the first two the independent variables and the last the dependent variable. This does not necessarily mean we assume that school enrollment is caused by age and year of birth, but that causes of school enrollment vary with age and year of birth and that school enrollment does not affect age or year of birth. We can observe from the data in Table 7-1 that school enrollment *decreases* with increasing age, and *increases* with later year of birth—that is, increases with time. Thus our model in the abstract is:

$$y = f(t, a)$$

where y = percent enrolled in school,
 t = time (year of birth),
 a = age.

We will further specify this relationship by stating three separate functions, one for each age group.

$$y_i = f_i(t_i),$$

where y_i = percent enrolled for age group i,
 t_i = time (year of birth) for age group i,
 f_i = function describing the dependence of enrollment on time for age group i.

(*Note:* i takes three values: 1 for 14 and 15, 2 for 16 and 17, 3 for 18 and 19.)

We have separated the two independent variables, and we intend to use different equations for each age group—for two reasons: (1) Age and time are independent of each other—that is, if we assume that data were collected with equal accuracy from all cohorts, we do not expect that year of birth will affect whether a cohort gets to age 16. (2) The second reason has to do with why we might expect different functions for the relations between time and school enrollment for the different age groups. Each age group is subject to different influences on its school enrollment. The 14- and 15-year-olds are in most states required by law to be in school and prohibited by law from full-time employment. This would lead us to expect most of them to be in school, as the data show they are, and we would also expect the changes over time to be small. The 16- and 17-year-olds are old enough to be employed and are not required to be in school but for the most part have not graduated from high school, while the 18- and 19-year-olds are likely to have finished high school. Since both of these groups are free to choose whether to enroll in school or not, factors such as increasing affluence, increasing demand for educated workers, and increasing availability of educational facilities, which have changed over time, should affect them more than the 14- and 15-year-olds. If there has been a greater increase in the desirability of higher education than in the desirability of a high-school diploma, we would expect that the increase in enrollment of 18- and 19-year-olds will be more rapid than the increase in enrollment of 16- and 17-year-olds. If, however, there has merely been an increase in desirability of education at all levels, these two groups will increase at about the same rate.

We now must specify the form of the relationship $y_i = f_i(t)$. For all three age groups, the trend is generally upward. Between 1947, when the first of the cohorts reached age 14 and 15, and 1965, when the last set of data was collected, there were no major social upheavals such as wars or depressions which would lead to abrupt changes or discontinuities in the rate of increase in educational enrollment over time. Equations that are continuous and describe a smooth upward trend are therefore appropriate. We will use the linear and the logarithmic functions. We could try a parabola, but there is no indication in the data of a downward trend following the upward trend, nor is there any theoretical reason for expecting a reversal of the trend, so we will not.

The fact that the dependent variable is in terms of percents means that both the straight line and exponential models will ultimately be unsatisfactory as predictions of future school enrollments, since there is an asymptote of 100 percent. The problem of having a theoretical upper limit of 100 could be solved by using the actual numbers of people enrolled in a given year rather than percentages. This, however, would introduce another variable into the model, the variable of size of cohort, which depends on birth rate in year of birth and is itself a function of many factors that are not of direct concern at the moment. Although this type of model is frequently used to make projections, our use will be primarily to interpret the relationship between the variables as shown in the data we have.

The variable of time is measured by year of birth. Since we are concerned with the intervals between times rather than the absolute value of year, we can transform the time variable into the series 1, 2, . . . , 10 instead of using the much more cumbersome series 1923–33, 1934–35, . . . , 1964–65.

Neither the variables nor the relationships involve an assumption of randomness, which means that the natural variability of the data will have to be attributed to "error."

Translation Diagram 7-1

DATA	MODEL

Variables

Percent of population of a given age enrolled in school in a given year ⟶ y, a continuous variable ranging from 0 to 100

Age group; 14 and 15, 16 and 17, and 18 and 19 ⟶ i, a discrete variable with three values: $i = 1$ corresponds to 14 and 15 years old, $i = 2$ corresponds to 16 and 17 years old, $i = 3$ corresponds to 18 and 19 years old.

Year of birth, two-year intervals, from 1932–33 through 1949–50 ⟶ t, a continuous variable ranging from 1 to 10.

Relationships

A. General relationship
  1. School enrollment increases with time ⟶
  2. School enrollment decreases with age
  3. The rate of increase in school enrollment over time is different for different age groups

A. General equation
  $y_i = f_i(t); \quad i = 1, 2, 3$

B. Possible interpretations
  1. Rate of increase in school enrollment is linear ⟶
  2. Rate of increase in school enrollment is rapid at first, then slower, eventually reversing to become a decrease ⟶
  3. Rate of increase is rapid first, then slower but monotonic upward ⟶

B. Possible equations
  $y_i = m_i t + b_i$

  $y_i = m_i t + n_i t^2 + b_i$

  $y_i = m_i \ln t + b_i$

Estimation of Parameters. Since we are applying a set of models that already exist and are in common use, the techniques of parameter estimation are readily available. The techniques we will use is to fit each of the three equations to each of the three sets of data by the least-squares method. This method provides a set of simultaneous equations which, when solved for the parameters m, b, and n, will produce values that determine the line with minimum average distance from the actual data points. The equations for estimating m, b, and n can be found in most textbooks on statistical methods, particularly those oriented to economics and business applications.

For the simple linear model, the equations are:

I. $\sum Y_j = Nb + m \sum T_j$,
II. $\sum Y_j T_j = b \sum T_j + m \sum (T_j^2)$, (7-1)

where $j = 1, 2, \ldots, 10$; $T =$ time; $Y =$ percent school enrollment.

For the first-order nonlinear (parabolic) model, the equations are:

I. $\sum Y_j = Nb + m \sum T_j + n \sum (T_j^2)$,
II. $\sum Y_j T_j = b \sum T_j + m \sum (T_j^2) + n \sum (T_j^3)$, (7-2)
III. $\sum Y_j T_j^2 = b \sum (T_j^2) + m \sum (T_j^3) + n \sum (T_j^4)$.

And for the exponential model, the equations are:

I. $\sum Y_j = Nb + m \sum (\ln T_j)$,
II. $\sum Y_j T_j = b \sum \ln T_j + (\ln T_j)^2$. (7-3)

The results of solving the equations simultaneously for each model applied to each age group appear in Table 7-2. Table 7-2 also shows the results of comparing the expected values for the percent enrolled in school with the actual values. Note that for the linear function, the procedure of estimating parameters and comparing observed and predicted data is simply a linear regression analysis.

Table 7-2

Parameter Estimates and Fit of Linear and Logarithmic Models

| | MODEL | | | |
| | LINEAR $y = mt + h$ | | LOGARITHMIC $y = m \ln t + b$ | |
Age Group	Parameter Estimates	Correlation with Actual Data (r^2)	Parameter Estimates	Correlation with Actual Data (r^2)
14 and 15	$y = .72t + 92.24$	.90	$y = 3.09 \ln t + 91.51$	.98
16 and 17	$y = 2.18t + 68.89$	.97	$y = 8.16 \ln t + 68.19$	.93
18 and 19	$y = 2.50t + 24.49$	.96	$y = 8.33 \ln t + 24.70$	.89

Interpreting the Model. The first thing to note in Table 7-2 is that for the two older groups, the linear model fits best, while for the youngest group the log model fits best. We noted earlier that a linear relationship needs a theoretical interpretation just as much as any other relationship; this is a good example, because intuitively one would expect the model associated with growth processes to fit what seems to be a growth process better than the linear model does. One of the interpretations of a linear relationship we suggested was that the data cover only a small part of a total process; this seems the most reasonable explanation here. In other words, it looks as though the process of growth in educational system has not started to taper off noticeably for the 16–19 year olds, who started at the beginning of the process, but it has for the 14- and 15-year-olds, who are toward the end of it.

This interpretation is supported by a comparison of the slopes of the straight lines for the two older groups; these parameters are almost the same, indicating that these two groups are changing at the same rate, and are only different because they start at different points. The slopes for both the straight line and the log curves for the 14- and 15-year-old group are quite different from these parameters for the other two groups, indicating that either this group is at a different point in the process or that there are different factors affecting the growth in educational enrollment in this group. Probably both interpretations are reasonable, since the proportion enrollment among 14- and 15-year-olds cannot grow much more, and these people have a different legal status as regards school enrollment. The similarity of the rate of change in enrollment for 16- to 17-year-olds and 18- to 19-year-olds is consistent with an interpretation that says that the value of staying in school relative to leaving has changed at about the same rate for high-school and post-high-school education. This interpretation must be offered with care, however, because the data are in terms of ages, and not everyone who graduates from high school does so at age 17.

A number of other approaches could be taken to develop models to fit and explain this set of data. One is multivariate regression analysis, in which we would use (for the linear case) a set of equations such as the following:

$$Y = at + b(\text{age}) + e,$$

where Y = percent school enrollment,
  t = time (year of birth),
  e = error.

The factor (age) must be entered as a dummy variable because it is not continuous. This model assumes that school enrollment depends simultaneously on time and age group rather than there being different relationships for the three age groups, and that school enrollment also depends on an error factor. The definitions of the variables and relationships are very similar to the models developed previously, except that this assumes a probabilistic rather than a deterministic relationship. If we suspected that there were an interaction between the independent variables, we might reasonably prefer a regression model in which an interaction term is explicitly included. The regression model would tell us how much of the variation in enrollment could be attributed to changes in time and age, but would not tell us so much about the shape of the relationship.

Which of these models will be most useful will depend, as indicated, on what other data are available and on the particular practical or theoretical uses to which the model will be put.

process models: diffusion

The time series analysis we have just described begins at the data point of the theory-model-data triangle, and it tries to develop the mathematical representation that fits best and then interpret it. In this section we will discuss a set of models that also treat change in a dependent variable as a function of time, but we begin at the theory point of the triangle and use theoretical assumptions to decide which mathematical equations are appropriate.

A diffusion model describes the way some characteristic spreads among the members of a population. Diffusion is often thought of in terms of a medical analogy; people catch a contagious disease from other people, and the progress of an epidemic depends on the power of the disease to infect and the rate at which people have contact with each other. Sociological examples of diffusion are the spread of rumors, of innovations, and of fads and fashions.

It is typical in discussions of diffusion processes to begin with a fairly well-developed model. We will start at a much simpler level so that the steps can be taken one at a time.

The general substantive problem can be stated quite simply. Given that a specified subset of a population knows or creates a message or rumor at the start of the process, and they proceed to communicate their knowledge to nonknowers with specified intensity and pattern of interaction (for example, random mixing and k tellings per unit of time), how will that information spread through the population? Various facts might be of interest. How many knowers are there after t time units? How much of the population will eventually get the word? What is the shape of the growth curve?

The intention of this model building is clearly developmental. Theoretical principles of diffusion are to be translated into mathematical form for more rigorous development. The mode of the work is deductive, although some efforts at building models of diffusion have profited by attempting to account for empirical evidence. Variables of the model might reasonably be conceived either as state variables (knower vs. nonknower), as discrete scales (numbers of knowers, and so on) or as continuous variables (the proportions of the population who are knowers, and so on). If the state-variable approach is taken, a Markov-chain type of model could be developed. Most approaches, however, have used scales, and either developed stochastic models concerned with the numbers of persons who are knowers or nonknowers or worked with deterministic models concerned with the proportions of the population in either category.

In general, the finite, stochastic systems are precise, whereas the deterministic models represent only approximations of the assumptions underlying the model. Coleman[1] has stated two advantages of stochastic, finite models over deterministic models. Those advantages have to do with (1) being able to determine the probability that a growth process might die out, and (2) being better able to test the models against empirical evidence. He then comments that ". . . these seem the *only* [sic] added advantages of the stochastic process. The deterministic model can . . . reflect the same basic process . . . much more simply."[5] We will use deterministic models in this chapter, hence variables will be continuous-scale variables. We will incorporate time into the model by treating the rates of change of other variables over time, hence by using differential equations. Feedback is specified for all but the first model, in that the state of the system at any given time affects the rate of change of the system.

Translation into Mathematics. Basic variables in the diffusion models include the size, N, of the population within which the diffusion is taking place; the number, a, of persons in the subset of the population who first start the rumor or message; the intensity, k, of communication (number of tellings per knower per unit time) and the resulting number of persons told, $n(t)$, and nonknowers, $m(t)$, at any subsequent time, t. As more complex models are considered, different subsets of knowers might be distinguished, with different intensities of communication.

To make our work as simple as possible, let us assume that N is very large, k is constant for all tellers, and we really are interested in the proportions of the population that know or do not know the message at time t. By considering proportions, we can use $a/N = p_0$ (the proportion of knowers at the start, or at time 0); $n(t)/N = p_t$ (the proportion of persons told by time t); and $m(t)/N = 1 - p_0 - p_t$. If we further simplify by assuming that new knowers are not behaviorally different from original knowers, we can combine original knowers and subsequent learners, so that p_t is the proportion of the population that knows the message by time t. Then p_t will equal the sum of p_0 and p_t as defined earlier, and the rest of the population, $q_t = 1 - p_t$, will be nonknowers. This last simplification will not be used in the first model, below, but will be helpful for subsequent models.

[4]James S. Coleman, *Introduction to Mathematical Sociology* (New York: The Free Press, 1964), p. 527.
[5]Coleman, *Introduction to Mathematical Sociology*, p. 527.

Translation Diagram 7-2 applies to the diffusion models.

Translation Diagram 7-2

THEORY	MODEL

Variables

Those who know a message:
   a) at the outset   → p_0
   b) at time *t*   → p_t
(Nonknowers are the appropriate complements)

Intensity of message transmission → k

Amount of time during which diffusion has proceeded → t

Relationships

Rate of spread of the message depends upon knowers, intensity, and time. → $\frac{dp}{dt} = f(p, k, t)$

What form $f(p, k, t)$ takes depends upon specific assumptions to be incorporated into the model.

For a very simple first model, consider the following assumptions:

1. Only the original knowers tell the message. New knowers do not transmit it. Later this assumption will be relaxed.
2. All tellers communicate with the same, constant intensity, k ($k > 0$) tellings per unit time. This assumption could also state that tellers average exactly k tellings for each time unit.
3. The knowers randomly mix with the population. This assumption is basic to almost all diffusion models, but it is problematic to the extent that people tend to interact in relatively separate cliques or interpersonal networks. For now, the simplification introduced by assuming random mixing will be of instructional value if not of predictive value.
4. The population is so large with respect to the process under study that q_t never gets small enough to restrict the supply of potential new knowers. Obviously this assumption is too simple, and it will be relaxed later.

From these assumptions we can establish the basic relation of the diffusion process. At each time unit, a fixed proportion of the population, p_0, will communicate randomly at a constant rate, k, with nonknowers. Thus the rate of increase in knowers will be constant. That amounts to saying

$$\frac{dp}{dt} = k. \tag{7-4}$$

We now have a complete set of statements connecting the general question with mathematical formulation.

What can be done with equation (7-4)? Two basic questions should be asked. (1) Is the process accelerating, constant, or decelerating? (2) What is the general equation describing the curve of p_t (the curve of the proportion of knowers over time)? To answer the first question, examine the second derivative of the process. If it is positive, zero, or negative, the process is accelerating, constant, or decelerating, respectively. Clearly, $d^2p/dt = 0$, so the process is constant. That is no surprise, since telling took place at a constant rate by a fixed number of people without running out of an audience.

The general curve is obtainable by integrating equation (7-4) in the following manner:

$$dp = k\,dt,$$
$$\int_0^T dp = \int_0^T k\,dt,$$
$$p\Big|_0^T = kt\Big|_0^T,$$
$$p_T - p_0 = kT,$$
$$p_T = p_0 + kT \tag{7-5}$$

Equation (7-5) indicates that one need only multiply the rate of transmission by the amount of time elapsed to determine the proportion of new knowers acquired from time 0. Add to that amount the original knowers to get the total proportion of knowers at time $t = T$.

The procedures above will now be followed, with less detail, for a series of slightly more realistic models. First, relax assumption 1 so that new knowers become tellers with the same intensity as the original set of knowers. If the other assumptions are left unaltered, then the rate of spread depends strictly upon the intensity of telling, k, and the number of tellers, or more conveniently, the proportion of tellers, p.

$$\frac{dp}{dt} = kp. \tag{7-6}$$

Differentiating equation (7-6) gives $d^2p/dt = k$. Since we assume that $k > 0$, the process is accelerating, which means that each time unit will accrue more new knowers than did the previous time unit.

132   Mathematical Sociology

Integrating equation (7-6) requires the following rearrangement of terms:

$$\frac{dp}{p} = k\, dt,$$

and recognition that the integral of $dp/p = \ln_e p$. Thus:

$$\frac{dp}{p} = k\, dt,$$

$$\ln_e p \Big|_0^T = kt \Big|_0^T,$$

$$\ln_e p_T - \ln_e p_0 = kT.$$

Rearranging and taking antilogs gives

$$p_T = p_0 e^{kT}, \qquad (7\text{-}7)$$

which is an accelerating, or *waxing exponential curve*. It and the other curves discussed are shown in Figure 7-2.

Clearly, equation (7-5) will eventually, and equation (7-7) will rapidly produce values of p greater than unity, yet a proportion cannot exceed that value. The problem results from assumption 4. As the proportion of knowers increases, eventually there will be a shortage of nonknowers to receive the message, and the diffusion process will taper off. In fact, the rate of diffusion should depend upon availability of nonknowers, q_t. If only original knowers are tellers (reinstituting the first assumption), but they are subject to the limitation of q_t, then

$$\frac{dp}{dt} = kq = k(1 - p). \qquad (7\text{-}8)$$

Differentiating equation (7-8) provides $d^2p/dt = -k$; hence the process is continually decelerating. Integration follows the procedure used earlier:

$$\int_0^T \frac{dp}{1-p} = \int_0^T k\, dt,$$

$$-\ln_e (1-p) \Big|_0^T = kt \Big|_0^T,$$

$$\ln_e (1 - P_T) = \ln_e (1 - p_0) - kT,$$

$$p_T = 1 - q_0 e^{-kT}. \qquad (7\text{-}9)$$

Note that as T increases, e^{-kT} decreases, so that the process begins at $1 - q_0$ and ends asymptotically at 1. This is a *waning exponential curve* [see Figure 7-2(c)].

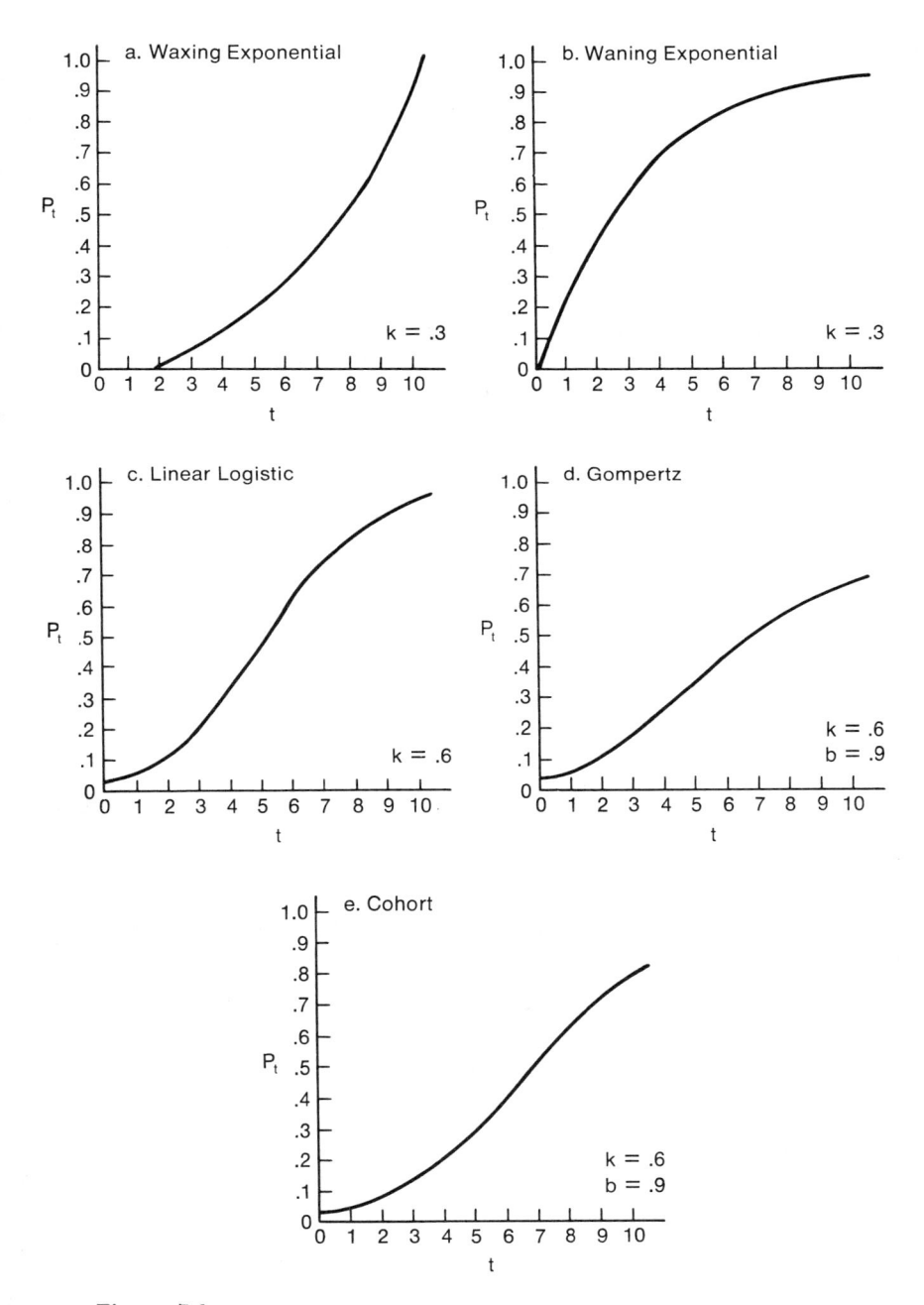

Figure 7-2

Types of diffusion curves

134 Mathematical Sociology

Suppose that the last two models are combined, so that new knowers become tellers (at the same rate as the original knowers) and tellings are restricted by available nonknowers. Then a new telling depends upon the chance that a knower encounters a nonknower:

$$\frac{dp}{dt} = kpq = kp(1-p). \tag{7-10}$$

Note that $p(1-p)$, or pq, is part of the binomial expansion, representing the probability of knowers encountering nonknowers. Other terms in the expansion are p^2 (knowers wasting time talking to each other) and q^2 (nonknowers communicating among themselves).

Differentiating (7-10) gives $d^2p/dt = k(1-2p)$. When $p < .5$, the second derivative is positive; when $p > .5$, it is negative. Therefore the process accelerates until half of the population has the word, at which point it begins decelerating. As with equation (7-8), equation (7-10) is asymptotic to 1.

Integrating equation (7-10) is similar to previous examples:

$$\frac{dp}{p(1-p)} = k\,dt,$$

$$\ln_e \frac{p}{1-p} \bigg|_0^T = kt \bigg|_0^T,$$

$$\ln_e \frac{p}{1-p_T} = \ln_e \frac{p_0}{q_0} + kT,$$

$$\frac{p_T}{q_T} = \frac{p_0}{q_0} e^{kT}. \tag{7-11}$$

Some algebraic manipulation, using $q_T = 1 - p_T$ again and letting a equal p_0/q_0, gives

$$p_T = \frac{1}{1 + \frac{1}{ae^{kT}}}. \tag{7-12}$$

Equations (7-11) and (7-12) are equivalent versions of the *linear logistic* curve. Its graph is found in Figure 7-2(d).

Note the equation (7-9) could have been written $q_T = q_0 e^{-kT}$, and both sides could be inverted to give

$$\frac{1}{q_T} = \frac{1}{q_0} e^{kT}. \tag{7-13}$$

Multiplying Equations (7-13) and (7-7) produces equation (7-11), assuming that the two *k* values in (7-13) and (7-7) sum to that in (7-11). Thus, as Dodd[6] has noted, the linear logistic curve is factorable into two separate processes: an accelerating effect as knowers increase and a decelerating effect as the available audience decreases. The logistic is one of the most common curves describing growth processes.

Further Development of the Model. Certain assumptions which remain in the model underlying the logistic curve are empirically questionable. We might reasonably ask the following questions.

1. *Is random mixing of the population reasonable?* One possible source of nonrandomness is the amount of social or geographic distance between a knower and various nonknowers with whom he might communicate. Another source of nonrandomness lies in clique or subgroup structuring within which communication occurs more readily than it does across group boundaries. The distance model has been developed to some extent by Rapoport,[7] although methods are somewhat more difficult than those discussed here, and general results are not obtained directly. Coleman[8] has used a different approach to explore the clique or group-structure type of model, with cliques of size two being the easiest to handle analytically.

    Because both of these approaches require different mathematical structures and produce results which are not expressible as simple curves, we will not explore them. It should be noted, however, that they represent a very desirable aspect of mathematical work. Originally, very simple models can be built which are easily handled. Then these models can be questioned in terms of the assumptions behind them. As one or more challenges occurs, more complex models can be developed. The initial work is often simple enough to get things started, and subsequent revision or reconceptualization proceeds by reasonable steps until a model of useful subtlety is developed. The eventual model may be much more complex than could have been visualized at the outset.

2. *Does a constant intensity of telling make sense?* One possible way to relax the constant-intensity assumption would be to assume that all tellers at any point in time have a systematically reduced intensity compared to tellers at the preceding time point. Thus, as a fad wears thin, all adherents (even new ones) may become less active spreaders. We will examine two such variations and take note of some others.

    Second, it may be that each cohort of new knowers (that is, all who got the word during the same time interval) experiences systematic waning of intensity. This is a more difficult model, without a direct solution. A discrete time model using difference equations has been calculated, so that some comparison is possible. It appears in Figure 7-2(e).

    A third possibility is that there is a distribution of individual intensities such that the proportion of knowers with a given intensity can be specified at any point in time. No attempt will be made to present such a model here, but the

---

[6]Stuart C. Dodd, "Testing message diffusion in harmonic logistic curves," *Psychometrika*, vol. 21 (June, 1956), pp. 191–205. See also Stuart C. Dodd, "Diffusion is predictable: Testing probability models for laws of interaction," *American Sociological Review*, vol. 20 (1955), pp. 392–401.

[7]A. Rapoport, "Nets with distance bias," *Bulletin of Mathematical Biophysics*, vol. 13 (1951), pp. 85–91.

[8]Coleman, *Introduction to Mathematical Sociology*, pp. 495–505.

same type of solution appears in some work with random nets[9] and has recently been applied to the mover-stayer model[10] described in Chapter 9.

The simplest way to handle a general, uniform reduction in intensity would be to make k a decreasing function of time. Suppose that, in successive time intervals, intensity reduces to a fixed proportion of the previous intensity. If intensity were k at t_0 ($k > 0$), it might be kb at time t_1, where $0 < b < 1$, kb^2 at time t_2, and so on. For such a process we can substitute kb^t for k in equation (7-10) (the differential form of the logistic curve) or any of the earlier, simpler curves.

$$\frac{dp}{dt} = kb^t p(1-p). \tag{7-14}$$

The second derivative is $d^2p/dt = kb^t(1 - 2p)$. Again, this changes from accelerating to decelerating as p passes .5. How does it differ from the logistic curve?

By the same procedures used before, we can integrate equation (7-14) to find

$$\frac{p_T}{1-p_T} = \frac{p_0}{1-p_0} \exp\left[\frac{k}{\ln b}(b^T - 1)\right].$$

By algebraic manipulation, the above expression can be written

$$p_T = \frac{1}{1 + \dfrac{1}{\dfrac{p_0}{q_0}\exp\left[\dfrac{k}{\ln b}(b^T - 1)\right]}}.$$

By letting $\ln_e c = k/\ln_e b$, we will have $e^{k/\ln b} = c$. Also, for simplification, let

---

[9] It has been demonstrated that, if the probability that a person will be contacted exactly k times, given that he has a "target intensity" of e, is a Poisson distribution, and if the distribution of target intensities in the population follows a particular gamma distribution, then the probability for the whole population of someone's receiving exactly k contacts is a "negative binomial" distribution. See A. Rapoport and W. J. Horvath, "A study of a large sociogram," *Behavioral Science*, vol. 6 (1961), pp. 279–291. Also, see T. J. Fararo and M. H. Sunshine, "*A study of a biased friendship net* (Syracuse, N.Y.: Youth Development Center, Syracuse University, 1964).

[10] Spilerman has suggested that if each person's transitions in the "mover-stayer" mobility model (see Chapter 9 for discussion of this model) follow a Poisson distribution, and individual rates of mobility follow a gamma distribution, then the proportion of the population making exactly k moves (in a specified time interval) follows a negative binomial distribution. See Seymour Spilerman, "Extensions of the mover-stayer model," *American Journal of Sociology*, vol. 78 (November, 1972), pp. 599–626. Clearly, the random-net and the mobility process models are using the same type of generalizing assumptions and producing the same type of probability process for quite different substantive problems.

$a = p_0/q_0 c$. Then,

$$p_T = \frac{1}{1 + \dfrac{1}{ac^{b^T}}}. \tag{7-15}$$

This curve [equation (7-15)] is the *Gompertz curve*. Note its basic similarity to the logistic [equation (7-12)]. In fact, the curves begin similarly, but the Gompertz tapers off sooner [Figure 7-2(d)]. Deteriorating intensity causes the diffusion process to slow down as time goes on. As $T \longrightarrow \infty$ in the logistic, $1/ae^{kT} \longrightarrow 0$, so that $p_T \longrightarrow 1$. In contrast, as $T \longrightarrow \infty$ in the Gompertz, $ac^{b^T} \longrightarrow a$, so that $p_T \longrightarrow 1/(1 + 1/a)$. In general, although a will be moderately large, p_T has an asymptote less than unity. The cohort curve [Figure 7-2(e)] asymptote is also less than 1.00, but the curve falls between the logistic (no waning of intensity) and the Gompertz (everyone's intensity wanes together).

It is difficult to explain theoretically why all knowers, regardless of when they first received the message, have the same amount of deterioration of intensity, for any given point in time. In an application quite different from message diffusion, Hernes[11] has demonstrated that the property of the Gompertz curve helps provide a good description of the cumulative proportion of people who have married for the first time at any given age. The effect of increasing p is to add social pressure to marry, the effect of decreasing q is to restrict the opportunity to find a spouse, and the deteriorating intensity describes a deteriorating marriageability with increasing age. In such an example it is quite reasonable to assume essentially the same rate of deterioration for all persons.

How might decreasing intensity be treated more realistically for diffusion processes such as rumor spreading? One set of variations, discussed by Bartholomew,[12] assumes that knowers will spread a message until (a) they have told a certain number of people (work done by Rapoport),[13] or (b) they have encountered sufficient stifling by trying to tell others who already know, that they cease telling. In the latter case, stifling could occur after one such encounter, or with a specified probability each time an individual is encountered who already knows the message[14].

---

[11]Gudmund Hernes, "The process of entry into first marriage," *American Sociological Review*, vol. 37 (April, 1972), pp. 173–182. See also D. W. Hastings and J. G. Robinson, "A re-examination of Hernes' model on the process of entry into first marriage for United States women, cohorts 1891–1945," *American Sociological Review*, vol. 38 (February, 1973), pp. 138–142.

[12]David J. Bartholomew, *Stochastic Models for Social Processes* (London: John Wiley & Sons, 1967), pp. 235–257. This volume is an excellent reference for stochastic processes.

[13]Bartholomew provides a number of references to the work of Rapoport and his associates in the area of random net theory. See p. 264.

[14]See Bartholomew's discussion of the work by Daley and Kendall. (Bartholomew, pp. 250–254). Also, D. J. Daley and D. G. Kendall, "Stochastic rumours," *Journal of the Institute of Mathematical Applications*, vol. 1 (1965), pp. 42–55.

138   Mathematical Sociology

A variety of facts about such models has been provided, both in stochastic form and in appropriate deterministic form. One notable aspect of these models is that, in strict stochastic form, they allow for stifling to prevent the process from occurring. If early conditions are accidentally just right, first knowers will manage to stifle each other before spreading can get under way. Clearly such an occurrence would be likely if diffusion occurred readily within small cliques but only with difficulty across clique boundaries.

problems

1. Here are some census data (1970) on the relationship of income to age for all males and females with any income during 1969. Try fitting a linear, an exponential, and a parabolic equation to these two sets of data. Decide which fits best, and give an interpretation for both the shape of the curve and the value of the parameters.

AGE	MALES, MEAN INCOME, 1969	FEMALES, MEAN INCOME, 1969
14–19	1,396	1,176
20–24	4,129	2,924
25–29	7,561	3,698
30–34	9,126	3,579
35–39	10,066	3,711
40–44	10,497	3,931
45–49	10,554	4,106
50–54	10,038	4,167
55–59	9,248	4,117
60–64	8,175	3,491
65–69	5,657	2,494
70–74	4,423	2,234
75+	3,485	1,978

2. Suppose a town library is moving to a new building. The library has 50,000 volumes and wishes to avoid costs of moving them, so it places an ad in the local newspaper requesting that patrons come in, check out a few books, and turn them in at the new building. Each day for one month, 100 different people come to the library to do just that, except that they check out only those books which interest them. The first day, all of them find five books they wish to check out. The second day, they take out fewer books because there are fewer left, and so on. In fact, the number of books checked out each day is a constant proportion of the number left in the old building. Assuming that all books are turned in at the new building immediately, develop a model for describing the number of books in the new building as a function of time (number of days). Is the curve an exponential curve, a power curve, or a logarithmic curve? If necessary, work out the series of numbers of books moved, day by day, and fit possible curves to this series.

3. Hamblin, et al. [*A Mathematical Theory of Social Change* (New York: John Wiley & Sons, 1973)] present a number of diffusion processes. Read their discussion, then attempt to find your own examples of diffusion processes. If possible, look for examples for which data are available, such as in government publications, almanacs, and so on, then fit an appropriate curve.

CHAPTER 8

computer simulation and renewal processes

The process models we discussed in Chapter 7 have the form of two-variable equations in which a dependent variable is a function of time. This makes time appear as the "independent" variable. In the present chapter we will present two models that not only predict changes in a dependent variable over time but also try to represent the underlying process. This means that there are other variables besides time and the dependent variable, and the models are correspondingly more complicated than those in the previous chapter.

*a computer simulation
of interpersonal choice*

The basic problem in this section will be to illustrate process models using a detailed analysis of a simulation of interpersonal choice developed by Farr and Leik.[1] This work is chosen partly because it is a simulation rather than a direct mathematical model. Also, it contains nonlinear equations for some of the relationships.

The primary purpose in constructing the computer simulation was to express certain aspects of interpersonal choice which were not well handled by existing theories. In particular, the intent was to develop a model based on the following four considerations. First, the relationship between an individual's tendency to act and how much conversation he actually contributed in any given group, as expressed in earlier works by Leik[2] and discussed in Chapter 3 of this book. Second, a simple assumption about voluntary increase or decrease in a person's getting together with other people, depending upon how satisfied that person is with his share of the conversation. Third, an attempt to adjust the involvement of all individuals with various sets of others so that the entire system will simultaneously seek optimal associations for each person. Such optimization must be within the constraints imposed by the expectations of other people; that is, the optimizing requirements for those others will limit any individual's freedom to optimize. It is possible for such a system to be in constant flux, although it was initially assumed that the more probable result would be eventual stability. Fourth, it was assumed that any or all of the individuals in the system could decide to avoid interaction altogether. Thus, any individual could eventually drop out by developing a zero probability of getting together with any set of others in the system.

Because this model was concerned with the development of interpersonal grouping, it was necessary that time be included. However, the specific amount of time which any grouping required was not relevant to the theoretical ideas. It was therefore preferable to treat time implicitly by the iterative process of the simulation. Thus, the state of the system at any given time would imply changes in individual probabilities as a consequence of satisfaction of the individuals with what they were experiencing. These changes would then be reflected in changes in the overall grouping process, which would alter the satisfaction of the individual members. This altered satisfaction could then cycle back to new changes in probabilities, new groupings, and a continuation of the adjustment process through successive iterations.

[1] These excerpts, drawn from "Computer simulation of interpersonal choice," by Grant Farr and Robert K. Leik, are reprinted from *Comparative Group Studies*, vol. 2, no. 2 (May, 1971), pp. 125-148 by permission of the Publisher, Sage Publications, Inc. For general discussions of simulation see Harold Guetzkow, ed., *Simulation in Social Science: Readings* (Englewood Cliffs, N.J.: Prentice-Hall, Inc., 1962) and John T. Gullahorn and Jeanne E. Gullahorn, "Some computer applications in social science," *American Sociological Review*, vol. 30, no. 3 (1965), pp. 363-365.

[2] Robert K. Leik, "Type of group and the probability of initiating acts," *Sociometry*, vol. 28, no. 1 (1965), pp. 57–65; and "The distribution of acts in small groups," *Sociometry*, vol. 30, no. 3 (1967), pp. 280–299.

142 Mathematical Sociology

It was assumed that the specific results of any particular grouping *caused* a given amount of satisfaction or dissatisfaction for each member, which *caused* readjustments in the members' behavior, which caused new grouping, and so on. It was necessary, therefore, to write equations which led from probability distributions to specific groupings to satisfactions to new probabilities. Because small changes in probabilities, satisfactions, and other aspects of the model could cause important changes in the system, it was necessary to use continuous relationships on the continuous variables. For reasons which will become evident in the discussion, some of these relationships had to be nonlinear. This was not anticipated at the time the modeling began, because there was nothing specific at the theoretical level which indicated nonlinear forms. As various alternative expressions were considered, it became evident that the theoretical statements should specify nonlinear adjustment for some of the relationships; hence the model contains nonlinearity.

Rather than attempt to present a translation diagram (the model is fairly complex), we will start with the simple diagram shown in Figure 8-1. It may help when building complex models to make such a diagram of the theoretical system which is to be modeled before beginning to write equations. This is parallel to a computer programmer's drawing a flow diagram before beginning serious programming, in order to assure himself of necessary feedback loops, proper chains of implication, and other demands of the job.

The model attempts to avoid certain difficulties with most theoretical approaches to interpersonal choice. One of those difficulties is that most theories are concerned with only dyads or possibly with triads. Usually the analysis pertains to one actor's decision only. It was specifically desired for this model to treat the decisions of each actor as dependent upon the system which developed from everyone's decisions taken together. Therefore the rest of the system necessarily must be considered variable, whereas most theories consider the rest of the system constant for the sake of analysis. There are exceptions to this objection, so the reader should not assume that all theoretical endeavor in this field is unnecessarily narrow. Nevertheless, the specific intent of making the total system dependent upon individual behaviors has clear implications for the model being developed.

The second major problem which most approaches to interpersonal choice encounter is in the availability of alternatives outside the immediate focus of analysis. It was not desired to specify alternatives beyond the possibility of interacting with the individuals simulated, but those alternatives should be represented by the possibility of each individual's deciding to avoid further interaction in the system. Thus all probabilities of interaction within the system could go to zero.

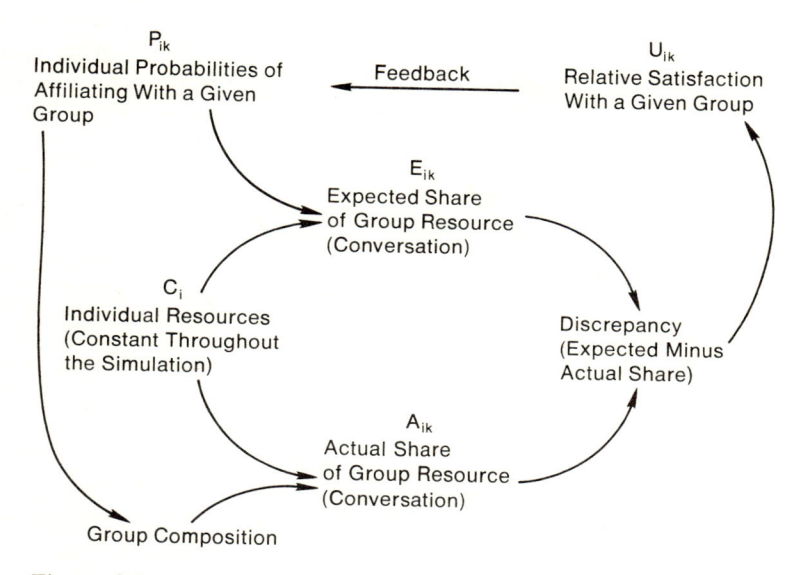

```
                    P_ik                                    U_ik
        Individual Probabilities of    Feedback    Relative Satisfaction
        Affiliating With a Given    ←———————       With a Given Group
        Group
                                    E_ik
                                 Expected Share
                                 of Group Resource
                                 (Conversation)
                C_i
        Individual Resources                        Discrepancy
        (Constant Throughout                        (Expected Minus
        the Simulation)                              Actual Share)
                                    A_ik
                                 Actual Share
                                 of Group Resource
                                 (Conversation)
            Group Composition
```

Figure 8-1

Diagraming the model

A second aspect of the problem of alternatives is that for each possible group which might form, there should be alternative groupings of the same population which an individual might prefer. The problem was therefore conceived as making a person's choice or avoidance of specific other actors dependent not only upon the extent of satisfaction received from that interaction context, but also upon the attractiveness or repulsiveness of potential relationships elsewhere in the system.

There remains one further question before specific discussion of the form of the model. Why choose computer simulation rather than direct mathematical solution? The preceding comments about the requirements for the model should indicate that a fairly large number of probabilities, groups, amounts of satisfaction, and other related variables will have to be considered in the model. Furthermore, the state of one set of such variables at a given time will influence change of state of another set of variables in subsequent time. The entire process becomes very complex. It was therefore decided that direct solution would either be entirely too difficult or would require too much simplification of the theoretical ideas incorporated in the model. The approach of computer simulation allows the desired mutual interdependency and potential indeterminacy of the model within the general principles of interpersonal selection or rejection. By programming the computer to adjust each set of variables depending on the previous state of the system according to the flow diagram in Figure 8-1, it was possible to determine step-by-step system change without the undue restraints of requiring direct mathematical solution.

Translation into Mathematics. The initial equation in the simulation is exactly that discussed in Chapter 4 for the distribution of acts in small groups. That equation relates the individual resource of talkativeness to the probability that an individual will talk in a group of specified composition:

$$A_{ik} = \frac{C_i}{\sum_i \delta_{ik} C_i}. \tag{8-1}$$

A_{ik} is actor i's probability of talking in group k, C_i is i's individual (and constant) tendency to talk, and δ_{ik} is an operator which indicates whether actor i is in group k. It has the value 1 if i is in k and the value 0 otherwise. Note that this equation simply states that as others in the group are more active on the average, any individual will get a relatively smaller share of total group activity, and vice versa. The relationship can pertain to groups of any size, in that larger groups simply have more members, hence more C values incorporated in the denominator. For discussion of the initial work leading to this equation, see Chapter 3.

The basic equation, equation (8-1), was used because it indicates the most probable amount of conversation which any individual will be allowed to contribute to a group discussion. There is evidence, furthermore, that if people do not get sufficient opportunity to talk they will be very dissatisfied with their participation in the group. Perhaps, as well, if they talk too much because of unusual group demands for their contributions, they may be uncomfortable and dissatisfied. Whatever the consequence for satisfaction, it was necessary to express the actual share of group conversation allotted to any member so that it could be compared with the expectation that that person had for his behavior in social groups. The discrepancy between expectation and actual share, then, would be a basis for establishing satisfaction and subsequent adjustment of participation.

Note that the flow diagram as indicated in the preceding remarks requires expectations as well as actual participation in order to assess satisfaction. The work which led to equation (8-1) was not concerned with expectation. It is necessary, therefore, to ask whether there is any theoretical basis for establishing an expected rate of participation for individuals in group conversation.

Clearly it would be unrealistic to assume that all individuals would be satisfied with exactly the same degree of participation. Some, for example, seem content to sit quietly and listen attentively while others talk. Others cannot be satisfied unless they are granted a very large share of attention from the group. The theoretical basis for establishing some form of expectation was the concept of a *generalized other*, which is derived from the writings of George Herbert Mead[3] and others in the symbolic interactionist tradition. For Mead, each person forms a conception of how others in general behave (in conversational groups, for the purposes of this model). Such a conception necessarily depends on experience with those others, and a kind of abstracting from a multitude of specific experiences to form a generalized notion.

The generalized-other concept was formulated for the model in the following way. For each individual, note how much time he spends in interaction with specific others and what C values those others have. If each other's C value is weighted by the amount of interaction experienced with that other, and these weighted values then averaged so that the person most often encountered looms largest in the average, a generalized C can be obtained which will represent the degree of activeness of the average other encountered. Someone who spends most of his time with hesitant people will develop a generalized other represented by a small average C, whereas someone who interacts mostly with very active others will develop a high average C representing the generalized other.

Mathematically the requirement for a set of expectations for the individuals in the system is satisfied by multiplying the C for each person in the system by the probability that actor i will interact with that person, then dividing by the sum of those probabilities of interacting.[4] The variable just defined will be designated C_i^*. There is one departure at this point from the implication of Mead's writings. The conceptualization of a generalized other's tendency to initiate behavior is changed in the model each time the individual participation in various groups changes. That is, each cycle of the reiterative process recomputes C_i^* based upon the latest interaction probabilities. A more accurate treatment of Mead's writings would probably retain information from earlier cycles, although possibly at a reduced weighting in the overall computation.

To translate C_i^* into an individual's expectations for his participation in a particular group requires consideration of group size. If an individual is participating in a dyad, equation (8-1) will contain his C value in the numerator and his plus one other C value in the denominator. For triadic discussion groups, there will be his plus two other C values in the denomina-

---

[3]See, for example, Anselm Strauss, ed., *The Social Psychology of George Herbert Mead* (Chicago: University of Chicago Press, 1956).

[4]Although the value of C_i^* represents a psychological expectation, the manner of computing also represents a mathematical expectation.

tor. In general, for groups of size N, the denominator contains his C value plus $(N-1)$ other C values. If those others are to be generalized others in the Meadian sense, then an expression for each actor's expectations in a group of size N will be his C value divided by his C value plus $(N-1)$ (other members) times C_i^* (his generalized C). The expected participation rate would therefore be the same for all groups of the same size, although actual participation will depend upon the particular other participants in a given group:

$$E_{ik} = \frac{C_i}{C_i + (N-1)C_i^*}. \tag{8-2}$$

To determine whether the individual is satisfied or dissatisfied with the group in which he is participating, it is necessary to compare his actual share of the action with his expected share. A simple difference indicates this discrepancy, but a linear function of that difference would not be a very realistic representation of relative satisfaction. The problem posed by a linear relationship is the assumption that a large discrepancy in favor of the individual talking *more* than he expected is "good." In fact, too much talking may be embarrassing, stressful, or otherwise aversive. Similarly, excessive leadership or dominance or influence or other group-based properties of this sort could be quite disconcerting to an individual not so prepared.[5] The implication of these comments is that a more appropriate function would be, for example, parabolic. A parabolic function would imply that as discrepancy increased in absolute value, aversion would increase. A parabola is provided by a quadratic function, so we need only square the discrepancy between actual and expected participation and use the result as an indicator of aversion.

Equation (8-3) indicates the parabolic relationship between the discrepancy of actual shares and expected shares and the resulting dissatisfaction U_{ik}. The subscript of the variable U indicates, as in equations (8-1) and (8-2), which actor and which group are under consideration.

$$U_{ik} = (A_{ik} - E_{ik})^2. \tag{8-3}$$

A problem occurs with a simple squared discrepancy; for many people it would be desirable to be *somewhat* more active than one expected to be without having to be excessively so. Consequently, it may be desirable to

---

[5]Research has shown that people are evaluated by others less favorably as they depart from average or "appropriate" shares of interaction. Assuming that we are all aware of such a tendency, we would shun such departure to the extent that we value approval from co-participants. See, for example, Donald P. Hayes and Leo Meltzer, "Interpersonal judgements based on talkativeness: I. Fact or artifact?," *Sociometry*, vol. 35, no. 4 (1972), pp. 538–561.

effect a transformation of the parabola so that its minimum point is associated with a rate of participation somewhat above expectation but relatively near it. One variation of the simulation involves such an adjustment in a manner which provides for a fairly large increment if expectation is very small, but a proportionately smaller increment if expectation is already quite large. This implies that someone who expects to carry 50 percent of the group discussion would not care to carry much more, whereas someone who would expect only 10 percent of the discussion might be quite happy to carry 25 percent or so. This difference in the program will be referred to as the presence or absence of a bias factor. Equation (8-4) shows the bias factor incorporated in equation (8-3):

$$U_{ik} = [A_{ik} - (1 - B_{ik})E_{ik}]^2, \tag{8-4}$$

where $B_{ik} = D(1 - E_{ik})^2$.

Note that the value of B_{ik} accompanying equation (8-4) will be smaller as the individual's expectation becomes closer to 1 or 100 percent of group participation. Furthermore, the decrease in B is nonlinear, being rather slow for small values of E but decreasing very rapidly as E gets beyond 50 percent. The multiple D was arbitrarily given the value 2.0 in the original model. It adjusts the value of B so that an intuitively appropriate reduction in E in equation (8-4) would occur. If actual data were available to test the model, it would be necessary to determine a best-fitting value of this parameter rather than arbitrarily choosing 2. Note that if equation (8-4) were written with the form of B expressed completely, it would be a very complex expression in that it would contain a square of a squared difference. This compounded nonlinearity was one reason for preferring simulation to direct solution. Directly solving such an expression would be extremely difficult.

A glance back at Figure 8-1 will indicate that most of the model is at this point ready. Given that a group has formed, there is now a way of determining actual share in conversation [equation (8-1)], expectation for share in conversation [equation (8-2)], and relative satisfaction based on discrepancies between those two [equation (8-3) or equation (8-4)]. The remaining problem is how to get the group formed in the first place. The first form of the model was developed as what was called a *host* model. The model assumes that each individual has his own location, such as his home, and that social activity is carried on only in these locations. The probability that any set of individuals would interact as a group was expressed simply as the product of the probabilities that the individual members would be at any given locus. Note that this approach means that grouping is treated as a random consequence of individual tendencies to go to different places where they might encounter others. Although this sounds particularly nonsociological, it incorporates the possibilities that subsets of the population could have high probabilities of going to one or two particular places so that their small group would form readily at a favorite place of meeting. There is, however, no scheduling process built into the model. The problems implied by this lack of scheduling are discussed briefly later.

The probability that an individual will stay at his own locus can be represented by P_{ii}, and the probability that individual i will go to locus k represented by the probability P_{ik}. For a random beginning it can be assumed that all $P_{ik} = 1/n$, where n is the number of people in the population. If n were very large, we would need to use some kind of subgrouping initially in order to get sufficient probabilities to allow the process to operate at all. For this simulation, only five people were represented in the total population. Therefore, the initial values were .2 for all actors at each locus. A second P_{ik} distribution was also used, to provide initial structure rather than random behavior. This nonrandom structure is shown in Table 8-1.

Table 8-1

Nonrandom Initial P_{ij} Values

		LOCUS j			
PERSON i	1	2	3	4	5
1	.4	.4	.2	0	0
2	.3	.4	.2	.1	0
3	.1	.2	.4	.2	.1
4	0	.1	.2	.4	.3
5	0	0	.2	.4	.4

Based on the P_{ik}, the following probabilities were computed: the probability that an individual would be alone at his own locus, the probability that he would be there with each other individual when the remaining three were not present, the probability that he would be there with each pair of others when the remaining two were not present, probabilities for comparable sets of four including the host, and the probability that all five were at his locus. No group was considered at a locus if the host were not there. The probabilities for groups of 2, 3, 4 or 5 were based on the simple products of the probabilities of the others' being or not being at that locus, hence represent joint occurrence of independent events. This amounts to saying that no prearrangements were made, but that individuals simply drifted from place to place looking for interesting action.

Once a group was specified at a given locus and its probability computed, the aversion of each individual in the group to that group (U_{ik}) was computed and weighted by the probability of the group's occurrence. For any individual at any locus, such weighted aversions were added to provide total aversion to that locus. Note that the emphasis is placed on avoiding a *location* rather than a particular *individual*. This is consequently not a person-person choice model, but rather a group affiliation model.

Having computed total aversion to each locus for a given individual, the simulation routine normalized the aversions so that probabilities could be adjusted to retain involvement of each individual in the system. Thus, although the parabolic aversion function could have no negative values, representing attraction, the normalized aversions were given a mean value of zero so that negative values represented attraction to that locus and positive values aversion to that locus. Normalized aversions were then multiplied by a constant to keep them in reasonable scale for the probability system, then subtracted from the original P_{ik} values, producing new probabilities of going to the other loci or staying at one's own locus. At this point new group probabilities were computed along with new aversions, and again P_{ik} values were readjusted. The entire routine for the initial simulation attempt was thus a random distribution of individuals with a built-in system of readjustment according to expectations as compared with actual experiences at each of the loci of the system.

In order to operate such a simulation, it is necessary to establish values for the C_i. Note that the use of the C's is such that only proportionality matters. Multiplying C distributions by any constant would have no effect on results. To provide runs in which all persons were somewhat different and runs in which there was the possibility of at least dyads that were relatively similar, two sets of C values were used. The first set was 1, 2, 3, 4, 5; so that no two individuals were alike and there were no extremely divergent cases. The second set was 1, 1, 2, 3, 3. This set provided two identical dyads and one intermediate individual. Initial runs were consequently of four types: each of two distributions of C values with bias and each of two distributions of C values without bias in expectation. Each run was for 100 iterations.

Testing and Extending the Model. No formal hypotheses had been posed when the development of the model was undertaken. Nevertheless some informal expectations were held about the implications of the kind of grouping process represented in the model. In particular it was expected that individuals with equal or similar C values would eventually get together in the same group. For the C distribution containing two 1's, a 2, and two 3's, that expectation meant that the individuals with $C = 1$ should form a subgroup and those with $C = 3$ should form a subgroup, and that the case of $C = 2$ would be an interesting indeterminant problem. For the other C distribution it was anticipated that those $C = 1$ and 2 would get together as would those with $C = 4$ and 5, and again 3 would represent an intermediate indeterminant case.

One implication of these informal expectations is that there would be subgroupings rather than all five members constituting a single group. A second implication is that the intermediate case has the greatest chance of being an outcast. Possibly, for the 1, 2, 3, 4, 5 distribution, the intermediate case could become an intermediary between the extreme pairs. If so, there would be a greater chance for complete grouping in this distribution, since the intermediary could act as a cohesive force.

Note that these informal expectations constitute a basis for checking the intuitive validity of the model. However, it has been stated earlier in this book that developing models to represent theories provides a way of determining the implications of those theories in more precise manner. Thus at this point the model builder is trying to use informal expectations from the theory as a basis for determining whether the model makes sense, while at the same time using the model to determine what the theory implies. Obviously, there is a kind of circularity here from a formal analysis standpoint. If the implications of the model do not agree with expectations, either the model does not represent the theory adequately or those expectations were inappropriate. In order to avoid circularity, it would be most appropriate to use the model to explore for conditions which would produce what was expected as well as conditions which would violate those expectations, allowing the model in this manner to specify further what implications the theory really has.

At this point one major difficulty with simulations becomes evident. There are the following variables in this relatively simple model: a six-person by six-locus matrix of probabilities, the probabilities of any sized group of whatever composition forming at each locus, the actual and the expected share for each person's participation in each of those groups, the resultant discrepancies in share of conversation leading to relative satisfaction or dissatisfaction with each locus, hence the eventual greater or lesser probability that any particular set of individuals will get together at whatever locus. Clearly it is not possible to consider all of these facts when asking how well the model performs; there would simply be too many aspects to judge at one time. Consequently, since the main concern of the model was the manner in which groups form, two simple indexes were devised to indicate grouping.

Five probabilities were recorded, consisting of the probability that the first and second individuals, the second and third, the third and fourth, the fourth and fifth, and finally the fifth and first would spend time together regardless of locus. These probabilities were computed at the one-hundredth iteration of the simulation. Other pair probabilities would not be independent of those used, and would not add useful information unless special disjoint subgroupings were discovered. In the latter event a within-group mean would have been needed versus a between-group mean. To simplify the interpretation of this mean probability across various pairs, all pair probabilities falling below .25 were eliminated under the assumption that they represented more or less irrelevant aspects of grouping patterns rather than major groupings.

A second index concerned the stability of the grouping process. The mean number of changes in the sign of the slopes of the pair probabilities was computed over one hundred iterations. Although this computation could easily have been programmed directly, it was made visually from graphs of the pair probabilities produced by the program. The implication of such an index is that if grouping progressed smoothly and monotonically then there would be no changes in the sign of the slope. On the other hand, pairs which had a history of oscillating attraction, separation, and so on would consequently have unstable pair probabilities, represented by a large number of changes in the sign of the probability curve. These two indexes plus the graphs of the pair probabilities over the one hundred iterations were sufficient to get some idea of the grouping process which the model created.

A total of eight initial runs of the simulate were made. These runs were a combination of random or nonrandom initial P matrix, bias or no bias in the satisfaction parabola, and two different distributions of C values. Two of the runs, those with no bias but with random initial probabilities, had no power to produce viable groups. All individuals became isolates over time. Regardless of the C distribution, there evidently is not a sufficient basis for attraction or repulsion to cause stable enough grouping that expectations and experiences can balance. The mean number of inversions in the slopes of the probability curve for these two runs was zero, which indicated that there was no temporary formation of groups which then later decayed. Instead, the process was what might be called monotonic decay.

Another aspect of the runs was that the introduction of bias caused considerable fluctuation in the grouping process. The mean number of inversions in the probability curve was relatively high for all bias runs. Thus, the implication of bias in expectation for participation would seem to be a continual moving in and out of various groupings looking for a more ideal circumstance. In the runs without bias but with a nonrandom initial P matrix, individuals 2 through 5 formed a complete grouping in that they all had a probability of 1 of going to the same locus. Individual number 1, however, became an isolate in both cases. Thus, the initial eight runs show that a random, nonbiased beginning will not form groups at all, a nonrandom, nonbiased process will form partial groups but no disjoint subgroups, and the introduction of bias creates sufficient fluctuation that the stability of grouping is problematic.

Incorporating the Idea of Social Pressure. One distinct advantage in using computer simulation is that one need only change the program in order to incorporate a new idea in the theory. The results of the initial runs suggested one particular problem with the kind of grouping process represented in the model. Individuals with high C values could invade groups of lower-C-valued persons, giving the high individual a biased share of the interaction without providing any means for the lower-valued numbers to defend themselves against the invasion. What was needed, it seemed, was some way to represent the fairly common social phenomenon of rejecting an undesirable person. This notion of rejection necessitated representing a group evaluation of any member and exertion of pressure against that person if he upset a desirable structure. Therefore, the idea of social pressures was examined.

For each group at a given locus, each individual's discrepancy (basis for dissatisfaction) was already computed and weighted by the probability of that group's forming. To operationalize social pressure against individual i, then, it was possible to compute the dissatisfaction of all others with groups which included i at locus k compared to their dissatisfaction with all groups *not* including i at that locus, weighted by probabilities of i's being or not being included. If the other four actors showed greater dissatisfaction when actor i was present than when he was absent, then social pressure was exerted against i by augmenting i's dissatisfaction with locus k. Conversely, greater satisfaction when i *was* present resulted in a reduction of i's dissatisfaction with locus k, which can be interpreted as pressure to become a more frequent member of groups at k. By computing pressure for or against each individual at each locus, the routine allowed personal attraction to or rejection of a locus, as before, to be augmented or offset by others' attempts to attract or reject him.

As before, the runs which had random beginning and no bias were unable to produce grouping. Again, the curves showed monotonic decay. Random runs with bias produced complete grouping. That is, one group eventually formed which involved all five persons at the same locus with probabilities of unity. The process of formation was by no means smooth, however. The graphs indicated that the subset 1, 2, 3, formed early and that persons 4 and 5 nearly destroyed the system when they entered later before sufficient adjustment to their presence could occur. Nonrandom runs without bias produced fairly straightforward total groupings (person 1 omitted in one case) similar to the earlier runs without social pressure. Nonrandom runs with bias produced a group of person 1 through 4 for the population involving all different C values, but no group whatsoever for the 1, 1, 2, 3, 3 distribution of C values.

The introduction of social pressure had the following implications. With one exception, all groups formed as they had without social pressure, except that some new persons were included in earlier partial groupings. Apparently adding social pressure had the consequence of preventing unduly fast entry of extreme C values into existing groups, thus allowing a broader base of stability. Of course, if all five persons end up in the same group, the only difference which social pressure could make would be in the orderliness of the process. With fixed individual tendencies, eventual expectations and actual participation rates must be the same if a complete grouping is to occur. It becomes evident in examining the results of the model that the individual actor is represented as a person who is adaptable to virtually any circumstance provided he has sufficient time to adjust his expectations to actuality. Thus any pair or larger group could form in the model if that pair interacted over a long enough period of time to allow each member to adapt expectations to what actually occurred in the conversation.

A "No-Host" Model. Because some of the runs described thus far took initial downward trends in the pair probabilities to the point where recovery was virtually impossible, it was thought desirable to avoid the excessive loss of interaction time which the host model imposes on the system. That loss can be represented as follows. When not at home, an individual goes to some other locus with a specifiable probability. If the other host is not home, he has wasted his time, for no group can form. Similarly both he and a third person may go to this locus but overlap only by chance with the host's being home. They may be there together without the host, but the routine ignores such no-host assemblies. As a result, time spent waiting or wandering greatly exceeds time spent in interaction, a most wasteful model indeed.

To avoid waiting for a host, the no-host model assumes a set of loci, such as taverns or clubs, at which individuals interact without requiring any specific person to be present. To maintain comparability with the "host" version of the simulate, the number of loci is still the number of persons in the population. All other aspects of the routine are the same as before, except that random initial P_{ik} cannot be used, since everything would be in immediate balance.

In contrast to the earlier versions of the model, the "no-host" version provided stable groupings with little difficulty in formation for all runs. Even the previously problematic situation of a nonrandom beginning with bias for the 1, 1, 2, 3, 3 distribution produced grouping in the new version of the model. Apparently the loss of potential interaction which occurred under the random-grouping model was part of the difficulty experienced in the earlier runs. In sociologically relevant terms this difference suggests that social scheduling processes are crucial to successful grouping.

One run in the no-host version nearly created two disjoint subgroups. Individuals 4 and 5 were just beginning to interact apart from the other three by the one-hundredth iteration. It was possible that this single run could have provided the anticipated splitting of the set of five individuals into groups of relatively similar basic tendencies. In three of the other runs either number 4 or number 5 was incorporated into a group including numbers 1, 2, and 3 at the expense of the other high-C-value person. These three were nonrandom bias runs, which would indicate that the initial nonrandom character of the system (putting them into higher-than-average interaction with each other) coupled with the preference for a slightly larger than equitable share of the group's attention has created a competitive situation which worked to the advantage of one of them. The other in each case became an isolate. It is possible that the one run which nearly developed a four-five dyad avoided that competition before it had reduced the four-five interaction to such a low point that no return was feasible.

One final question was considered in the use of the model. Examination of all runs indicated that person 3 was always included if groups formed. In fact, person 3 was always one of the first pair to stabilize in any of the groups. As was anticipated at the outset, then, individual 3 served a kind of intermediary function. It was possible that such an intermediary function was basic to the fact that the population did not split into opposing dyad and triad groupings. Perhaps absence of such an intermediary would greatly change some of the results.

A Final Attempt. The question remains: is it possible, given the present simulate model, for two or more distinct subgroups to develop? To approach this problem directly, a series of runs was made using the "no-host" model with initial C values of 1, 2, 2, 3, 6, 7, 7, 8. This eight-person population, it was thought, would provide the program with enough of an initial bifurcation to insure the formation of two distinct subgroups. Use of an eight-person population, too, has eliminated the intermediary position. This middle position, as noted above, seemed to keep the population together.

The four runs were: social pressure—with bias; social pressure—without bias; without social pressure—with bias; and without social pressure—without bias. Results were less than expected, in that there still was no bifurcation of the groupings. As before, groupings were formed in some of the runs, but there was at most only one group per run. Also as before, the bias factor seemed to be important in the formation of the groups. In the two runs without bias, no groups at all were formed; but in both runs with bias, a group formed after much instability. It is of interest to note that the two groups that do form on the bias runs always include individuals 1, 2, 3, and 4.

Why didn't a bifurcated system develop? There may be several reasons, but the basic problem may be that the general nature of the model precludes any distinct subgrouping. The model is based on the assumption that each individual will attempt to maximize his momentary self-interest in selecting a group in which to participate. While this model has certain advantages, it makes groupings temporary and tenuous, with each individual moving in or out of the group as he finds other possible groups more to his liking. Since the model is based on minimizing aversion, any location to which a person is not going at any given time will usually seem more attractive, since he will have no current aversion to it. This "grass is greener on the other side" aspect of the model results in individuals' spreading their participation widely, but thinly, over available loci until something particularly attractive is encountered. Groups which could be reasonably satisfactory, but not ideal, are consequently broken up before they stabilize. With bias present, this tendency to look elsewhere is likely to cause high-C individuals to keep on the move, while social pressure makes their presence at any particular locus somewhat uncomfortable. An implied consideration for making the model more compatible with the operation of "real" groups is some kind of group identification function. Such a function would provide already existing groups a degree of inertia and of attraction for the members which would increase over time if the group continued together. Consequently, loci not currently used would in general be *less* attractive than current ones.

A final difficulty with the model is that a person will choose groups that satisfy his expectation without regard for group size. It might be more reasonable, other things being equal, to assume that people prefer smaller groups to larger ones. Work by James[6] on free-forming groups suggests that dyads are by far the most common size of group.

Five basic conclusions were drawn from the simulation work described here:

1. The situation of random structure and no bias does not generate viable groups. Sociologically this implies that *either* preexisting structure *or* motivation to obtain a "better share" or both will be needed to engender grouping processes. Structure without bias might be representative of such primary groups as family and friendship structures of long standing. No structure, coupled with bias, is essentially a competitive situation with equal beginning for participants. A number of interesting sociological considerations may be derived from this conclusion.
2. Bias (or a motivating factor *re* inequitable share) induces unstable grouping processes. The bias factor could have been made large enough to defeat all grouping, suggesting that if a process rests upon bias, careful controls, perhaps of a normative nature, are needed to prevent destruction of the system.
3. Social pressure, as incorporated here, is a stabilizing factor. It *reduces* the likelihood of forcing extreme persons into oblivion, as incongruous as that sounds, by preventing too rapid changes in the system, hence allowing more orderly adaptation of expectations to changing reality.
4. Social scheduling processes are crucial to successful grouping. However, they may be represented in a model, they clearly have strong influence on the development and maintenance of stable groups.

[6]John James, "The distribution of free-forming small group size," *American Sociological Review*, vol. 18, no. 5 (1953), pp. 569–570.

5. Some form of group identification (or possibly identification with a particular locus) appears essential if all individuals are to affiliate with a group, and also if subgroups are to form. Many questions could be raised about the validity of aspects of the simulate, but if this final conclusion is valid, it amounts to saying that short-range self-interest cannot produce stable social groupings for all members of a population.

Other Implications and Other Models. Although the model just discussed was not entirely satisfactory for the purposes for which it was created, it does illustrate certain implications of the ideas about group formation which gave rise to it. Also, as was seen, those specific mathematical implications suggest necessary revisions of the theoretical ideas in order to produce certain kinds of behavior in the model which intuitive understanding of social grouping suggests should occur. Two questions remain to be examined. The first is whether the model developed in this case might be applicable to other spheres of substantive theory than the question of friendship groupings. The second is whether other models might provide a better basis for looking into the development of such friendship groups.

Regarding other applications of the model, it is interesting to note that a basic assumption in experimental work on coalition formation is that each partner in a coalition will expect to get that share of the payoff which is represented by his contributed share of coalition power. If this relationship, first expressed by Gamson,[7] is expressed mathematically, it produces exactly the same kind of equation as (8-1). One of the problems of the simulation was that some sort of group identification appeared essential if individuals were to remain affiliated with a particular group. If, on the other hand, one were asking about strictly rational coalition formation for the sake of maximizing one's payoff in a monetary payoff situation, perhaps the model would be quite appropriate.

Note one distinct difference between the coalition situation and the friendship grouping situation. In the former, a total coalition (that is, all persons forming a single coalition) provides no competitive advantage. It presumably would not occur if individuals were trying to follow the Gamson criterion of a minimal winning coalition. Such a criterion requires that partners in the coalition have as little total power as is needed to control the situation for which the coalition is formed. Thus, applications of this simulation model to a problem of coalition formation would require some notion of a minimal group necessary for control of a situation. This, however, sounds surprisingly similar to saying that people prefer smaller groups to larger ones. Thus, incorporating a preference for small-group interaction into the friendship-formation model might in fact make it quite appropriate for the coalition problem.

[7] William Gamson, "A theory of coalition formation," *American Sociological Review*, vol. 26, no. 3 (1961), pp. 373–382.

One further difference between friendship formation as expressed in the simulation and the question of coalition formation is that the theories of coalition assume that the individual is after a maximal share of the payoff. That means, in terms of the kind of simulation presented here, that expected share of conversation based on previous experience would probably have to be changed to maximum share of payoff. However, the bias factor introduced into the model could well accommodate a desire for as large a share as possible in light of the experience the individual has had in previous coalition relationships. In short, it would appear that the same kinds of principles developed in the friendship-formation model, equation (8-1) in particular, could be built into a developmental model of coalition formation.

Regarding other models which might be appropriate for the question of friendship formation, there are many possibilities. Most of the material of Chapters 4 and 5 is directly relevant to this question. Among the more common theories of friendship and interpersonal choice are those which deal with balance, or variations of that notion such as interpersonal similarity or cognitive dissonance as a consequence of disagreement between individuals. These models are treated in graph-theory form in Chapter 4 and extended to the question of clique formation as treated by matrix algebra.

One final comment should be made about the work discussed in this chapter. It was indicated at the outset that simulation is preferable when the mathematical form becomes so complex that direct solutions are difficult. It is also, of course, an easy way to observe the process of development rather than simply determining such things as points of equilibrium, stable states, and other special cases in the overall problem. A related aspect of using simulation should be evident in comparing this chapter with the other chapters. When direct solutions are required by the nature of the model, then a greater concern with the mathematics of the model becomes necessary. It is possible in simulation work to be relatively cavalier about mathematical neatness.

So long as the mathematical expressions can be put into computer-program form, the computer can worry about the outcome of those expressions. The person constructing the model need only worry about casting it into a program and interpreting the results. Thus simulation puts more stress on the developmental process and on the translation from theory to mathematical form of the various parts of the model, whereas direct-solution models necessarily place considerable stress on the overall fitting together of the mathematics in a way which allows determinant answers. Perhaps most theorists who wish to avoid excessive mathematical training should start with simulation. Then, of course, it is necessary either to be a good computer programmer or to be able to explain one's requirements to a programmer. It may be a moot point whether it will be easier to acquire programming sophistication or mathematical sophistication.

a model of birth control processes

As the second model in this chapter we will consider a way of answering the following question: How much can a given birth control procedure reduce the number of babies that would have been born if that procedure was not used? The particular model to be discussed was developed by Keyfitz.[8] It represents a growing field of formal models dealing with factors influencing the birth rate and the size or composition of the population generally.

The Substantive Problem. If we focus attention on a couple who are capable of having children, we may consider these questions. How long is it likely to take for the woman to become pregnant if no precautions are exercised? Once pregnant, how long will it be before she has completed the cycle of giving birth and returning to the state of being susceptible to becoming pregnant again? Taken together, these questions imply asking: What is the expected length of a total cycle from conception to birth to becoming fertile again to the next conception? Subsequently, what is the expected length of the cycle if some birth control method is employed? With the answers to these questions, some interesting and surprising facts about the effects of contraception, abortion, or other control methods can be deduced.

Translation into Mathematics. The source of the model is not exactly a theory, nor is it data. It is a mathematical formalization based on our general knowledge of the cyclic process we wish to model. In more-or-less formal terms, it can be assumed that there is a fixed probability of the woman's becoming pregnant during any given month if she (1) is not pregnant at the beginning of the month, and (2) is not sterile, either permanently or temporarily (owing, for example, to just having delivered a baby). If she becomes pregnant, and does not abort, miscarry, or deliver prematurely, then there will be nine months while she is carrying the baby that she cannot become pregnant again. Also, there is a postpartum period of temporary sterility of up to eight months or so. Thus she is out of the susceptible-to-pregnancy category for, say, 17 months. That time, plus the time it took to become pregnant in the first place, is the total time needed to produce one baby and return to being able to become pregnant again.

Now consider some procedure which either reduces the probability of her becoming pregnant or reduces the waiting period (gestation plus postpartum sterility). A reduction in the probability of becoming pregnant should increase the number of months it takes to become pregnant, but it

---

[8]Nathan Keyfitz, "How birth control affects births," *Social Biology*, vol. 18 (June, 1971), pp. 109–121.

will not affect the delay of approximately 17 months once pregnancy has occurred. Of course, a perfect contraceptive (for example, not having intercourse) would produce an infinite time to pregnancy. Less efficient methods will result in some finite total time to pregnancy, hence in a finite total time to produce one baby and return to being able to become pregnant again. This total time *with* contraception can be compared to total time *without* contraception to deduce the amount of reduction in the number of babies born that use of the contraceptive method has accomplished.

On the other hand, assume that pregnancy was terminated by abortion. If abortion occurs during the second month and there is an additional month of postpartum sterility, then no baby is born but the woman returns to the susceptible-to-pregnancy category about 14 months sooner than she would have if she had not had an abortion. A second pregnancy will occur, on the average, that much sooner for her.

It should be evident that we are working from empirical knowledge, although not data in the sense of a series of specific observations and measurements. The attempt is to deduce what mathematical forms would describe the empirical process as we know it. The principal variable is the *state* of a woman: susceptible (to pregnancy), pregnant, or sterile. For simplicity, it will be assumed that the amount of time spent pregnant and the amount of time spent sterile following delivery or abortion are empirically specifiable quantities rather than being treated as part of the random process. Consequently, the only random aspect of the problem concerns passing from the susceptible state to the pregnant state versus remaining susceptible (that is, not becoming pregnant). We need to calculate mean passage times through the cycle of pregnancy and back to susceptibility. In general, such a model is called a *renewal process*.

Because the basic model is so simple, a translation diagram is hardly needed. We have the probability, p, that a susceptible woman becomes pregnant during a given month. The probability of her not becoming pregnant is $1 - p$. If she becomes pregnant during the first month, she does so with probability p. If not, she may become pregnant during the second month with probability p times the probability that she did not conceive during the first month. Hence, the probability of pregnancy in month 2 is $(1 - p)p$. If she escaped pregnancy for two months, then became pregnant in month 3, the probability is $(1 - p)^2 p$. In general, the probability of pregnancy occuring in month r is

$$p^{(r)} = (1 - p)^{r-1} p. \tag{8-5}$$

If this series is a valid probability process, than it should sum to one over all possible months. That sum is

$$\sum_{r=1}^{\infty} (1 - p)^{r-1} p = p + (1 - p)p + (1 - p)^2 p + \cdots. \tag{8-6}$$

Let $p = 1 - q$, and rewrite equation (8-13) as

$$\sum_{r=1}^{\infty} q^{r-1}(1-q) = 1 - q + q(1-q) + q^2(1-q) + \cdots$$
$$= 1 - q + q - q^2 + q^2 - q^3 + \cdots$$
$$= 1 - q^{\infty}$$
$$= 1.$$

As is evident, all terms cancel except 1 and the last power of q, which approaches zero as the power approaches infinity. Since the sum is unity, the process is properly defined.

How many months will pass, on the average, before pregnancy occurs? To obtain an answer, we need to recognize that if each particular number of months, r, is multiplied by the probability of pregnancy during that rth month, $(1 - p)^{r-1} p$, then the average number of months to pregnancy will be given by the sum of those products. This is no different from calculating an expected value for any variable by multiplying each possible value of the variable by its probability of occurrence, then adding over the range of the variable. Mean time to pregnancy is thus

$$\sum_{r=1}^{\infty} r(1-p)^{r-1} p = p + 2(1-p)p + 3(1-p)^2 p + \cdots . \qquad (8\text{-}7)$$

Again, substituting $1 - q$ for p allows rewriting equation (8-7) in more convenient form:

$$\sum_{r=1}^{\infty} r q^{r-1}(1-q) = 1 - q + 2q(1-q) + 3q^2(1-q) + \cdots$$
$$= 1 - q + 2q - 2q^2 + 3q^2 - 3q^q + \cdots$$
$$= 1 + q + q^2 + \cdots .$$

To solve for this series, let T stand for the sum, and remember that $q^r \to 0$ as $r \to \infty$.

$$T = 1 + q + q^2 + \cdots ,$$
$$qT = q + q^2 + q^3 + \cdots ,$$
$$1 + qT = 1 + q + q^2 + \cdots ,$$
$$1 + qT = T.$$

Solving for T gives $T = 1/(1 - q) = 1/p$. Consequently, the mean number of months it takes for a woman to become pregnant is $1/p$. If $p = .2$ (a 20 percent chance of becoming pregnant each month without contraception), then mean time to pregnancy would be $1/.2 = 5$ months.[9] If we are considering only one woman, it may seem a bit strange to say that the average time it takes her to get pregnant will be five months, since there normally will be so few pregnancies that an average seems questionable. As a collective process, though, the mean time states that, if all women are described by the same process, then the average time to pregnancy will be five months, although some women will conceive more quickly or less quickly. Either interpretation is proper, however.

Assume that the number of months until delivery and the number of months of postpartum sterility are random variables averaging a total of S months. Recurrence time (from first being susceptible to first becoming susceptible again after delivery) would be $1/p + S$, or 22 months if gestation averaged nine months and postpartum sterility averaged eight more. These appear to be reasonable figures for human populations.

Efficiency of Abortion as Birth Control. What is the comparable recurrence time if abortion is used to stop pregnancy? First, note that pregnancy follows the same distribution whether or not abortion is to be used; it takes an average of $1/p$ months to become pregnant. If the number of months until abortion after pregnancy occurs, and the number of postabortion months of sterility are random variables averaging a total of a months, then recurrence time given abortion is $1/p + a$. Reasonable figures might be $p = .2$, again, and $a = 3$, as suggested earlier, so that $1/p + a = 8$ months.

The number of abortions needed to fill the time normally used for one live birth can be calculated by a ratio of recurrence times.

$$N = \frac{1/p + S}{1/p + a}. \tag{8-8}$$

For the example used so far, the number of abortions needed to "replace" one live birth is $22/8 = 2.75$. Intuitively it might seem that one abortion prevents one birth, but we have just discovered that it takes nearly three abortions to replace that one birth. In fact, the main consequence of abortion is to increase the number of pregnancies to be expected.

The reciprocal of N in equation (8-8) can be considered the effectiveness of abortion as a birth control device. In this instance, one abortion uses up only eight out of 22 months of the usual recurrence time, or only about 36 percent. It should be evident that, if S and a are fixed, efficiency increases

[9]The values of p and other empirically determinable factors in these models are taken from Keyfitz, who comments, "The constraints in the . . . calculation are about right for human populations that do not use contraception." Keyfitz, in *Social Biology*, 1971, p. 112. We presume that later constraints in the more complex models are also "about right."

only as p decreases. Such a conclusion suggests that possibly abortion would work best as a back-up for contraception rather than alone.

Suppose that a contraceptive method is available which has efficiency of e, meaning that the probability of becoming pregnant in any given month (assuming susceptible) is only $1 - e$ times the probability without that contraceptive, or $p(1 - e)$. For $e = .95$, and $p = .2$ as before, the monthly chance of pregnancy is $.2(.05) = .01$. This value may replace p in the series computed previously, since it acts as a probability just as p did alone. Recurrence time is therefore $1/p(1 - e) + S$ for women who give birth, and $1/p(1 - e) + a$ for those who use abortion. Again, the ratio of these values determines the number of abortions needed to prevent (take as much time as) one birth, and the reciprocal is the effectiveness of abortion and contraception together. For the figures used previously, it will require only 1.14 abortions to prevent one birth, making abortion 88 percent effective in using up the recurrence time of a single birth when 95 percent efficient contraceptive methods are used.

General Use of the Model. Any single method of birth control can be evaluated by the preceding model. Contraception alone, for example, will produce a recurrence time of $1/p(1 - e) + S$, as shown above. Comparison with a couple using no precaution means comparison with a recurrence time of $1/p + S$. For relatively unreliable methods, contraception has very little overall effectiveness. If $p = .2$, $S = 17$, and $e = .50$ (50 percent efficient contraception), the recurrence times are 27 months with contraception and 22 without. Consequently, the expected rate of birth (in births per month) has gone from 1/22 to 1/27, or from .045 to .037. Birth rate reduction is, in fact, only about 19 percent when contraception efficiency is 50 percent.

Assuming that the values of $p = .2$ and $S = 17$ are reasonable estimates for populations not using contraception, we can derive a simple formula for computing the proportion reduction in birth rate as a function of efficiency of a contraceptive method. Using R to indicate reduction, that formula would be (after some algebraic simplification)

$$R = 1 - \frac{(1-e)(1+pS)}{1+(1-e)pS}$$
$$= 1 - \frac{4.4(1-e)}{1+3.4(1-e)}. \qquad (8\text{-}9)$$

Figure 8-2 shows the curve of proportional reduction in the birth rate as a function of efficiency of contraception, assuming no other birth control method is used.

Although much more can be done with models of this sort (Keyfitz provides other extensions of the basic model[10]), we will not pursue them

[10]Keyfitz, in *Social Biology*, 1971.

Figure 8-2

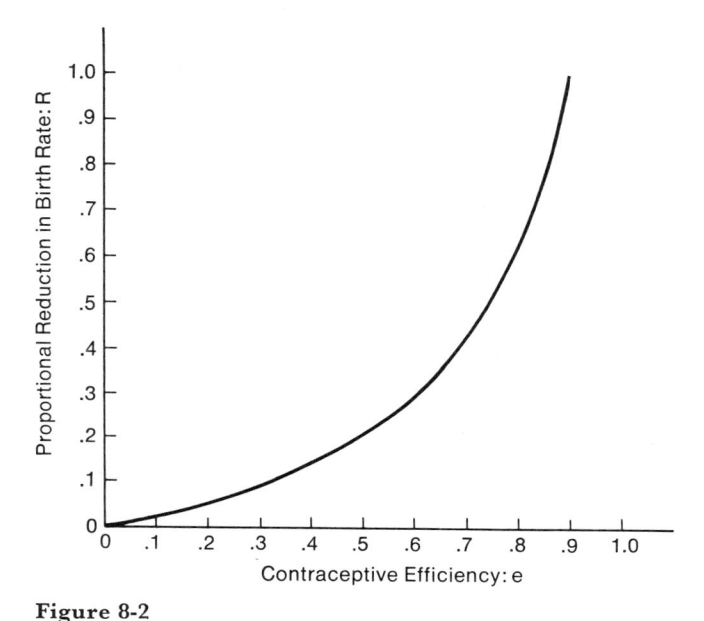

Effects of contraceptive efficiency on birth rates

Based on Keyfitz model. The curve is close to but not exactly a circle.

further. It should be clear that renewal processes are very useful models for social processes. They form a convenient and important part of the tools of mathematical sociology.

problems

1. Develop a computer simulation which begins by randomly pairing people from a total group of, say, ten, who have either pro or con views on a single topic. If they agree when they meet, then increment their future chances of meeting slightly. If they disagree when they meet, let either one of them change to the other's viewpoint with some (small) probability. If they reach agreement, treat their future interaction probability the same as for those who initially agreed. If they continue to disagree, reduce their chances of meeting again. Will the group split over time into two separate camps? Will you always retain both opinions? Can you develop a mathematical model for this problem instead of a computer simulation? How would you proceed?

2. Assume that two contraceptive devices are available to the residents of Town X. One has efficiency of .4, the other has efficiency of .8. Construct a model in which one-third of the women of X use no contraceptive, one

third use the one with lower efficiency, and one third use the more efficient device. Assume that age, marital status, and so on are comparable for the three groups of women. Will the total effect on fertility be the same as the effect of everyone using the .4 procedure? (The value .4 is the mean efficiency for the contraceptive practices of the women.)

3. Develop a flow diagram for a simulation of a small-group discussion. It might help to read the Bales (1953), Horvath, and Fisek references given in Chapter 3 to help you think about the problem.

4. Try doing a computer simulation of one of the process models in Chapters 7 through 10.

CHAPTER 9

markov processes
and occupational mobility

Stochastic processes deal with events that occur randomly over time. Although there are a large variety of stochastic processes, one kind, Markov chains (alternatively referred to as Markov processes), seems particularly useful to sociologists. In the next few pages, we will present a brief review of some of the basic concepts, operations, and systems of notation for Markov processes, as a preparation for the models in the next three chapters.[1]

a brief introduction to markov processes

In order to be appropriate for representation by a Markov process an event must occur randomly over time, and the probability with which it occurs

---

[1]For more information on Markov processes, see J. G. Kemeny, J. L. Snell, and G. L. Thompson, *Introduction to Finite Mathematics*, 2d ed. (Englewood Cliffs, N.J.: Prentice-Hall, Inc., 1966), pp. 194–200 and 271–290 (a brief, simple explanation); D. J. Bartholemew, *Stochastic Models for Social Processes* (New York: John Wiley & Sons, 1967), or a textbook on stochastic processes.

166 Mathematical Sociology

must be a function of the immediately preceeding event. To illustrate, consider the hypothetical Professor Smith. Dr. Smith can either go out to lunch with his colleagues or remain in his office over the lunch hour to eat a sandwich at his desk. While he enjoys eating out, he does not feel he can afford the time and money to do this every day. It works out that he eats out with probability .80 if he stayed in his office the previous day, but he has only a probability of .40 of eating out if he ate out the previous day. What he did two, three, or more days previously makes no difference to his decision. This situation meets the requirements of a Markov process.

First, there are a set of *states*, the possible events, which are mutually exclusive and exhaustive. The states of this system are "in" and "out," and we must assume that Smith is one or the other but not both during any one lunch hour. Second, the probability of moving from a particular state to another in one time interval remains constant; that is, the probability that Smith will eat out today if he stayed in yesterday is always .80, regardless of whether "yesterday" and "today" are January 6 and 7, May 12 and 13, or November 1 and 2. Third, the probability of moving from one state to another depends on what the first state is; there is a different probability he will move from "in" to "out" than from "out" to "out." The consequences of meeting these three requirements is that the state of the system at any time depends only on its state at the immediately preceeding time and a constant transition probability.

Ways of Representing Markov Processes. One of the common ways of representing states and transitions in a Markov process is with tree diagrams, as shown in Figure 9-1. The branches of the tree represent the possible states on any given day, and the probability that a given branch is taken is written on the branch. We can picture Smith as standing at one node of the tree and "deciding" to take one or the other of the branches available. His choice looks different if he is standing at the "in" node rather than at the "out" node. Thus, if we know what Smith did yesterday, we can tell what the probability of his being in or out today is. Furthermore, *all* we need to know is what he did yesterday and the two sets of probabilities. Note that the probability of "in" is always equal to one minus the probability of "out," because Smith must be somewhere during the lunch hour.

Yesterday   Today

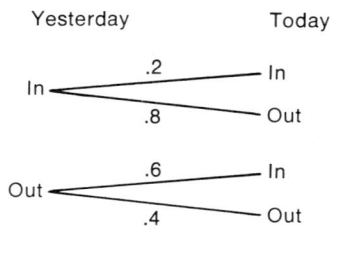

In ──.2── In
   ──.8── Out

Out ──.6── In
    ──.4── Out

Figure 9-1

Tree diagram for one-step transitions in a Markov process

Although we have assumed that the probability of being in or out today depends only on what happened yesterday, we are also equipped to predict the probability that Smith will be in tomorrow, the day after tomorrow, or any day after that, by extrapolating from Figure 9-1, as shown in Figure 9-2. If we know that Smith was in yesterday, we see that the probability he will be in tomorrow is the probability of going from "in" to "in" to "in" plus the probability of going from "in" to "out" to "in", which is $(.2)(.2) + (.8)(.6) = .52$. Similarly, the probability he is out tomorrow is $(.2)(.8) + (.8)(.4) = .48$. These add up to one, because he must be either in or out tomorrow. All these probabilities are conditional on his being in yesterday; if we knew he was out yesterday the probabilities would be different. In order to make predictions, we must know where he was yesterday (unless we assume the system is in equilibrium, as explained below).

An alternative representation of a Markov process is a transition diagram, as illustrated in Figure 9-3. This shows the various possible events and the probabilities of movement among them in one time interval. This form of representation makes very clear the distinction between remaining in the same state and changing to a different state; it does not show so clearly as the tree the predictions that can be made for longer time intervals.

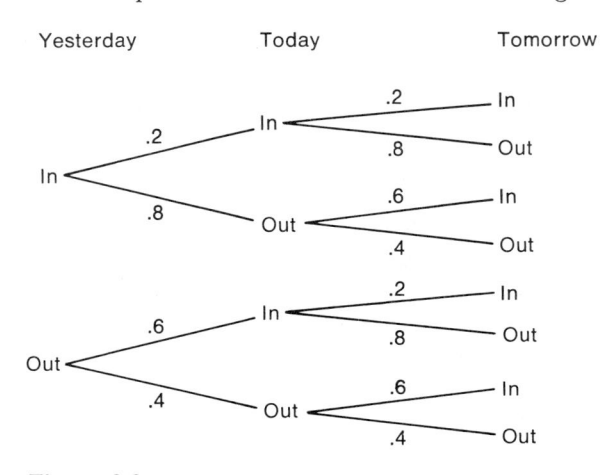

Figure 9-2

Two-step tree diagram for a Markov process

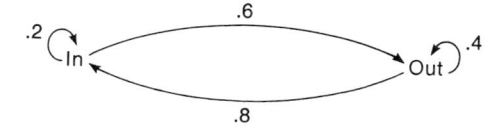

Figure 9-3

Transition diagram for a Markov process

The standard mathematical representation of a Markov process is as a matrix, with the events at one time forming the rows, and the events at the next time the columns. Figure 9-4 shows a matrix for our example. The ijth entry indicates the probability of moving from state i at time t_n to state j at time t_{n+1}. The rows must always add up to one. We pointed out in Chapter 4 that matrix notation and graphs (a tree is a kind of graph) can be used to represent the same relationships in many cases. This is true for the tree and matrix notations for Markov processes, also. For example, if the matrix M in Figure 9-4 is squared, we get

$$M^2 = \begin{array}{c} \\ \text{in} \\ \text{out} \end{array} \begin{array}{c} \text{in} \quad \text{out} \\ \begin{pmatrix} .52 & .48 \\ .36 & .64 \end{pmatrix} \end{array}.$$

In M^2, the columns represent events on day 0 and the rows represent events on day 2; the entries in M^2 are exactly what we found when we calculated the probabilities of transition between yesterday and tomorrow using the tree diagram in Figure 9-2. This is because the arithmetical operations required to square the transition matrix are identical to the operations required to go through the tree twice and add the probabilities; if this does not seem intuitively obvious, convince yourself it is so by working through some examples.

Similarly, to find the probability of a transition from "in" to "out" between day 0 and day 3, we simply find M^3, and the probability of moving from state i to state j in n days is the ijth entry of M^n. The matrix that shows the transition probabilities between day 0 and day 1 is a *one-step transition matrix*, M^2 is a *two-step transition matrix*, M^n is an *n-step transition matrix*, and so on. The ijth entry in M^n is usually written $p_{ij}^{(n)}$, meaning the probability of moving from state i to state j in n time periods. Technically, the one-step transition probabilities should be written $p_{ij}^{(1)}$ but for convenience the superscript is usually omitted.

As one can see from the discussion above, the most abstract mathematical notation for a Markov process is a conditional probability equation of the form:

$$p_{ij}^{(1)} = \Pr(\text{state } j \text{ on trial } n+1 \mid \text{state } i \text{ on trial } n).$$

Yesterday   Today

          In   Out

In $\begin{pmatrix} .2 & .8 \\ .6 & .4 \end{pmatrix}$

Out

Figure 9-4

One-step transition matrix for a Markov process

As this indicates, the mathematics of conditional probability is important to working with Markov processes.

Aggregation and Equilibrium. If we can justifiably make the assumption that Professor Smith is typical of his department in his eating habits, and if we know the proportion of people who were out to lunch on any particular day, we can predict what the proportion will be of people in or out any successive day, as follows:

Let the vector $V_0 = (P_{1,0}, P_{2,0})$ represent the distribution of the population between states on day 0. The capital P's are the proportion in state 1 (in) and state 2 (out) at time 0. Then, $P_{1,0} + P_{2,0} = 1$ (everyone must be either in or out), and furthermore

$$V_1 = V_0 M.$$

That is, the vector describing the distribution of the population among states at time t_{n+1} is the product of the vector of distribution among states at time t_n times the transition matrix. If we know, for example, that the day before classes begin (day 0) everyone in Smith's department is in his or her office at noon, we have:

$$V_0 = (1.0, 0)$$

and

$$V_1 = V_0 M = (1.0, 0) \begin{pmatrix} .2 & .8 \\ .6 & .4 \end{pmatrix} = (.2, .8).$$

Thus we can predict that 20 percent of the faculty will be in at noon on the first day of classes. Likewise, we can find:

$$V_2 = V_1 M = V_0 M^2 = (.52, .48),$$
$$V_3 = V_2 M = V_0 M^3 = (.39, .61),$$
$$V_4 = V_3 M = V_0 M^4 = (.44, .56).$$

That is, the distribution of population among states at any time can be calculated either by multiplying the previous time's vector of distribution by the transition matrix, or by multiplying the appropriate power of the transition matrix and the initial distribution vector.

Note that as the powers of the matrix M get larger, the difference in distribution from day to day gets smaller. Eventually, a Markov process such as the one here illustrated will reach *equilibrium*. At equilibrium, although individuals shift from state to state as time passes, the proportion of individuals in each state does not change over time. That is,

$$M^{n+1} = M^n \quad \text{and} \quad V_{n+1} = V_n \quad \text{when } n = \infty.$$

Since $V_{n+1} = V_n M$, this means that at equilibrium

$$V_{eq} = V_{eq} M,$$

where the subscript "eq" refers to the characteristics at equilibrium. In our example, this means

$$(P_{1,eq}, P_{2,eq}) = (P_{1,eq}, P_{2,eq}) \begin{pmatrix} .2 & .8 \\ .6 & .4 \end{pmatrix},$$

or

$$P_{1,eq} = .2 P_{1,eq} + .6 P_{2,eq},$$
$$P_{2,eq} = .8 P_{1,eq} + .4 P_{2,eq}.$$

This provides a set of two equations in two unknowns, which when solved for $P_{1,eq}$ and $P_{2,eq}$ (and keeping in mind that $P_{1,eq} + P_{2,eq} = 1$) gives $V_{eq} = (.43, .57)$. We can see that our system was fairly close to equilibrium after four days.

The properties of equilibrium have some interesting characteristics. One is that the equilibrium distribution is in no way dependent on the initial distribution; no matter what happened on day 0, by the time the system is in equilibrium the distribution will be the same. Also, at equilibrium the rows of the transition matrix M^n ($n \longrightarrow \infty$) are identical to each other and each row is the same as V_{eq}; in other words, no matter what state a given individual in the population starts in, the probability he will be in a given state at equilibrium is the same as for any other individual in the population. As we will see later, these properties are sometimes useful, sometimes troublesome, in using and interpreting Markov models.

A different kind of Markov process is one that has one or more *absorbing states*. An absorbing state is one that has a zero probability of transition to any other state. Once an individual enters the state, he never leaves. An example of a transition matrix for a Markov process with an absorbing state is

$$\begin{array}{c} \\ A \\ B \\ C \end{array} \begin{array}{c} A \quad B \quad C \\ \begin{pmatrix} 1.0 & 0 & 0 \\ .4 & .2 & .4 \\ .8 & .1 & .1 \end{pmatrix} \end{array}.$$

In this model, state A is an absorbing state; states B and C are not. A Markov process may have more than one absorbing state. At equilibrium, the distribution of the process for the matrix above will be:

$$V_{eq} = (1.0, 0, 0).$$

In other words, since there is a nonzero probability of entering state A and a zero probability of leaving it, if the process goes on long enough everyone will eventually be "absorbed" into state A. For this model,

$$M^n_{\text{as } n \to \infty} = \begin{pmatrix} 1 & 0 & 0 \\ 1 & 0 & 0 \\ 1 & 0 & 0 \end{pmatrix}.$$

In Markov models of demographic processes, death is considered an absorbing state. The population for such a model would be one cohort, and although each individual may pass through a number of states such as health or illness, eventually all the members of a cohort will be dead.

Stochastic models such as Markov-process models are in many ways particularly well suited to problems posed by the data and theories of the social sciences. First, they can be applied to data that have not been gathered by measuring techniques that result in tidy scales corresponding exactly to the real number system. Sociological data are much more likely to appear as categories, ordered or unordered, that correspond nicely to states in a Markov process. Second, the probabilistic assumption often suits both theory and data about human behavior better than a deterministic assumption. Third, the Markov assumption permits incorporation of time in a relatively simple way.

markov models of mobility

Social mobility is a subject of perennial interest to sociologists and one that readily suggests itself for models describing movement between states over time. We have chosen two approaches to models of mobility—an early one by Blumen, Kogan, and McCarthy[2] and a more recent one by McFarland.[3] Both the Blumen, Kogan, and McCarthy book and the McFarland article are concerned with *intra*generational social mobility—that is, with the movement of one person from one job or status to another, not with mobility from one generation to another. Some of the other applications of stochastic models to mobility consider *inter*generational mobility, but these present more complicated problems of measurement and interpretation.

Blumen, Kogan, and McCarthy begin their construction of a model with a set of data. After moving from data to model, they test the model and

[2] Isadore Blumen, Marvin Kogan, and Philip J. McCarthy, *The Industrial Mobility of Labor as a Probability Process* (Ithaca, N.Y.: Cornell University Press, 1955).
[3] David D. McFarland, "Intragenerational social mobility as a Markov process: Including a time-stationary Markovian model that explains observed declines in mobility rates," *American Sociological Review*, vol. 35 (June, 1970), pp. 463–475.

find it wanting in important respects. At this point they call on theory to provide a revision of the model, moving from theory to model, then testing the model again. The revised version is greatly improved, but still presents some problems. This work thus goes in both directions on the theory-data-model triangle.

Developing the Model. The data that Blumen, Kogan, and McCarthy use are from government statistics collected between 1947 and 1949, at one-quarter intervals (every three months), on the current occupation of a one-percent sample of all workers covered by social security since 1937. Occupations were grouped into categories; for some purposes there are ten categories and for other purposes there are fewer. Figure 9-5 shows the coding categories, which are in terms of industry rather than in terms of social class or prestige as in many sociological studies. There is thus no inherent rank order in the set of categories. A worker may leave the system by entering an occupation that is not covered by social security or by ceasing to work because of retirement, death, or whatever. With the addition of a category to represent being outside the system, this describes a closed system of states (occupations) with information about the state occupied by each individual at twelve different times.

Figure 9-5

Meaning of code group designations

INDUSTRY CODE GROUP	INDUSTRIES THEY INCLUDE
A	Farms, Agricultural Service, Forestry and Fisheries
B	Mining and Construction
C	Food and Kindred Products, Tobacco, Textile Mills, Apparel, Lumber, Furniture and Fixtures, Paper and Applied Products
D	Printing and Publishing, Chemical Products, Petroleum Products, Rubber Products, Leather Products, Stone and Clay Products
E	Ordinance, Primary Metals, Fabricated Metals, Machinery, Electrical Equipment, Transportation Equipment, Professional and Scientific Equipment, Miscellaneous Manufacturing
F	Transportation, Communication, and Utilities
G	Wholesale and Retail Trade
H	Banks, Insurance, and Real Estate
J	Service, Amusement, and Professions
K	Government and Unclassified

The variables in the model are the occupations of individuals and the time intervals. Time is represented as having twelve values, corresponding to the moment at which the data are gathered. A second set of variables is the age and sex of the individuals. The population is divided into categories by sex and by four-year age groups. The model is then developed separately for each category. In the discussion that follows, we illustrate how the model is developed for one age-sex category; Blumen, Kogan, and McCarthy, of course, did the same for all the other age-sex categories, with the intention of comparing the results across categories.

There are two ways in which populations can be compared using this approach. The first is by seeing if the same general process seems to work for all of them; if it turns out that the Markov assumption seems to fit some age categories but not others, for example, then we have an interesting item of information about the relationship between age and mobility. For the categories in which the general process seems to operate as a Markov process, we can then compare the parameters for the different populations.

The parameters are derived from the data. From the occupations of individuals at two successive time intervals we can determine the proportion of individuals in any occupation at one time who were in any other occupation at an earlier time. This set of proportions is translated into a set of conditional probabilities of being in state j at time $n + 1$ given occupancy of state i at time n. These are the parameters of the Markov process.

Given these variables and parameters, Blumen, Kogan and McCarthy proceed to construct a simple Markov model using the parameters (proportions of people in occupation i at time n and j at time $n + 1$) as the entries in the transition matrix. This requires two basic assumptions about the relationships between the variables: (1) The probability of an individual's being in state i at time $n + 1$ depends only on the state he occupied at time n and a transition probability (the Markov assumption), and (2) the transition probabilities are constant for all time periods. The latter is referred to as the *stationarity assumption*; this is a *stationary Markov process*. In addition there is an implicit assumption: (3) the population is homogeneous. In other words, we have to assume that the same matrix describes all the people in a given age-sex category.

Translation Diagram 9-1 applies to the simple Markov model.

Estimating the Parameters. With these assumptions we can use the data to estimate the elements m_{ij} of the transition matrix, M. Blumen, Kogan, and McCarthy do this by developing a one-quarter (three-month) transition matrix based on the sum of all one-quarter transitions. There are eleven three-month intervals, since we have twelve data points. The mean one-quarter transition matrix looks like that shown in Table 9-1, for males aged 40–44.

Translation Diagram 9-1

DATA   MODEL

Variables

Occupations; eleven categories $\longrightarrow$ States; $S_1, \ldots, S_{11}$

Time; twelve measurements at $\longrightarrow$ Time $T_1, \ldots, T_{12}$
three-month intervals

Parameters

Age and sex $\longrightarrow$ Separate populations
Proportion of those in $\longrightarrow$ matrix M, with m_{ij} such that
occupation i during the $m_{ij} = \Pr[S_j \text{ at } T_{n+1} | S_i \text{ at } T_n]$
previous time interval who
are now in occupation j.

Relationships

Markov assumption $\longrightarrow \Pr[S_i \text{ at } T_{n+1}] = \sum_{j=1}^{11} \Pr[S_j \text{ at } T_n] m_{ji}$

Table 9-1

One-Quarter Transition Matrix for Males, 40–44. (Based on the sum of all one-quarter observations)

CODE GROUP OF ORIGIN	A	B	C	D	E	F	G	H	J	K	U
A	.826	.028	.018	.009	.009	.018	.018	.009	.000	.000	.064
B	.001	.824	.011	.006	.008	.008	.023	.004	.010	.003	.104
C	.000	.013	.885	.004	.006	.006	.016	.001	.005	.000	.063
D	.000	.007	.003	.921	.007	.004	.016	.002	.002	.000	.038
E	.000	.006	.005	.003	.928	.004	.010	.002	.005	.001	.036
F	.000	.014	.006	.002	.007	.901	.009	.001	.006	.001	.053
G	.000	.012	.010	.005	.008	.004	.879	.002	.010	.001	.069
H	.001	.014	.002	.003	.008	.001	.011	.896	.009	.002	.054
J	.000	.020	.009	.004	.012	.007	.037	.003	.822	.000	.085
K	.000	.121	.040	.024	.064	.032	.040	.000	.008	.484	.186
U	.001	.047	.031	.009	.021	.015	.056	.008	.026	.003	.782

(CODE GROUP OF DESTINATION)

Source: From Isadore Blumen, Marvin Kogan, and Philip J. McCarthy, *The Industrial Mobility of Labor as a Probability Process* (Ithaca, N.Y.: Cornell University, 1955), p. 60. By permission of the publisher.

From the estimated one-quarter transition matrix, the probability of moving from any given occupation to any other occupation in t time intervals is found by raising M to the tth power. The authors chose a two-year, or eight-quarter interval to determine whether the same quarterly transition rates reproduce the longer-term changes in occupation accurately. Since the data cover twelve time intervals, it is then possible to compare the estimates in M^8 with the actual transition probabilities for observed eight-quarter intervals. Blumen, Kogan, and McCarthy do this for several sets of data. For the males aged 40–44 (the group described in the Table 9-1 above), the results are as indicated in Table 9-2. The most useful comparisons are the observed transition probabilities and the expected probabilities (based on M^8) for the main diagonal. Since the entries in a row always sum to one, the magnitude of errors in the main diagonal gives an indication of the magnitude of the rest of the errors for that row. The main diagonal, of course, shows the probability that there will be no change in occupation over the two-year period.

As is obvious from Table 9-2, the predicted entries on the main diagonal are always smaller than the actual entries. In other words, the simple Markov

Table 9-2

Comparison of Expected and Observed Eighth-Order Matrices for Males, 40–44

CODE GROUP OF ORIGIN		A	B	C	D	E	F	G	H	J	K	U	NUMBER OF OBSERVATIONS
A	Exp.	.217	.108	.087	.046	.063	.075	.119	.036	.030	.002	.216	
	Obs.	.500	.075	.000	.000	.025	.025	.125	.000	.000	.000	.250	(40)
B	Exp.	.003	.277	.075	.038	.066	.047	.144	.022	.054	.004	.268	
	Obs.	.001	.649	.022	.006	.031	.021	.041	.006	.009	.003	.210	(1,360)
C	Exp.	.002	.080	.412	.030	.052	.039	.116	.012	.040	.002	.214	
	Obs.	.001	.026	.681	.030	.020	.025	.043	.005	.009	.001	.159	(1,593)
D	Exp.	.001	.054	.035	.526	.053	.028	.102	.015	.025	.002	.155	
	Obs.	.000	.017	.013	.749	.015	.020	.064	.007	.010	.001	.103	(987)
E	Exp.	.001	.052	.042	.025	.568	.031	.080	.013	.034	.003	.152	
	Obs.	.000	.019	.026	.013	.749	.021	.040	.005	.009	.004	.113	(2,309)
F	Exp.	.002	.079	.052	.019	.054	.452	.089	.013	.040	.003	.196	
	Obs.	.000	.025	.009	.004	.023	.756	.029	.002	.007	.002	.143	(908)
G	Exp.	.001	.079	.067	.035	.060	.035	.427	.017	.052	.003	.225	
	Obs.	.000	.029	.030	.014	.029	.013	.693	.006	.028	.002	.156	(2,517)
H	Exp.	.003	.082	.038	.027	.058	.021	.100	.423	.049	.004	.199	
	Obs.	.000	.028	.007	.000	.014	.002	.042	.745	.035	.000	.126	(427)
J	Exp.	.002	.098	.069	.032	.076	.044	.171	.021	.242	.002	.244	
	Obs.	.001	.030	.023	.016	.050	.018	.069	.007	.573	.000	.214	(888)
K	Exp.	.002	.151	.100	.057	.132	.071	.154	.018	.052	.006	.255	
	Obs.	.000	.143	.104	.117	.156	.169	.013	.013	.117	.013	.156	(77)
U	Exp.	.003	.124	.104	.043	.089	.058	.186	.027	.070	.004	.293	
	Obs.	.002	.090	.063	.024	.047	.033	.142	.026	.043	.004	.526	(2,810)

Source: From Blumen, Kogan, and McCarthy, p. 63. By permission of the publisher.

model underestimates the extent to which people will remain in the same occupation for a long time. The tables comparing observed and expected values on the main diagonals for the other data groups (males of other ages, and females for all ages) have the same feature. On the other hand, there are no systematic discrepancies among the other entries, except for their being too large. The only consistently erroneous feature of the model is its underestimation of the main diagonal.

Revising the Model. Since the simple Markov model produces a large and consistent discrepancy between its predictions and the actual data, Blumen, Kogan and McCarthy attempt to revise it. Table 9-2 says that people are less likely to move than the model predicts. If they do move, however, the model doesn't do too bad a job of predicting where they will go. This consideration led the authors to try assuming that there are two kinds of individuals: those who never move from their original occupations (called *stayers* in the new model) and those who do move (called *movers*). The movers will move according to a set of probabilities governed by the Markov assumption, while the probability matrix describing behavior of the stayers will have 1's on the main diagonal and zeroes elsewhere (that is, it is an identity matrix). The whole population is described by a matrix that combines the two separate matrices. Obviously, the more stayers there are in a population, the larger will be the entries on the main diagonal of higher powers of the transition matrix describing the population as a whole.

Translation diagram 9-2 applies to the mover-stayer model.

Translation Diagram 9-2

THEORY   MODEL

Variables

Occupations   ⟶ $S_1, S_2, \ldots, S_{11}$ (as before)
Time   ⟶ $T_1, T_2, \ldots, T_{12}$

Parameters

Two sets of transition probabilities ⟶ Transition matrices P, I and M as defined below

The proportions of people in different occupations who are stayers ⟶ A matrix S as defined below

Relationships

Assumption: The population can be divided into movers and stayers. For each subset, a stationary Markov assumption holds. ⟶ Conditional probability statements as given below for each matrix

The matrices listed in the translation diagram have the following properties.

1. Matrix P describes the whole population, with element $p_{ij} = $ Pr [Any worker is S_j at $T_{n+1} | S_i$ at T_n].
2. Matrix I describes the stayer population, and is the identity matrix. Thus, Pr [Any stayer is in S_j at $T_{n+1} | S_i$ at T_n] $= 1$ if $i = j$, and 0 otherwise.
3. Matrix M describes the mover population, with element $m_{ij} = $ Pr [Any mover is in S_j at $T_{n+1} | S_i$ at T_n].
4. Matrix S contains element s_{ij} such that $s_{ij} = 0$ if $i \neq j$, and $S_{ij} = $ the proportion of workers in state i who are stayers if $i = j$.

Development of the Revised Model. Given the matrices defined above, Blumen, Kogan, and McCarthy point out that $P = S + (I - S)M$, meaning that the probability of any person's being in any occupation, given his occupation at a previous time, is equal to the probability of his being a stayer (in which case we know he doesn't move) plus the probability of his being a mover (which is $I - S$) times his probability of making the indicated move. To find the transition probabilities for two quarters, one can use $P^{(2)} = S + (I - S)M^2$, and for three quarters the equation becomes $P^{(3)} = S + (I - S)M^3$, since only M changes with longer sequences. In general, the equation is

$$P^{(t)} = S + (I - S)M^t. \qquad (9\text{-}1)$$

One interesting difference between this model and the simple Markov model is in their characteristics at equilibrium. Because the rows of the equilibrium matrix for a simple Markov process are identical, the simple (first) model would require us to predict that after a long enough time, anyone starting in any occupational category would have exactly the same chance of winding up in some particular other category as would someone who started out in that category. On theoretical grounds, this is not an acceptable consequence. It is reassuring, therefore, to discover that the modified probability process does not lead to an equilibrium matrix with identical rows.

The M^t portion of equation (9-1) does approach a matrix with identical rows. However, multiplying that matrix by $(I - S)$ will change the rows differentially to the extent that the occupational states have different proportions of movers. Even if the proportion of movers were constant for all states, adding the matrix S will augment the main diagonal without changing the off-diagonal elements of $(I - S)M^t$. Consequently, the modified process is not a true Markov process; the probability that a person is in state i depends not only on his location at the previous moment and a constant transition probability, but also on whether he is a mover or a stayer. The movers and stayers can each be described by a Markov process (a degenerate one in the case of the stayers), but the combination is not a Markov process.

Estimating Parameters. In this model, as in the next chapter, a problem arises of estimating parameters for states that are unobservable but are assumed to exist and to influence the process. Since the movers are assumed to behave according to a Markov process, however, it can also be assumed that at equilibrium this portion of the population can be described by a matrix with identical rows. Blumen, Kogan, and McCarthy use this property to help estimate the probability of being a mover or a stayer, and the transition probabilities for movers.

To estimate the parameters, the authors use the following procedure.

STEP I. *Find the equilibrium matrix for movers*

1. Assume that the process is in equilibrium after eight quarters. This assumption means that there is a matrix $M_{eq} = M^8$ in which the entries in column j, the probabilities of moving *into* state j, are independent of state of origin and are constant.
2. To find a population of movers, look at all individuals who show a change in code group between any two quarters of eighth order (that is, between first and eighth quarter, second and ninth, and so on). Call this population N_m. Everyone in N_m is certainly a mover, but not all movers are in N_m. Some may have moved and then moved back to their original location. Table 9-3 gives an example from Blumen, Kogan, and McCarthy using data for males aged 40–44.

Table 9-3

Parameter Estimation for Mover-Stayer Model

CODE GROUP j	COLUMN 1 m_j	COLUMN 2 P_{jj}	COLUMN 3 S_j
A	.003	.500	.499
B	.107	.649	.607
C	.083	.681	.652
D	.046	.749	.737
E	.080	.749	.727
F	.062	.756	.739
G	.168	.693	.632
H	.028	.745	.738
J	.059	.573	.547
K	.007	.013	.006
U	.358	.526	.261

Column 1: Estimated fraction of movers who are expected to be in each of the eleven code groups at equilibrium. Estimates based on fraction of workers showing change over eight quarters who end in code group j.

Column 2: Observed percent of workers starting in code group j who are also in that group after eight quarters.

Column 3: Estimated fraction of workers in each code group who are stayers.

Source: Based on data from Blumen, Kogan, and McCarthy, for males aged 40–44. By permission of the publisher.

3. For each code group j, find the fraction of those workers showing any change over eight quarters who wound up in state j.

$$\hat{m}_j = \frac{\text{number with } j \text{ as destination}}{N_m}. \qquad (9\text{-}2)$$

4. The value of $\hat{m}_j$ is an estimate of the entries in the equilibrium matrix for movers.

STEP II. *Find the percent of stayers in each code group*

1. Look at the population of workers who have *not* changed code group between any two quarters of eighth order. Some of these are stayers, but some are movers who have moved and then moved back to their original location.
2. Note that we already have an estimate of the likelihood that a mover will move into any given code group j: $\hat{m}_j$. We can use this value to estimate the number of movers who have moved out and then back to j. From column 1 of Table 9-3 we see that .080 of all movers should be in code group E at equilibrium. In column 2 we note that .749 of all workers who started in E also ended in E. Thus, for code group E, we should expect that, since

$$\hat{p}_{EE}^{(8)} = S_E + (1 - S_E)\hat{m}_E,$$

from equation (9-1), then

$$.749 = S_E + (1 - S_E).080,$$

$$S_E = \frac{.749 - .080}{1 - .080} = .727. \qquad (9\text{-}3)$$

In other words, 72.7 percent of workers who start in group E are stayers, leaving 27.3 per cent movers. The same procedure may be applied to all the other groups, with results as indicated in column 3 of Table 9-3.

In general,

$m_j =$ the proportion of all movers who will end up in group j. Because we are assuming equilibrium, this proportion does not depend upon the origin group of the movers.

$p_{jj}^{(8)} =$ the proportion of all people who start in group j that will end up also in group j, assuming that equilibrium is obtained in eight quarters.

$S_j =$ the proportion of people in group j who are stayers, and, from equation (9-1),

$$p_{jj}^{(8)} = S_j + (1 - S_j)m_j. \qquad (9\text{-}4)$$

3. The entries in column 3 of Table 9-3 provide an estimate of S, the matrix of stayers. These are the diagonal elements in S; all nondiagonal elements are zero.

STEP III. *Estimate the one-step transition matrix for movers*

In order to find the one-step transition matrix for movers, we can can combine S, as estimated in step II, with the observed one-step transition matrix for movers. The latter is simply the average of moves over one quarter for any worker who ever moves. From equation (9-1) we should be able to write

$$p^{(1)}_{\text{obs}} = \hat{S} + (I - \hat{S})\hat{M},$$

so that

$$p_{ii} = \hat{S}_i + (1 - \hat{S}_i)\hat{m}_{ii} \qquad (9\text{-}5)$$

and

$$p_{ij} = (1 - \hat{S}_i)\hat{m}_{ij}. \qquad (9\text{-}6)$$

Solving for estimates of the entries in M gives

$$\hat{m}_{ii} = \frac{p_{ii} - \hat{S}_i}{1 - \hat{S}_i} \qquad (9\text{-}7)$$

and

$$\hat{m}_{ij} = \frac{p_{ij}}{1 - \hat{S}_i}, \qquad (9\text{-}8)$$

where the p_{ii} and p_{ij} values are from the observed one-step transition matrix. For the sample population, males aged 40–44, the results of carrying out the estimation procedure are shown in Table 9-4.

Table 9-4

Estimated One-Quarter Transition Matrix For "Movers" (Males, 40–44)

CODE GROUP OF ORIGIN	A	B	C	D	E	F	G	H	J	K	U
A	.652	.055	.036	.018	.018	.036	.036	.018	—	—	.128
B	.002	.551	.027	.015	.021	.019	.058	.009	.024	.007	.265
C	.001	.038	.670	.012	.017	.016	.047	.003	.016	.002	.180
D	.002	.027	.011	.699	.028	.014	.060	.008	.008	—	.143
E	—	.024	.017	.012	.734	.015	.036	.006	.019	.004	.133
F	.002	.052	.022	.006	.025	.621	.036	.005	.024	.005	.203
G	.000	.032	.026	.015	.020	.011	.673	.006	.026	.002	.188
H	.003	.054	.006	.013	.029	.003	.042	.603	.035	.006	.207
J	.001	.045	.021	.008	.027	.015	.081	.008	.607	←	.187
K	—	.122	.040	.024	.065	.032	.040	—	.008	.481	.187
U	.001	.064	.042	.013	.028	.020	.076	.010	.035	.004	.705

Heading for destination columns: CODE GROUP OF DESTINATION

Source: From Blumen, Kogan, and McCarthy, p. 136. By permission of the publisher.

Testing the Model. A test of the revised model can be obtained by estimating the movement of *all* workers between any two nonadjacent quarters according to Equation (9-1). The authors chose a four-quarter interval so that the test does not duplicate the time interval used for the

Table 9-5

Comparison of Selected Elements[a] from Expected and Observed Eleventh-Order Matrices for Males, 40–44

CODE GROUP OF ORIGIN		SAME CODE GROUP	CHANGE IN CODE GROUP	CHANGE TO U	NUMBER OF OBSERVATIONS
A	Exp.	.500	.304	.196	
	Obs.	.454	.273	*.273	(11)
B	Exp.	.646	.200	.154	
	Obs.	.625	.134	*.241	(336)
C	Exp.	.682	.182	.136	
	Obs.	.622	.180	*.198	(415)
D	Exp.	.747	.150	.103	
	Obs.	.684	*.170	*.146	(247)
E	Exp.	.751	.142	.107	
	Obs.	.685	*.149	*.166	(590)
F	Exp.	.750	.148	.102	
	Obs.	.694	.123	*.183	(229)
G	Exp.	.691	.165	.144	
	Obs.	.627	*.167	*.206	(635)
H	Exp.	.743	.154	.103	
	Obs.	.678	*.166	*.156	(115)
J	Exp.	.576	.247	.177	
	Obs.	.527	.212	*.261	(207)
K	Exp.	.013	.598	.389	
	Obs.	.000	*.773	.227	(22)
U	Exp.	.550	.450	—	
	Obs.	.484	*.516	—[b]	(672)

*An asterisk indicates that the "observed" element is greater than the "expected" element.

[a]Entries under the heading "same code group" are the main diagonal elements in the matrices; entries under "change to U" are the elements in the U columns of the matrices; and entries under "change in code group" are the sum of all row elements except main diagonal and U.

[b]Not applicable.

Source: From Blumen, Kogan, and McCarthy, p. 124. By permission of the publisher.

equilibrium estimates or the one-step transition matrix estimates. Table 9-5 presents the estimated and the observed four-quarter transition probabilities.

Blumen, Kogan, and McCarthy found that for most of their samples, as indicated for males aged 40–44, in Table 9-5, the new model somewhat underestimates the number of people in the same code group after four quarters. They also found that the predictions derived from the modified probability process fit well for quarters of eighth order and somewhat overestimate the number of people remaining in a given code group after eleven quarters. However, the fit of the model to the data is greatly improved over the original simple Markov model. The authors suggest as possible reasons for less than perfect fit:

1. The assumption that there are some people who literally never move (the stayers) is probably inaccurate. After all, even people who don't want to move do occasionally get sick, die, experience extreme changes in the job market, and so on.
2. The assumption that the process is in equilibrium after eight quarters may be inaccurate.

With these observations in mind, the modified model appears to be a great improvement over the simple Markov model, both theoretically and in the way it fits the data. A more recent and somewhat contrasting approach to the same general problem is taken by David D. McFarland. His work follows directly from that of Blumen, Kogan, and McCarthy.

McFarland's Mobility Model. After examining several possible answers to the challenges left by the work of the previous authors, McFarland proposed that the next step should be to examine the possible *theoretical* assumptions that could correspond to the inadequacies of their model, rather than attempting to play with that model to try to "fit" it better to existing data. In other words, having gone from model to data and back again in the first step, the next step should be to go from model to theory and back rather than continuing on the model-data side of the triangle. McFarland suggests that we should examine the major assumptions of the model, keeping in mind the question: which is most questionable on sociological grounds?

The reasoning behind the return to theoretical considerations concerns a property that mathematical models share with all theories. If several assumptions are combined to derive a prediction, and if that prediction is not confirmed, any of the assumptions may be false and hence all are suspect. To the extent that the predictions derived from the modified model proposed by Blumen, Kogan, and McCarthy are unsatisfactory, any of the original assumptions are candidates for change.

The major assumptions of the mover-stayer model are:

1. Stationarity, that is, the process is the same at all points in time.
2. The Markov assumption that the probability of movement for any individual depends only on his immediately previous location and a constant transition probability, for movers. That probability is zero for stayers.
3. Homogeneity, at least of the two separate populations of movers and stayers. This assumption implies that all members of a population (for example, all stayers) are affected by the process in the same way. McFarland suggests that it is the homogeneity assumption that is most open to question on sociological grounds, and in fact it is this assumption that Blumen, Kogan, and McCarthy had partially revised by introducing the two subpopulations of movers and stayers.

In sociological terms, the stationarity assumption can be interpreted as meaning that no great differences in the social structures involved in employment (the job market, the ways people find and lose jobs, and so on) occur during the period in which the data were collected, and that people of different ages are affected similarly. The Markov assumption can be interpreted as meaning that an individual's relevant history can be captured adequately by knowing his current job. That job would imply such things as his level of skills, his attachment to geographic location, etc. The Markov assumption also permits us to assume that experience in a given occupation affects the probability of entering another occupation. All of these assumptions make some sociological sense.

The assumption that all individuals are alike, however, makes less sense, according to McFarland. He points out that the decline in mobility rates over time (an aspect of the data that neither form of the previous model predicts) does not necessarily require an explanation involving corresponding reduction in mobility probabilities; it can be explained by assuming that the population is heterogeneous. We can assume that people are different in that some get stuck in an occupation and others are highly likely to move. Furthermore, the getting stuck or moving may have to do with different qualifications possessed by the workers and required by the jobs. Under this assumption, we can also allow for people who move a lot until they find the "right" occupation, and do not move after that. McFarland suggests that the population can be composed of *individuals*, each of whom behaves in accord with his own Markov process, but the sum of which is not a Markov process.

Translation Diagram 9-3 might suit this approach.

Translation Diagram 9-3

THEORY → MODEL

Variables

Same as B, K, and M. ⟶ Same as B, K, and M.

Parameters

As many patterns of moving as there are individuals. ⟶ Transition matrices, $P(m)$, one per person.

Relationships

Stationarity holds for all individuals. Markov assumption applies to each individual. ⟶ For each individual, the equation is the same as from B, K, and M.

To develop a matrix, Q, which shows the transition probabilities for the population as a whole, define the following:

$N_0(m)$ is a diagonal "initial location" matrix for person m. It contains all zeroes except a value of 1 in the main diagonal entry of the row indicating the occupation person m is in at time zero. Then,

$N_0(m)P(m)$ is the one-step transition probabilities for person m out of the occupation he started with. To obtain the one-step matrix for the whole population, it will be necessary to sum $N_0(m)P(m)$ over all m. Unfortunately, such a sum will not contain probabilities. It will require dividing each entry by the number of persons who started in the row of that entry. The sum of the individual initial location matrices will help.

$N_0 = \sum_m N_0(m)$ is that sum, and is itself a diagonal matrix. Then,

N_0^{-1} is also a diagonal matrix, with entries equal to the reciprocals of the diagonal elements in N_0. This is the necessary matrix for normalizing the sum of the $N_0(m)P(m)$ into a probability matrix. Thus

$$Q = N_0^{-1} \sum_m N_0(m) P(m), \tag{9-9}$$

and

$$Q^{(t)} = N_0^{-1} \sum_m N_0(m) [P(m)]^t. \tag{9-10}$$

Theoretical assumption 1, stationarity, is somewhat questionable, especially if the process is used to describe mobility over a long period of time. Assumption 2, the Markov assumption, makes some sense sociologically. For example, persons from lower-class background who graduate from college have occupations much more like other college graduates than like other persons of lower-class origin, indicating that more information about such a person's immediate future is contained in the information we have about his immediate past than about his more distant past. On the other hand, information about a person's social class background, education, religion, and so on continues to be relevant to his occupational status, suggesting that a large number of "states," and consequently a large number of parameters, may be required to fit the model more precisely to mobility data.

To find the equilibrium distribution for McFarland's model, one needs first to find the equilibrium distribution for each individual, which can be designated

$$P^*(m) = [P(m)]^k \quad \text{as } k \longrightarrow \infty.$$

Then

$$Q^* = N_0^{-1} \sum_m N_0(m) P^*(m). \tag{9-11}$$

Although the $P^*(m)$ matrices have identical entries in each column, Q^* does not, thus eliminating one undesirable feature of the simple Markov model, the identical rows.

It should be noted that the mover-stayer model of Blumen, Kogan, and McCarthy also eliminates the necessity of predicting that everyone has an equal chance at every occupation, but at the price of assuming that some people (the stayers) have a zero probability of ever moving. McFarland's model assumes that any individual may move at some time, but at the price of introducing too many parameters to make estimation procedures feasible with the model as stated. As is often the case, accuracy and theoretical reasonableness are purchased at the price of parsimony and ability to estimate parameters.

Markov models appear widely as representations of change processes involving movement of people among positions; the positions may be occupations, residences, or adoption of innovations.[4] An interesting variation on the basic assumption that people move from one position to another is provided by White,[5] who suggests that an appropriate model for mobility within an organization is to think of jobs as moving from one person to another. According to his model, when a person quits a job for some reason, a vacancy is created which then moves through the occupational hierarchy as individuals are promoted or fired.

problems

1. In Professor Smith's department, it can be observed that some people arrive at faculty meetings on time and others arrive late. Smith has made the following observations.

    On the average, people who were late for any meeting will be late for the next meeting 60 percent of the time; people who were on time for any meeting will be late for the next meeting 50 percent of the time.

    From the past records for the year, he finds that 74 percent of the people who were late to the first meeting were late to the tenth meeting, while only 38 percent of the people who were on time to the first meeting were late to the tenth meeting.

---

[4]Some examples: R. Ginsberg, "Semi-Markov processes and mobility," *Journal of Mathematical Sociology*, vol. 1 (1971), pp. 233–263; R. McGinnis, "A stochastic model of social mobility," *American Sociological Review*, vol. 33 (1968), pp. 712–722; P. A. Morrison, "Duration of residence and prospective migration: evaluation of a stochastic model," *Demography*, vol. 4 (1967), 553–561; B. Singer and S. Spilerman, "Social mobility models for heterogeneous populations," in H. Costner, ed., *Sociological Methodology 1973–1974* (San Francisco: Jossey-Bass, 1974), pp. 356–401; S. Spilerman, "Extensions of the mover-stayer model," *American Journal of Sociology*, vol. 78 (1972), pp. 599–627.

[5]H. C. White, *Chains of Opportunity* (Cambridge: Harvard University Press, 1970).

Over the ten meetings, 50 percent of the people were late to all ten meetings, and 20 percent were on time for all ten meetings.

Does a Markov model fit this set of facts? Does a mover-stayer model fit better than a simple Markov model? Find the I, S, M, and P matrices for a mover-stayer model.

2. Is it possible that a mover-stayer model would describe the distribution of acts in a small group? What kinds of data would be required to test such a model?

3. Apply the mover-stayer model to voting behavior. How would you describe the movers in terms of the political process? How would you describe stayers?

CHAPTER 10

*value conflict
in two-person interaction*

The approach to the construction of models that is illustrated in this chapter is somewhat different from many of the models discussed so far. This chapter's approach is very closely tied to both the development of an experimental situation in which to collect data and to the development of theory. The axioms of the model represent both the conditions of the experiment and assumptions about fundamental social-psychological processes. In this respect it is like models used by mathematical psychologists.[1] The model presented here is similar to the Blumen, Kogan, and McCarthy model in the last chapter in that it has to deal with the empirical problem of deficient diagonals in a transition matrix; in this situation, too, people seem to stay where they

[1] A person who is interested in finding out about mathematical psychology might start with Richard C. Atkinson, Gordon H. Bower, and Edward J. Crothers, *An Introduction to Mathematical Learning Theory* (New York: John Wiley & Sons, 1965).

are more than a simple Markov model predicts.[2] This chapter also illustrates a situation in which no standard techniques existed for estimating parameters, and a technique had to be developed to meet the needs of the particular model. Finally, the chapter illustrates the general procedures for developing a model; first, deciding which of several alternative general assumptions seem to fit best, then estimating the parameters for the best set of general assumptions, then using the values of the parameters to compare several populations or conditions.

theory and data

Sociologists often assume that a complex set of motives, expectations, habits, values, and so on underlies interaction between people. This means that any one act—for example, an offer to help another person—can result from a wide variety of these factors. Also, the history of the interaction can make any particular act have a variety of meanings. An offer to help which follows a history of cooperation is a different action from an offer to help following a history of quarreling. A research challenge is presented by the unobservable quality of many of the theoretically important concepts such as values and expectations. It is difficult to explain how processes involving these things work if one can only observe resultant behavior.

The experiment that produced the data we will be using in this chapter was addressed to this challenge. Since the model is closely related to the experiment, we will describe the experiment first.[3]

Experimental Procedure. A pair of subjects were seated in a laboratory with a screen between them so they were unable to see each other. On a table in front of each was a small box with four switches and two lights. The subjects were instructed that they would be asked to choose between the right-hand switch and the left-hand switch 50 times or trials. On each of the 50 trials, the subject could gain or lose a small amount of money, depending on which of the switches he chose and which one his partner chose. The amount gained or lost varied according to the scoring system; there were three experimental conditions, each with a different scoring system. Two of

[2] A different approach to a "deficient diagonal" is presented by James S. Coleman, *Models of Change and Response Uncertainty* (Englewood Cliffs, N.J.: Prentice-Hall, Inc., 1965).

[3] B. F. Meeker, "Value conflict in social exchange: a Markov model," *Journal of Mathematical Psychology*, vol. 8, no. 3 (August, 1971), pp. 389–403, describes the experiment and the revised (value-conflict) model.

these involved a prisoner's-dilemma type of payoff matrix:[4]

		SUBJECT 2	
		A	B
SUBJECT 1	A	+2¢, +2¢	−3¢, +3¢
	B	+3¢, −3¢	−2¢, −2¢

and in the third the subject's decision had no effect on his own score:[5]

		SUBJECT 2	
		A	B
SUBJECT 1	A	+2¢, +2¢	0, +2¢
	B	+2¢, 0	0, 0

In one of the two prisoner's-dilemma conditions, the A choice was labeled "For the Group" and the B choice was labeled "For Myself," and the emphasis on group score was repeated in the instructions in which the experimenter pointed out that the group's scrore was higher if both subjects chose "For the Group." In the other prisoner's-dilemma condition and the no-cost condition, the choices were merely labeled "A" and "B," and no hints were given as to which choice was more appropriate. This provided one condition in which there was neither a cost associated with the A choice, nor a group orientation; this was the no-cost individual condition (NCI). In one of the prisoner's-dilemma conditions, there was a cost associated with the A choice and no group orientation; this was the prisoner's dilemma-individual condition (PDI). In the third condition, there was both a cost associated with the

---

[4] The scoring systems for charts 1(a) and 1(b) are examples of a *prisoner's dilemma* payoff matrix; the experiment is not a prisoner's dilemma game, however, since there is no possibility of retaliation. A discussion of the prisoner's dilemma and other game theoretical concepts can be found in R. Duncan Luce and Howard Raiffa, *Games and Decisions* (New York: John Wiley & Sons, 1957), esp. Chap. 5, and discussion of some ways these concepts can be applied to sociological theory in B. F. Meeker, "Decisions and exchange," *American Sociological Review*, vol. 36 (June, 1971), pp. 485–495. It is not necessary to have a background in game theory or prisoner's-dilemma literature to understand the present chapter.

[5] The scoring sheets the subjects saw were not in matrix form, but rather in the form of statements: "If I choose A and he chooses A, I gain 2 cents and he gains 2 cents," and so on.

A choice and a group orientation; this was the prisoner's dilemma-group condition (PDG). Each pair of subjects made 50 choices in one of the three conditions.

In addition, each subject was informed that after he had made his choice on each of the 50 trials, he would see a light telling him which choice his partner had made, and that *his partner would never see any indication which choice he himself had made*. In other words, he could see whether his partner had helped him or not, and if he didn't reciprocate the partner would never know.

The final feature of the experiment that established the "moral dilemma" was that the partner was actually instructed in advance (although the subject did not know this) to choose the helpful response (the A switch is the helpful response, as you can tell by looking at the scoring sheet) on all 50 trials. This meant that the subject knew that his partner had helped him and that the partner would not know if the subject reciprocated. In two of the scoring charts, the choice that reciprocates the partner's help (the A switch) is the one that gives the *subject* less money; he must thus choose between his own highest score and reciprocating his partner's choices.

Results. Each of the 50 trials represents a choice between reciprocating and nonreciprocating. When the reciprocating choices made by all the subjects in each of the three conditions are counted, the means and variances are as shown in Table 10-1.

Table 10-1

Means and Variances, Number of Reciprocating Choices

	MEAN	VARIANCE	N SUBJECTS
NCI	38.8	167.03	9
PDI	24.4	236.88	20
PDG	33.9	191.89	15

When we look at the means, we find that the mean number of reciprocating choices in NCI is higher than in PDI. In other words, as we would expect, when there is no particular benefit to be had from not reciprocating, the subjects are more likely to reciprocate. We also see that when the partner is presented as a fellow member of a "group," his help is reciprocated more (the mean for PDG is higher than for PDI). We also note that the mean numbers of reciprocating choices in PDG and NCI are very similar; this raises the question—are these situations in fact the same, or are there differences between them that do not show up in the simple aggregation of choices into means?

When we examine the variances we note that they are quite high in all three conditions; apparently the "dilemma" is being resolved in different ways by different individuals. This high within-condition variance is intriguing, because there is no variance within conditions in the independent variables (scoring system and behavior of partner).

Sociological theorists[6] have argued that reciprocity is a universal social norm or value, requiring that people return help for help or at least not harm someone who has given them help. This argument is based in part on the additional assumption that reciprocity is rewarding because it motivates others to continue to offer help. In this experiment, however, the subject need not reciprocate his partner's help in order to motivate the partner to continue to help him. In fact, the only "rational" thing for the subject to do is not to reciprocate because that results in higher reward for him at no cost. On the other hand, if he believes that reciprocity is a universal requirement of social behavior, he is in a state of conflict between getting as much as he can of something he wants and conforming to the norm of reciprocity which he also values. In addition, there are other norms he could consider: competition or maximizing the difference between his own and the other's outcomes (which would require that he not reciprocate), altruism or social responsibility (which would require that he reciprocate), and maximizing the group outcome (which might require either, depending on the relative gains to the group from each). There is a set of values consistent with each act, and while some may be consistent with both sets, others are in conflict.

The set of values that is consistent with one act will be called a *value state*. In the experiment there are two value states, one consisting of reciprocity, altruism, and possibly group orientation, and a second consisting of self-interest and competition. For convenience, the first will be referred to as the *reciprocating state*, the second as the *rational state*.

We will not specify the exact psychological nature of value states; they may be thought of as values, norms, motives, expectations, or utilities. The concept probably comes closest to the sociological concept of norm because a value state is an idea about what the right behavior is in a given situation, but it does not necessarily describe actual behavior.

We will begin with the simplest form of Markov model for this situation. This assumes that people will adopt either the value state associated with reciprocity or that associated with rationality, and that behavior will be consistent with value state. Instead of a translation diagram we will develop the translation by making a set of formal definitions and assumptions, and using them as bases for axioms of the mathematical model.

---

[6]For an example: Alvin Gouldner, "The Norm of reciprocity: A preliminary statement," *American Sociological Review*, vol. 25 (April, 1960), pp. 161–178.

Value states are assumed to have the following properties:

Assumption 1. All states are available to all actors, and each actor occupies one and only one state at any given time.
Assumption 2. The state the actor occupies determines his behavior.
Assumption 3. An actor may change his value state at any time; however, he is more likely to remain in his current state than to change.

Translation into Mathematics. To begin with, we define a *random event*, $E_{i,n}$; $i = 1, 0$; $n = 1, 2, \ldots, 50$. $E_{1,n}$ means the subject chooses A on trial n (reciprocates). $E_{0,n}$ means the subject chooses B on trial n (does not reciprocate).

The probability that event $E_{1,n}$ occurs (that is, the probability that the subject chooses to reciprocate on trial n), given that event $E_{1,n-1}$ occurred (that is, that he reciprocated on the previous trial) is:

$$p_{11}^{(1)}.$$

Likewise, the probability of $E_{1,n}$ given $E_{0,n-1}$ is $p_{01}^{(1)}$, and the probability of $E_{0,n}$ given $E_{0,n-1}$ is $p_{00}^{(1)}$.

Figure 10-1 shows a tree diagram for this model.

Assumption 4. $P_{ij}^{(1)}$ is a constant.

This assumption is the fundamental Markov assumption, and from it and the definitions a number of consequences can be derived. For example:

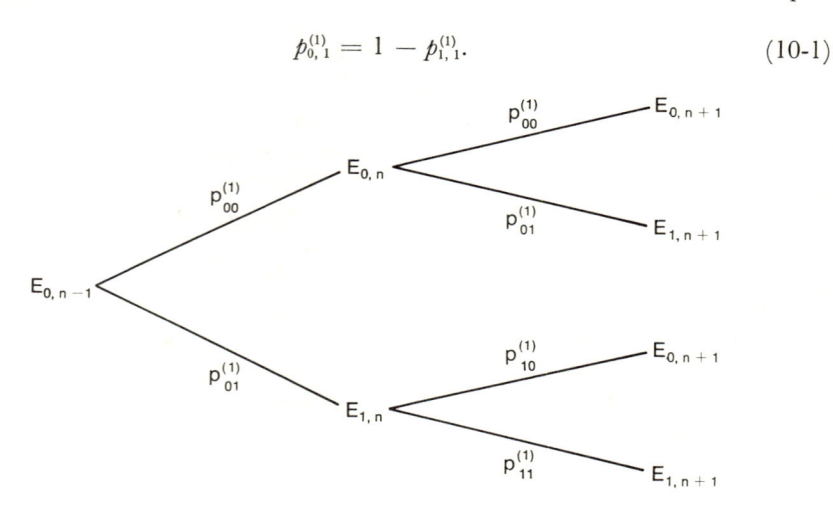

$$p_{0,1}^{(1)} = 1 - p_{1,1}^{(1)}. \tag{10-1}$$

Figure 10-1
Tree diagram for model I

(This is because the probability of reciprocating and the probability of not reciprocating must add to one, as the subject must do one or the other).

$$p_{0,0}^{(2)} = p_{0,0}^{(1)} p_{0,0}^{(1)} + p_{0,1}^{(1)} p_{1,0}^{(1)}. \qquad (10\text{-}2)$$

The transition matrix for the Markov process just defined is:

$$M = \begin{bmatrix} P_{00} & P_{01} \\ P_{10} & P_{11} \end{bmatrix}. \qquad (10\text{-}3)$$

Estimating the Parameters. The fundamental parameters of this model are the transition probabilities $p_{ij}^{(1)}$. These may be estimated directly from the data, as follows.

For each subject, we have a protocol of 50 responses, which we can code as 0 (nonreciprocating) or 1 (reciprocating) to correspond with the notation on the transition probabilities. For each protocol, we can count the number of ones and the number of ones followed by ones and ones followed by zeroes, and the number of zeroes followed by zeroes and zeroes followed by ones. We can then find the percent of ones that are followed by ones and the percent of zeroes followed by ones, and so on; $p_{00}^{(1)}$ is estimated by the percent of zeroes followed by zeroes, and $p_{11}^{(1)}$ by the percent of ones followed by ones.

If we take one subject's protocol as an example, we have:

00001011101111100000101010000000011000000000000000

Number of 1's, 14; number of 0's, 36; probability of E_0, .78.
number 1's followed by 1, 7; percent 1's followed by 1, 50; $\hat{p}_{11}^{(1)} = .50$.
number 0's followed by 0, 28; percent 0's followed by 0, 80; $p_{00}^{(1)} = .80$.

We will make the simplifying assumption that all the subjects in one condition (PDI, PDG, or NCI) are characterized by the same parameter, and estimate three sets of parameters, one for each condition, but adding up the numbers for all subjects in each condition. We obtain the estimates in Table 10-2.

Table 10-2

Parameters for Model I

	NCI	PDI	PDG
$\hat{p}_{11}$	.86	.78	.81
$\hat{p}_{00}$	.51	.80	.59

Test of the Model. As a preliminary test of the adequacy of the Markov assumption in this situation, we can compare the estimated transition probabilities with what we could expect if there were no tendency to repeat a response—that is, if the probability of an event were independent of the event that occurred on the previous trial.

From Table 10-1 we can get the probability of event E_0 occurring on any trial; this is simply the average number of nonreciprocating choices per trial. These probabilities can then be compared with the conditional probabilities of E_0 on the previous trial, and so on. Table 10-3 shows the proba-

Table 10-3

Probabilities of E_0, unconditional

	NCI	PDI	PDG
$P(E_0)$	.22	.51	.32

bilities which are to be compared with Table 10-2. In all three cases the Markov assumption seems justified; the probability of repeating is greater than would be expected if the occurrence of E_0 were independent of the event on the previous trial.

For a further test of the model, we will use the property that led to equation (10-2), which gave us the transition probability for a two-trial sequence. We do this by squaring the one-trial matrix. The data below are from the PDG condition.

$$M = \begin{matrix} \\ E_{1,n-1} \\ E_{0,n-1} \end{matrix} \begin{matrix} E_{1,n} & E_{0,n} \\ \begin{pmatrix} .81 & .19 \\ .41 & .59 \end{pmatrix} \end{matrix}, \tag{10-4}$$

$$M^2 = \begin{pmatrix} .74 & .26 \\ .57 & .43 \end{pmatrix}. \tag{10-5}$$

Thus, $\quad p_{11}^{(2)} = .74 \text{ and } p_{00}^{(2)} = .43 \tag{10-6}$

We can test whether the description is accurate by comparing these theoretical probabilities from M^2 with the actual proportion of 1's followed by 1 after two trials, 0's followed by 0's after two trials, and so on, which we find by counting three-trial sequences just as we counted two-trial sequences to get Table 10-2. Table 10-4 shows the proportions for PDG in matrix form for easy comparison with M^2.

When Table 10-4 is compared with the theoretical values in M^2, it appears that the model, like the simple Blumen, Kogan and McCarthy model,

Table 10-4

Actual Two-Step Response Dependencies, PDG

$$\begin{array}{c c} & \begin{array}{cc} E_{1,n} & E_{0,n} \end{array} \\ \begin{array}{c} E_{1,n-2} \\ E_{0,n-2} \end{array} & \begin{pmatrix} .81 & .19 \\ .39 & .61 \end{pmatrix} \end{array}$$

understimates the tendency to repeat a choice; subjects are more likely to continue making the same response over a three-trial sequence than our model predicts.

As a test of the amount of discrepancy between the theoretical and the actual distributions, we can calculate the theoretical and actual numbers of choices in each cell of the matrix and compare these using a chi-square test. Table 10-5 shows these distributions.

Table 10-5

Predicted and Actual Distribution of E_0 and E_1, PDG Two-Step Sequences

	PREDICTED	OBSERVED
$E_{1,n-1}E_{1,n}$	376	411
$E_{1,n-1}E_{0,n}$	133	98
$E_{0,n-1}E_{1,n}$	137	95
$E_{0,n-1}E_{0,n}$	104	146

We find that chi-square is 42.26, which, with two degrees of freedom, has a probability of less than .01 of occurring if the two columns actually represent random variations from the same distribution. We can thus conclude the model does not accurately describe this aspect of the data.

revised model

To revise the model, we take a strategy similar to Blumen, Kogan, and McCarthy's; we hypothesize a set of underlying unobservable states that are probabilisticially connected to observable behavior. These states are once again value states, but instead of assuming that value state determines behavior, we make two different assumptions.

Assumption 2 (*revised*). Value state influences but does not determine behavior.
 (a) An actor in the reciprocating state will choose to reciprocate more often than he chooses not to reciprocate.
 (b) An actor in the rational state will choose not to reciprocate more often than he chooses to reciprocate.

The next assumption is based on theoretical considerations about the possible effects of behavior on values, as well as of values on behavior.

Assumption 3.
(a) If an actor makes a choice that is consistent with his value state (that is, chooses to reciprocate when he occupies the reciprocating state or chooses not to reciprocate when he occupies the rational state), he will not change his value state.

(b) If an actor makes a choice that is inconsistent with his value state (that is, chooses not to reciprocate when he occupies the reciprocating state, or chooses to reciprocate when he occupies the rational state), he may or may not change his value state following his choice.

Assumptions 3(a) and 3(b) make use of some general ideas from the set of social psychological theories known as balance, or dissonance[7]. In these theories, it is assumed that an individual faced with some kind of cognitive conflict or inconsistency experiences discomfort, and is under pressure therefore to change some element of his cognitive structure. In Assumption 3(b), the inconsistency is between his value state (which says to do one thing) and his behavior (which he observes to be the opposite thing).

Since the subject experiences discomfort when his behavior is inconsistent with his value state, he may change his value state to be consistent with his own past behavior. On the other hand, since there is also some psychological cost involved in changing a value state (admitting he was wrong), he will not always change after an inconsistent choice. This means that if the subject is forced to make a series of decisions between reciprocating and not reciprocating, he will show a tendency to repeat the same choice over and over, but if he changes once from, say, reciprocating to not reciprocating, he may initiate a series of nonreciprocating choices. The only way a change of value state can occur is after he has made a choice that is inconsistent with his value state.

Assumptions 1 to 3 may be translated into the axioms of a Markov process as follows:

Assumption 1 becomes:

Axiom 1. There are two states, reciprocating (referred to as S_1) and rational (referred to as S_0). There are two responses, E_1 (reciprocating) and E_0 (nonreciprocating). On any trial n, the subject occupies one state and gives one response.

$$P(S_{0,n}) = 1 - P(S_{1,n}), \qquad (10\text{-}7)$$
$$P(E_{0,n}) = 1 - P(E_{1,n}). \qquad (10\text{-}8)$$

Assumptions 2(a) and 2(b) become:

Axiom 2(a). If the subject is in state S_1 on trial n, he will give response E_1 on that trial with probability p: $(p > 1 - p)$.

$$P[E_{1,n} | S_{1,n}] = p. \qquad (10\text{-}9)$$

---

[7]See footnote 2 to Chapter 4 for reference to some of this literature.

Axiom 2(b). If the subject is in state S_0 on trial n, he will give response E_0 on that trial with probability r: $(r > 1 - r)$.

$$P[E_{0,n} | S_{0,n}] = r. \tag{10-10}$$

Assumptions 3(a) and 3(b) become:

Axiom 3(a). If the subject is in state S_1 on trial $n - 1$ and gives response E_1, he will continue to be in state S_1 on trial n.

$$P[S_{1,n} | S_{1,n-1} E_{1,n-1}] = 1. \tag{10-11}$$

If the subject is in state S_1 on trial $n - 1$ and gives response E_0, he will change to state S_0 on trial n with probability θ.

$$P[S_{0,n} | S_{1,n-1} E_{0,n-1}] = \theta. \tag{10-12}$$

Axiom 3(b). If the subject is in state S_0 on trial $n - 1$ and gives response E_0, he will continue to be in state S_0 on trial n.

$$P[S_{0,n} | S_{0,n-1} E_{0,n-1}] = 1 \tag{10-13}$$

If the subject is in state S_0 on trial $n - 1$ and gives response E_1, he will change to state S_1 on trial n with probability ψ.

$$P[S_{1,n} | S_{0,n-1} E_{1,n-1}] = \psi \tag{10-14}$$

Figure 10-2 gives a tree diagram for these assumptions, and Table 10-6 shows the transition matrix.

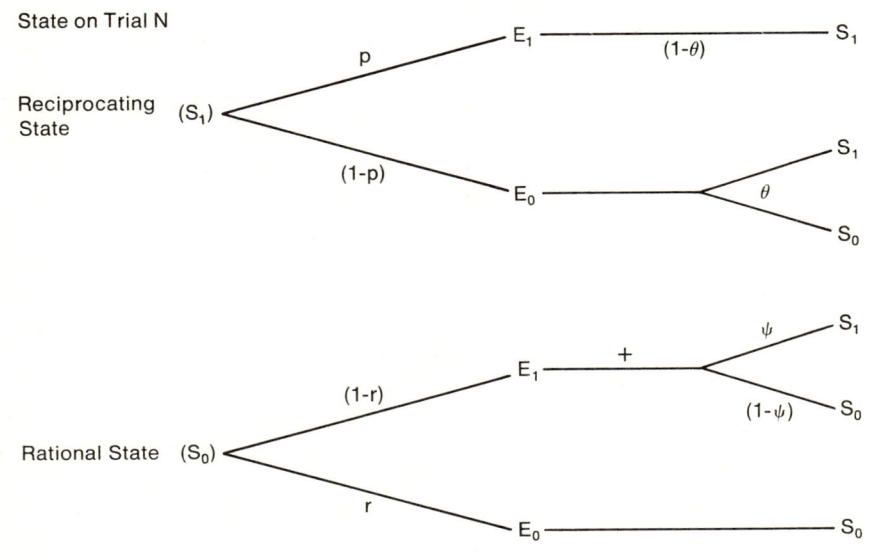

Figure 10-2

Tree diagrams for assumptions 1 to 3

Table 10-6

Matrix of Transition Probabilities

TRIAL n	State	S_0	S_0	S_1	S_1
	Behavior	E_1	E_0	E_1	E_0
TRIAL $n-1$					
State	Behavior				
S_0	E_1	$(1-\psi)(1-r)$	$(1-\psi)r$	ψp	$\psi(1-p)$
S_0	E_0	$(1-r)$	r	0	0
S_1	E_1	0	0	p	$1-p$
S_1	E_0	$\theta(1-r)$	θr	$(1-\theta)p$	$(1-\theta)(1-p)$

In this revised version, the variables are the value states and acts, the former being underlying mental states and the latter observable behavior. The relationships are defined by equations (10-9) through (10-14). If one thinks of the combination of value state and act on each trial as one state, this constitutes a Markov process. However, transitions between value states only or between acts only do not form a Markov process, as each depends on the other as well as on the previous state of the same variable.

Estimating the Parameters. The four parameters of the model now are p, r, θ, and ψ. For purposes of estimating the parameters, the last 40 trials from each subject were used—for two reasons. First, the subject must recognize the conflict between rationality and reciprocity, and he cannot do this until he has learned that his partner will usually choose the "helpful" response. Second, the procedure used to estimate parameters requires us to assume that the system is in equilibrium, and eliminating the first ten trials makes this assumption more reasonable.

Since the state S_1 and S_0 are not directly observable, estimation of the parameters presents some problems. We cannot merely count the proportion of repeats and switches from S_1 to S_0, because we don't know when the subject is in state S_1 and when he is in S_0. The estimation was accomplished by using a process of iteration, similar to what is known as a Bayesian analysis. It is based on the properties of conditional probabilities; it starts by making an assumption about the value of a probability and uses the logic of conditional probabilities to estimate how much in error the original estimate was.[8]

To begin with, it was assumed that if a subject made two E_1 responses in a row, he was in state S_1, and if he made two E_0 responses in a row, he was in state S_0. This assumption is, of course, inaccurate, because it will include in the sample of subjects in states S_1 some who are actually in S_0 and vice versa. However, for the moment, we will assume that the number of subjects inaccurately classified by this procedure is minimal. If it is assumed that two E_1

---

[8]Kemeny, Snell, and Thompson, *Introduction to Finite Mathematics*, pp. 158–64; Feller, W., *An Introduction to Probability Theory and Its Applications*, 2d ed., vol. 1 (New York: John Wiley and Sons, 1957), p. 114.

responses indicate that the subject occupies state S_1, then p, the probability that he will make a response consistent with the reciprocating state, may be directly estimated by finding the proportion of E_1, E_1 sequences followed by E_1 on the next trial. (Table 10-7 gives three- and four-step dependencies, which are called for by this procedure.)

Table 10-7

Three-Step and Four-Step Response Dependencies, 40 Trials per Subject

	NCI	PDI	PDG
$p[E_{1,n}\|E_{1,n-1}E_{1,n-2}]$	.90	.85	.89
$p[E_{0,n}\|E_{0,n-1}E_{0,n-2}]$	.72	.92	.69
$p[E_{1,n}\|E_{0,n-1}E_{1,n-2}E_{1,n-3}]$	.72	.49	.50
$p[E_{0,n}\|E_{1,n-1}E_{0,n-2}E_{0,n-3}]$	.46	.39	.47

Thus, we assume that

$$P[S_{1,n}|E_{1,n-1}E_{1,n-2}] = 1 \tag{10-15}$$

and

$$P[S_{0,n}|E_{0,n-1}E_{0,n-2}] = 1; \tag{10-16}$$

then

$$\hat{p} = P[E_{1,n}|E_{1,n-1}E_{1,n-2}] \tag{10-17}$$

and

$$\hat{r} = P[E_{0,n}|E_{0,n-1}E_{0,n-2}]. \tag{10-18}$$

From the first two columns of Table 10-7, we find that $\hat{p}$ and $\hat{r}$ are:

NCI, $\hat{p} = .90, \hat{r} = .72$;
PDI, $\hat{p} = .85, \hat{r} = .92$;
PDG, $\hat{p} = .89, \hat{r} = .69$.

Next we face the problem of estimating the change of state parameters θ and ψ. If we know that the subject was in state S_0 on trial $n-1$, and that he made an E_0 response, we would know that he must remain in state S_0 on trial n [equation (10-13)]. If we knew that he was in state S_1 and made an E_0 response on trial $n-1$, we would know that on trial n he would still be in state S_1 with probability $1-\theta$, and would be in state S_0 with probability θ [equation (10-12)]. Since his response on trial n depends on his value state on trial n [equations (10-9) and (10-10)], we know that:

$$P[E_{1,n}|E_{0,n-1}] = P[S_{1,n-1}][\theta(1-r) + (1-\theta)p] \\ + P[S_{0,n-1}](1-r) \tag{10-19}$$

This equation may be combined with the assumption that the subject is always in S_1 after two E_1 responses, to give:

$$P[E_{1,n} | E_{0,n-1} E_{1,n-2} E_{1,n-3}] = \theta(1-r) + (1-\theta)p. \qquad (10\text{-}20)$$

Similarly, using the assumption that two E_0 responses in a row means that the subject is in state S_0,

$$P[E_{1,n} | E_{1,n-1} E_{0,n-2} E_{0,n-3}] = \psi r p + (1-\psi r)(1-r). \qquad (10\text{-}21)$$

Upon the application of some algebra, these become:

$$\hat{\theta} = \frac{P[E_{1,n} | E_{0,n-1} E_{1,n-2} E_{1,n-3}] - p}{1 - r - p} \qquad (10\text{-}22)$$

and

$$\hat{\psi} = \frac{\{1 - P[E_{1,n} | E_{1,n-1} E_{0,n-2} E_{0,n-3}]\} - r}{1 - r - p}. \qquad (10\text{-}23)$$

We have already obtained values for $\hat{p}$ and $\hat{r}$; the other quantities called for in equations (10-22) and (10-23) appear in Table (10-7). $\hat{\theta}$ and $\hat{\psi}$, obtained by solving (10-22) and (10-23), appear in Table 10-8, along with $\hat{p}$ and $\hat{r}$, and an

Table 10-8

Estimates of Parameters Using the Assumption that
$P[S_{1,n} | E_{1,n-1} E_{1,n-2}] = P[S_{0,n} | E_{0,n-1} E_{0,n-2}] = 1$

	$\hat{p}$	$\hat{r}$	$\hat{\theta}$	$\hat{\psi}$	$P[S_1]$
NCI	.90	.72	.29	.42	.80
PDI	.85	.92	.47	.69	.44
PDG	.89	.69	.67	.38	.62

estimate of the probability of being in state S_1 on trial n. $P(S_{1,n})$ was obtained using another property of Markov chains, the notion of equilibrium.[9] Assuming that the process is in equilibrium means that $P[S_{1,n}] = P[S_{1,n-1}]$. This in combination with (10-9) through (10-14) gives:

$$P[S_{1,n}] = P[S_{1,n}][p + (1-p)(1-\theta)] + P[S_{0,n}](1-r)\psi \qquad (10\text{-}24)$$

---

[9]This Markov process will exhibit statistical equilibrium because it is irreducible and aperiodic and all states are ergodic (that is, it is possible to get from any state to any other state in a finite number of trials). If the model had one or more absorbing states it would not have statistical equilibrium, since all subjects would eventually end up in an absorbing state. See Chapters 9 and 11 for more discussion of statistical equilibrium.

which, solved for $P[S_{1,n}]$, becomes

$$P[S_{1,n}] = \frac{(1-r)\psi}{(1-r)\psi + (1-p)\theta}. \tag{10-25}$$

The estimates that appear in Table 10-8 are, of course, inaccurate, because it was assumed that $P[S_{1,n}|E_{1,n-1}E_{1,n-2}] = 1$. Now that we have estimates for all the parameters and for $P[S_{1,n}]$, however, it is possible to estimate how much in error the first arbitrary assumption was—that is, what the probability of being in state S_0 after two E_1 responses actually is (if these values of the parameters are correct)—and furthermore to use this estimate of error to reestimate the parameters. The necessary equations and their derivations appear in the Appendix.

$P[S_1]$ can be estimated from (10-25). Eventually the estimates for the parameters that result from the application of this procedure should converge, which in fact they do. Table 10-9 shows the final values for the parameters after convergence.

Table 10-9

Values of the Parameters After Iteration Procedure

	$\hat{p}$	$\hat{r}$	$\hat{\theta}$	$\hat{\psi}$	$P[S_1]$
NCI	.91	.74	.29	.41	.80
PDI	.85	.92	.47	.69	.44
PDG	.89	.69	.67	.38	.62

For two of the conditions, PDI and PDG, the probability of a subject in the wrong state being included in the first sample used to estimate the parameters is .005 or less; for these conditions it is therefore assumed that the first estimates are accurate and that no further refinement is necessary. For NCI, the process of reiteration converges after three cycles.

Testing the Model. As a check on these estimation procedures, the theoretical probability of an E_1 (that is, the expected frequency of E_1 at equilibrium) and the expected probability of E_1 following E_1 and of E_0 following E_0, none of which were used in estimating the parameters, may be compared with the actual probabilities from the data.

The equations for deriving these theoretical probabilities appear in the Appendix.

As Table 10-10 shows, the fit between the predicted quantities and the observed quantities is quite close.

Table 10-10

Comparing Predicted and Observed Response Probabilities

	$P[E_1]$		$P[E_{1,n}|E_{1,n-1}]$		$P[E_{0,n}|E_{0,n-1}]$	
	Predicted	Observed[a]	Predicted	Observed[a]	Predicted	Observed[a]
NCI	.78	.79	.88	.88	.54	.55
PDI	.42	.46	.82	.81	.88	.85
PDG	.67	.69	.84	.83	.65	.63

[a]Last 40 trials for each subject.

Interpreting the Values of the Parameters. Several point should be noted in Table 10-9. (1) The value of p (probability of E_1 in reciprocating state) is pretty much the same for all three conditions, while the value of r (probability of E_0 in rational state) varies between conditions. (2) The value of θ (probability of change from reciprocating to rational after E_0) is highest in PDG, lowest in NCI. (3) The value of ψ (probability of change from rational to reciprocating after E_1) is highest for PDI, lower and about equal in PDG and NCI.

A value state is a hypothetical construct, and initially no assumptions were made about its properties except that it influences behavior and may change after inconsistent behavior. These assumptions produce a model that makes sense when applied to data from an experiment designed to meet the conditions of the theory, and we are now in a position to add more content to the hypothetical construct.

In the first place, consider the parameters p and r (probabilities of behavior consistent with value state) in the three conditions (see Table 10-9). These parameters indicate the influence the value state has on behavior. In all three conditions, p remains about the same while r varies. This indicates that one property of state S_0 (rational state) is that the influence of state on behavior will change with changes in the cost of the behavior and with experimental instructions, while a property of state S_1 (reciprocating state) is that the influence of value state on behavior is not affected by these changes. In this sense, state S_0 is indeed more "rational" than state S_1. It is also reasonable to think of state S_1 as primarily oriented to the behavior of the other person, since the behavior of the other subject is the same in all three conditions. In this sense, state S_1 is more "reciprocating" than state S_0. It is also clear that the two states are different in the way they influence behavior, not merely opposite in effect. This interpretation of state S_1 leads to the testable hypothesis that variations in the behavior of the other subject should have more effect on the parameter p than on r.

The parameters θ and ψ (probabilities of change of state after inconsistent response) measure the effect of *behavior* on *value state*. The strongest effect of behavior on state S_1 occurs in PDG, the weakest in NCI. If a high value of θ may be taken as an indication of high conflict between behavior and value state, E_0 conflicts more with state S_1 when there is a cost attached to E_0 (that is, a cost to the other person), and when there is a group orientation. For state S_0, the greatest conflict between E_1 and S_0 occurs in PDI—that is, when there is a cost (to the subject) attached to E_1 and no group orientation. The similar effects of E_1 on S_0 in NCI and PDG might be interpreted as meaning that the addition of a group orientation to the instructions decreases the "irrationality" of the E_1 response.

This analysis of the four parameters indicates that perhaps the effect of values on behavior and the effect of behavior on values are independent of each other; there may be, for example, a strong "temptation" to behave in a manner inconsistent with the value state, and either great or little effect of that behavior on the value state.

Another thing this analysis shows is that the NCI and PDG conditions, which in the mean number of E_1 responses are alike, are really quite different; the PDG conditions has relatively high intrapersonal conflict. It may be hypothesized that factors that tend to increase the importance of "group" values (for example, an increase in the cohesiveness of the group) should increase p and θ, and decrease ψ. Increase in both cost and cohesiveness simultaneously ("escalation" in the exchange of favors, for example) should produce a result like the difference between NCI and PDG—more internal conflict and higher probability of changing value states.

Evaluating the Model. One thing this model does is provide a way of analyzing some kinds of binary choice data by using properties of the data such as the sequencing of responses. It should be noted that in order to use it as a method of analyzing data, the data must meet some of the conditions of the model; for example, if the probability of an E_1 following two E_1's is not greater than the probability of E_0 following two E_1's, equation (10-26) may break down. The second thing this model does is make use of mathematics in theory construction. By hypothesizing an unobservable underlying state with some of the properties often assigned to values or norms, we can discover other properties of these states, as well as explore the usefulness of the original assumptions. The assumptions about the nature of the value states come from two sources in social-psychological theory; one is the idea that reciprocity is a fundamental principle of social interaction, and the other is the idea that people seek consistency among cognitive elements. The model thus ties together two branches of theory, and the interpretation of the parameters provides some information about the nature of value states.

In terms of empirical validity, this model seems to fit the data from one experiment well. It needs to be tested by application to more data, with more subjects and conditions. Note that since the assumptions of the model are designed to reflect the conditions of the experiment, if the experiment is changed the model will have to be revised. For example, assumption 3 says that response A is consistent with the reciprocating value state, and inconsistent with the rational value state. This depends on the subject's always thinking his partner has chosen response A. If the experiment were changed to provide the subject with information that his partner had chosen A sometimes and B sometimes, then assumption 3 would have to be revised. In other words, expanding the empirical adequacy of this model requires expanding the theoretical adequacy as well as collecting more data. This is an example of one of the ways a model can be used to tie theory and data together.

The assumption that there is a strain toward cognitive consistency has been used in other process models. An example is B. P. Cohen's model of conflict and conformity in the Asch situation[10]. In Cohen's model a subject is pictured as being in a state of conflict between giving an answer that reflects his own perception and giving an answer that conforms to the (incorrect) statement of others. The underlying state is his orientation to himself (consistent with the independent response) and his orientation to the others (consistent with conformity). The model hypothesizes that the underlying state influences behavior and that behavior influences the state by making it possible for a person to become "absorbed" permanently in the state consistent with his immediate past response. Once a subject has entered an absorbing state neither his response nor his underlying state ever changes. The data produced by a situation described by a Markov chain with absorbing states will look quite different from the data analyzed in this chapter, since each subject will eventually settle on one response exclusively.

A similar use of this type of assumption in the development of Markov models of decision making appears in work on status characteristics and expectation states by Berger et al.[11] In these models, the underlying states are the expectations people hold for the performance of themselves and other—particularly, the expectations for competence at a task. The observable behaviors are resolution of disagreement over task-related decisions. These models, like the Cohen model and the Meeker model, are closely tied to the experimental situation in which data are collected as well as to the construction of theory about fundamental social-psychological processes.

---

[10] Bernard P. Cohen, *Conflict and Conformity: A Probability Model and Its Application* (Cambridge, Mass.: The M.I.T. Press, 1963). Also Bernard P. Cohen and Hans E. Lee, *The Effects of Social Status upon Conflict Resolution* (forthcoming).

[11] Joseph Berger, Bernard P. Cohen, Thomas L. Connor, and Morris Zelditch, Jr., "Status characteristics and expectation states: A process model," in Joseph Berger, Morris Zelditch, Jr., and Bo Anderson, eds., *Sociological Theories in Progress*, vol. I (Boston: Houghton Mifflin Company, 1966); Berger, Conner, and Fisek, *Expectation States Theory*.

problems

1. Labeling theory suggests that once a label is believed by someone, subsequent behavior is determined by that label. Behavioral modification theory suggests that, to the contrary, if you can induce behavioral change, the self-label will follow suit. Apply the value-conflict model to reconciling these two approaches.
2. Based on the results shown in this chapter, what are the probable effects of varying rewards or costs in the labeling theory-behavior modification problem?
3. Does the following sequence of choices fit the value-conflict model? If so, estimate the parameters. If not, how did you establish that fact?

AAAABAAABBBBAAABBBBAABAAABBAAAABBBBBAAAABBAAAABBB

appendix to chapter 10

Equations for the Process of Parameter Estimation by Reiteration, Once an Initial Estimation Has Been Made by Making the Assumptions of Equations (10-15) and (10-16). To estimate the error in the first estimate, we use the transition matrix in Table 10-6. What we want is $P[S_{0,n} | E_{1,n-1} E_{1,n-2}]$. By the laws of conditional probability, this equals

$$\frac{P[S_{0,n} E_{1,n-1} E_{1,n-2}]}{P[E_{1,n-1} E_{1,n-2}]}. \tag{10-26}$$

The denominator of (10-26)—that is, the joint probability of two E_1's in a row—is the probability that the subject started at either $S_1 E_1$ or $S_0 E_1$ on trial $n-2$, and on trial $n-1$ was in either $S_1 E_1$ or $S_0 E_1$. Referring to the transition matrix (Table 10-6) and the fact that

$$P[S_{1,n} E_{1,n}] = P[S_{1,n}] P[E_{1,n} | S_{1,n}],$$

we find that

$$\begin{aligned} P[E_{1,n-1} E_{1,n-2}] &= P[E_{1,n-1} | S_{1,n-2} E_{1,n-2}] P[S_{1,n-2} E_{1,n-2}] \\ &\quad + P[E_{1,n-1} | S_{0,n-2} E_{1,n-2}] P[S_{0,n-2} E_{1,n-2}] \\ &= P[S_{1,n}] p^2 + P[S_{0,n}](1-r)[\psi p + (1-\psi)(1-r)]. \end{aligned}$$
(10-27)

The numerator of (10-26) is the joint probability of having two E_1's in a row and on the next subsequent trial occupying state S_0—that is, the probability of starting with either $S_0 E_1$ or $S_1 E_1$, and after two trials occupying either $S_0 E_1$ or $S_0 E_0$ without having passed through either $S_1 E_0$ or $S_0 E_0$ on the intervening trial. In fact, since there is zero probability of going from S_1E_1 to S_0E_1 or E_0, this is

$$P[S_{0,n}E_{1,n-1}E_{1,n-2}]$$
$$= \{P[S_{0,n}E_{1,n}|S_{0,n-1}E_{1,n-1}]P[S_{0,n-1}E_{1,n-1}|S_{0,n-2}E_{1,n-2}]$$
$$+ P[S_{0,n}E_{0,n}|S_{0,n-1}E_{1,n-1}]P[S_{0,n-1}E_{1,n-1}|S_{0,n-2}E_{1,n-2}]\}P[S_{0,n-2}E_{1,n-2}]$$
$$= (1 - \psi r)^2(1 - r)^2 P[S_0]. \tag{10-28}$$

Thus, the probability that a subject who was actually in state S_0 was included in the sample of subjects assumed to be in state S_1 is

$$P[S_{0,n}|E_{1,n-1}E_{1,n-2}] = \frac{P[S_0](1-r)^2(1-\psi r)^2}{P[S_1]p^2 + P[S_0](1-r)[\psi r p + (1-\psi r)(1-r)]} \tag{10-29}$$

Likewise,

$$P[S_{1,n}|E_{0,n-1}E_{0,n-2}] = \frac{P[S_1](1-p)^2(1-\theta)^2}{P[S_0]r^2 + P[S_1](1-p)[\theta r + (1-\theta)(1-p)]}. \tag{10-30}$$

For reestimating p and r, we can use a more general form of (10-17) and (10-18):

$$P[E_{1,n}|E_{0,n-1}E_{0,n-2}] = P[S_{1,n}|E_{0,n-1}E_{0,n-2}]p + P[S_{0,n}|E_{0,n-1}E_{0,n-2}](1-r) \tag{10-31}$$

and

$$P[E_{1,n}|E_{1,n-1}E_{1,n-2}] = P[S_{1,n}|E_{1,n-1}E_{1,n-2}]p + P[S_{0,n}|E_{1,n-1}E_{1,n-2}](1-r). \tag{10-32}$$

Solving these two equations simultaneously gives

$$(1 - \hat{r}) = \frac{P[E_{1,n}|E_{0,n-1}E_{0,n-2}]P[S_{1,n}|E_{1,n-1}E_{1,n-2}] - P[S_{1,n}|E_{0,n-1}E_{0,n-2}]P[E_{1,n}|E_{1,n-1}E_{1,n-2}]}{P[S_{0,n}|E_{0,n-1}E_{0,n-2}]P[S_{1,n}|E_{1,n-1}E_{1,n-2}] - P[S_{1,n}|E_{0,n-1}E_{0,n-2}]P[S_{0,n}|E_{1,n-1}E_{1,n-2}]} \tag{10-33}$$

and

$$\hat{p} = \frac{P[E_{1,n}|E_{1,n-1}E_{1,n-2}] - P[S_{0,n}|E_{1,n-1}E_{1,n-2}](1 - \hat{r})}{P[S_{1,n}|E_{1,n-1}E_{1,n-2}]}. \tag{10-34}$$

For reestimating θ and ψ we can use the following relationships [Note: equations (10-20) and (10-21) are special cases of these relationships in which $P[S_{1,n}|E_{1,n-1}E_{1,n-2}] = P[S_{0,n}|E_{1,n-1}E_{1,n-2}] = 1$, and the same reasoning leads to these that led to (10-20) and (10-21)]:

$$P[E_{1,n}|E_{0,n-1}E_{1,n-2}E_{1,n-3}] = P[S_{1,n-1}|E_{1,n-2}E_{1,n-3}][\theta(1-r) + (1-\theta)p]$$
$$+ P[S_{0,n-1}E_{1,n-2}E_{1,n-3}](1-r), \qquad (10\text{-}35)$$

$$P[E_{1,n}|E_{1,n-1}E_{0,n-2}E_{0,n-3}] = P[S_{0,n-1}|E_{0,n-2}E_{0,n-3}][\psi p + (1-\psi)(1-r)]$$
$$+ P[S_{1,n-1}|E_{0,n-2}E_{0,n-3}]p, \qquad (10\text{-}36)$$

which, when solved for θ and ψ, provide:

$$\hat{\theta} = \frac{P[E_{1,n}|E_{0,n-1}E_{1,n-2}E_{1,n-3}] - P[S_{1,n-1}|E_{1,n-2}E_{1,n-3}]p - P[S_{0,n-1}|E_{1,n-2}E_{1,n-3}](1-r)}{P[S_{1,n-1}|E_{1,n-2}E_{1,n-3}](1-r-p)}, \qquad (10\text{-}37)$$

$$\hat{\psi} = \frac{P[E_{0,n}|E_{1,n-1}E_{0,n-2}E_{0,n-3}] - P[S_{1,n-1}|E_{0,n-2}E_{0,n-3}](1-p) - P[S_{0,n-1}|E_{0,n-2}E_{0,n-3}]r}{P[S_{0,n-1}|E_{0,n-2}E_{0,n-3}](1-r-p)}. \qquad (10\text{-}38)$$

The theoretical probability of E_1 at equilibrium is

$$P[E_1] = P[S_1]p + P[S_0](1-r). \qquad (10\text{-}39)$$

And the theoretical two-step dependencies are

$$P[E_{1,n}|E_{1,n-1}] = \frac{P[E_{1,n}E_{1,n-1}]}{P[E_1]} \qquad (10\text{-}40)$$

and

$$P[E_{0,n}|E_{0,n-1}] = \frac{P[E_{0,n}E_{0,n-1}]}{P[E_0]}. \qquad (10\text{-}41)$$

The numerators of (10-40) and (10-41) are the denominators of (10-29) and (10-30), respectively.

CHAPTER 11

discrete-state continuous time models

In this chapter we present models that use a combination of kinds of variables: discrete states and continuous time. In addition, this is a set of models rather than a single model, developed to provide a way of handling a variety of theories using the kind of data most usually available to sociologists.

The model is taken from James S. Coleman's *Introduction to Mathematical Sociology*.[1] Coleman's model is inspired not so much by a single theoretical or empirical problem, but by a general kind of dilemma that the whole field of sociology faces: that most of the data that are available are in the form of measurements of qualitative attributes, while most theories that deal with processes speak as though variables were continuous. Furthermore, most

---

[1] James S. Coleman, *Introduction to Mathematical Sociology* (New York: The Free Press, 1964), chaps. 4 and 5.

mathematics, having been developed to suit the needs of physics and engineering, assumes continuous variables. One example Coleman gives is the well-known proposition from George C. Homans' book *The Human Group*[2] that the amount of liking between two people will increase if the amount of interaction between them increases, and vice versa. This means that if there is a small increase in interaction, there should be a small increase in liking, while if there is a larger increase in interaction, there should be a larger increase in liking. In mathematical terms, this can be expressed as a differential equation in which the rate of change of liking over time is a function of the rate of change of interaction:

$$\frac{d \text{ liking}}{dt} = a \frac{d \text{ interaction}}{dt}.$$

where a is a parameter describing the strength of the effect of interaction on liking. Simon[3] has carried out an analysis of Homans' theory using this approach, but the work has the same problem the Stinchcombe and Harris model discussed in Chapter 6 has, that there are no available data to which to apply the model developed. Coleman points out that there are studies that are applicable to the hypothesis that interaction affects liking; for example, among printers, men who work at a kind of job that requires that they interact with other workers are more likely to name a person in the same shop as a best friend than are printers who work at a kind of job that precludes much interaction with the other men in their shop.[4] In this case, the data support the hypothesis but are in the form of two dichotomous variables (interaction being measured by kind of job, and liking by whether or not a man names another in the same shop as best friend). The sociologist is forced to assume that some kind of process like that described in the differential equation is taking place unmeasured, to result in distributions of cases like the one actually measured, rather than being able to test the assumptions about the process directly.

A second problem with testing a theory like Homans' is that the hypothesis is expressed as a one-to-one relationship between liking and interaction, whereas we can probably assume that many other factors besides interaction affect liking. Thus, in picturing the process by which interaction affects liking, we must include a set of other factors, presumably random,

[2]George C. Homans, *The Human Group* (New York: Harper & Row, 1950).
[3]Herbert Simon, *Models of Man* (New York: John Wiley & Sons, 1957).
[4]Coleman, *Introduction to Mathematical Sociology*, p. 105.

acting independently of interaction, with some tending to increase liking while others tend to decrease it.

Translation into Mathematics. With these problems in mind, Coleman has developed a mathematical model that will incorporate (1) the idea of a process by which one variable affects another over time and (2) both causal and random sources of the relationship, and that (3) can be used with discrete-state data. A picture of the general model for one independent and one dependent variable looks like Figure 11-1, which shows a cross-classification of two dichotomous variables.

We develop the model by making the following assumptions:

1. There are N individuals, each of whom has one and only one state of each of the two variables (that is, each individual can be put into one of the four cells).
2. Any individual can change his state on the dependent variable at any time. Individuals do not change their states on the independent variable.
3. All individuals in a given state of the independent variable are alike in the probability that they will move to the other state of the dependent variable.

The first assumption means that we are to look at the way one variable affects another by examining the proportions of individuals in each cell of the cross-classification, and the proportions moving between cells. The second and third assumptions mean that each individual can be characterized by a transition intensity or transition rate, which is conceptualized as the probability that an individual moves from one state to another in an infinitesimally small time.

$$q_{12}\, dt = \text{Pr (individual moves from 1 to 2 in time } dt),$$
$$q_{21}\, dt = \text{Pr (individual moves from 2 to 1 in time } dt).$$

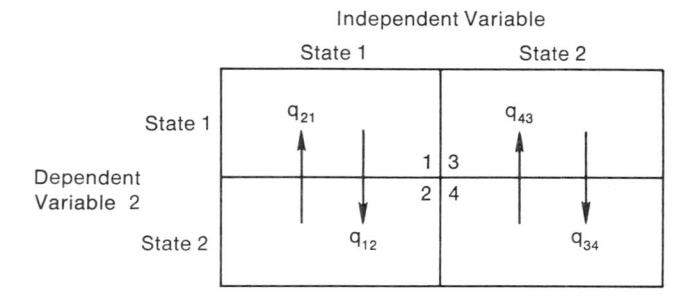

Figure 11-1

Continuous-time discrete-state model for one independent and one dependent variable

discrete-state continuous time models 211

If n_{1t} is the number of people occupying state 1 at time t, then

$$dn_{1t} = -q_{12}n_{1t}\, dt + q_{21}n_{2t}\, dt$$

or alternatively

$$\frac{dn_{1t}}{dt} = -q_{12}n_{1t} + q_{21}n_{2t}. \qquad (11\text{-}1)$$

This describes a Markov process; that is, the probability of being in any state is a function of the previous state and a constant transition probability. The transition probability, however, operates constantly over time and not at discrete points in time. This means that the equations expressing the expected number of individuals in a state must be written as differential equations with respect to time.

If, instead of one independent variable and one dependent variable, we wanted to describe a system in which there were two interdependent variables, we could use a model like the one in Figure 11-2. In this model, assumptions 1 and 3 are the same, and assumption 2 is changed to allow movement between states of both variables. This means that the number of people in state 1 at time t is a function of movement across as well as up and down, as expressed in the following:

$$\frac{dn_{1t}}{dt} = -(q_{12} + q_{13})n_{1t} + q_{21}n_{2t} + q_{31}n_{3t}. \qquad (11\text{-}2)$$

The q_{ij} are one of the basic parameters of the model, and much of the following mathematical work is devoted to finding ways to estimate them. If one could observe constantly, one could count the number of individuals moving and dividing by the length of time observed to estimate q_{ij} very simply.

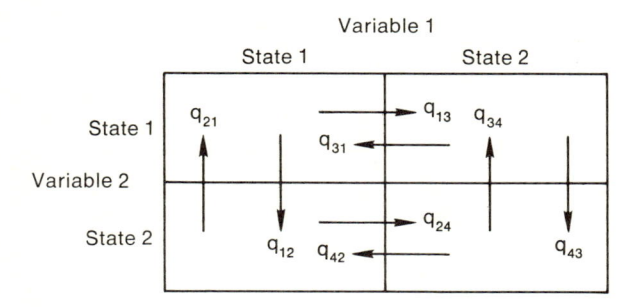

Figure 11-2

Continuous-time discrete-state model for two interdependent variables

212 Mathematical Sociology

However, most of the data available are not of continuous observations. Some data are only cross-sectional and have no information about changes, and even data that contain observations at several points in time will fail to catch all the moves. For example, an individual might move into state 1 from state 2, back into state 1, and into state 2 again between observations. This is actually three moves but would only be observed as one. The mathematical problem thus will be to find a way of estimating the transition rates, given that all moves cannot be directly observed.

However, defining the basic parameters q_{ij} answers only part of the needs of the model. Any theory that deals with the relationships between the two variables should suggest that the value of q_{ij} is affected by the causal relationship between the variables. It is also, as noted earlier, affected by random factors acting independently of the causal relationship between the variables. This can be expressed by a partitioning of the transition rates into causal and random factors. For the system described in Figure 11-1, this results in the following equations:

$$q_{12} = \epsilon_2, \quad q_{34} = \beta + \epsilon_2,$$
$$q_{21} = \alpha + \epsilon_1, \quad q_{43} = \epsilon_1. \quad (11\text{-}3)$$

Figure 11-3 shows this as a system, where α is the effect of the independent variable in one direction, β is the effect of the independent on the dependent variable in the other direction, and ϵ_1 and ϵ_2 are the random factors. The latter Coleman refers to as "random shocks"; they are all the extraneous things that push an individual from one state into another.

Note that a decision is required as to which direction the effects run; in Figure 11-3 it is assumed that state 1 of the independent variable causes

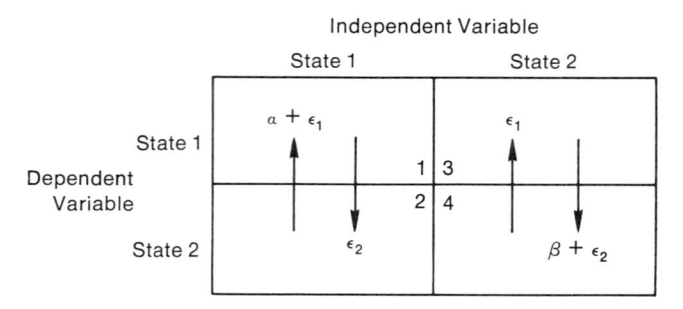

Figure 11-3

Model for one independent and one dependent variable, with transition rates partitioned into causal and random effect parameters, two-way effect assumed

discrete-state continuous time models 213

```
                    Independent Variable
                  State 1            State 2
              ┌─────────────────┬─────────────────┐
              │    a + ε₁       │      ε₁         │
      State 1 │      ↑    ↓     │       ↑    ↓    │
              │         1 │ 3            │         │
  Dependent   │─────────  │  ─────────────         │
  Variable    │         2 │ 4            │         │
              │      ↑    ↓     │       ↑    ↓    │
      State 2 │      ε₂         │       ε₂        │
              └─────────────────┴─────────────────┘
```

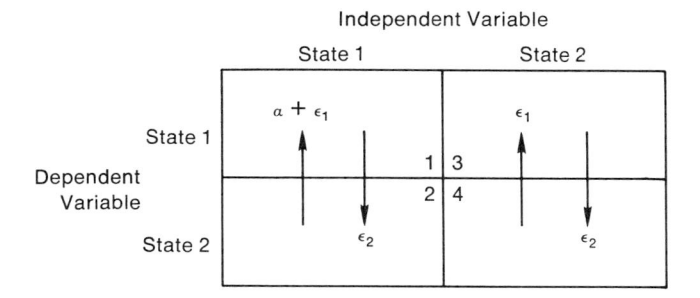

Figure 11-4

Model for one independent and one dependent variable with transition rates partitioned into causal and random effect parameters, one-way effect assumed

state 1 of the dependent variable, and that state 2 of the independent variable causes state 2 of the dependent variable. It is also possible to hypothesize a system that looks like Figure 11-4; here, there is a one-way instead of a two-way effect. Figure 11-4 shows a system in which having a positive state on one variable gives an added push toward a positive state on another, but in the absence of a positive state on the independent variable, only random factors are at work. The transition rates in the model of interdependent effects can likewise be partitioned into causal and random factors, as shown in Figure 11-5. Whether to use a model like Figure 11-3, Figure 11-4, Figure 11-5, or some other combination of hypotheses about causal effects depends on the theory to be tested, and the decision must be made before the parameters can be estimated.

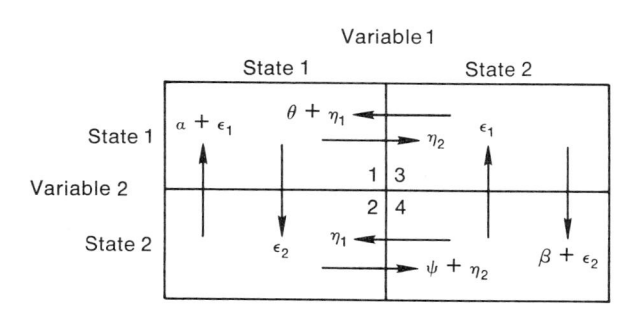

```
                         Variable 1
                  State 1            State 2
              ┌─────────────────┬─────────────────┐
              │ a + ε₁   θ + η₁ ←                 │
      State 1 │             ─── → η₂    ε₁        │
              │      ↑    ↓     │       ↑    ↓    │
              │         1 │ 3            │         │
  Variable 2  │─────────  │  ─────────────         │
              │         2 │ 4            │         │
              │      ↑    ↓     │       ↑    ↓    │
      State 2 │      ε₂    η₁ ←                    │
              │             ─── → ψ + η₂   β + ε₂ │
              └─────────────────┴─────────────────┘
```

Figure 11-5

Model for two interdependent variables, with transition rates partitioned into causal and random effect parameters, two-way effects of each variable on the other assumed

Translation Diagram 11-1

DATA	THEORY	MODEL
	Variables	
N individuals, cross-classified into a fourfold table →	Two dichotomous attributes →	n_{it}
Several points in time →	Time as a continuous variable →	t and dt
	Relationships	
	Individuals can change state at any time →	Transition rates q_{ij} and equations (11-1) and (11-2)
	a) One independent and one dependent variable →	Figure 11-1
	b) Two interdependent variables →	Figure 11-2
	There are both causal and random effects →	Equation (11-3) and counterparts for Figure 11-5 and other variations

In this model the source is both theory and data, and the direction is from both to model; the intention is to develop a general model that will include many sets of data and kinds of theories as special cases.

There are two kinds of variables, in addition to time: those referring to observable entities such as the dichotomous variables and the number and proportion of individuals in each category, and those referring to unobserved processes, such as the transition rates and the causal and random effect parameters. The q_{ij} are measures of probabilities, hence must stay between 0 and 1 in value. They are treated as dependent variables in a deterministic, differential equation.

There are also two kinds of relationships in this model. One set describes the process assumed to underly all the variations of the model, in which individuals can move between states at any time, with all individuals in one state being alike, and the probability of moving depending on the state occupied. These assumptions define a stationary Markov process with continuous time. This first set of relationships results in the use of differential equations such as (11-1) with respect to time. In the basic equations, the change in proportion of individuals in a given state is a dependent variable with the transition rate and time as independent variables.

The equations are nonlinear (as will appear shortly, they are basically exponential functions).

The second set of relationships are those that embody the theoretical assumptions about the effects of one of the dichotomous variables on the other, through the partitioning of the transition rates into causal and random effects. Here the transition rates are treated as dependent variables. The relationships allow some flexibility in answering questions of causal priority, as there are a number of variations in which different assumptions are made about the direction of effect. Note that the assumption that the effects of causal and random factors is linear and additive can be modified if need be to incorporate different theoretical assumptions without changing the other parts of the model. This system, like the other Markov processes we have examined, will reach an equilibrium at which the proportion of people in each category does not change.

estimating parameters

Panel Data. The major part of the mathematical work in the development of the model involves finding ways to estimate the q_{ij} or, if an absolute value cannot be estimated, the relative sizes of the q_{ij} for different conditions. In order to illustrate the derivations that follow, consider the data in Table 11-1, which were collected from a class of upper-level students in a sociology course.[5] In this course, some students make high grades (A) and

Table 11-1

Scores on Two Exams in a Sociology Course

		GIRLS SECOND EXAM					BOYS SECOND EXAM		
		A	B or less				A	B or less	
FIRST EXAM	A	6	16	22	FIRST EXAM	A	8	14	22
	B or less	19	59	78		B or less	6	72	78
		25	75	100			14	86	100

some make lower grades (B or less). Between the first exam and the second exam some students improved their performance, some went down, and others got the same grade on both exams.

To apply the model to this set of data we need to make the following assumptions. (1) The grade received on an examination reflects the current

[5]The percent of students in each category is from an actual class taught by one of the authors; the numbers have been changed to make computations easier.

216 Mathematical Sociology

state of the amount of effort the student is putting into the course, and (2) any student can change from "working hard" (which would be reflected by an A to "not working hard" (reflected by a B or lower). In other words, we assume that grade is determined by continuous work rather than by cramming or luck on a single exam, and we also assume that any student could change from doing A work to doing less than A work or vice versa at any time. If either of these assumptions is not justified, the model cannot validly be applied.

After assuming that the data meet the general conditions of the model, the next step is to decide which of the variations on the model is to be applied. We can safely assume that sex is an independent variable and grades a dependent variable, rather than assuming that grades can affect sex. This means the model will look like Figure 11-3 or 11-4. Next, we need to decide what assumptions to make about partitioning the transition rates. It seems most reasonable to use Figure 11-3 rather than assuming the transitions to be purely random for one sex but not for the other. Figure 11-6 shows the model we will apply.

To find values for the transition rates q_{ij}, we will need to define the following theoretical quantities:

n_{it} = expected number of people in state i at time t,
$n_{i0,\,jt}$ = expected number of people in state i at time 0 and in state j at time t.

The data provide direct estimates for these quantities, because we can observe how many people are in each state at each time. The rate at which people shift between states, however, cannot be directly estimated from the data. The reason is that the number of people in one state at the first observation and a different state at the second will not include those who have moved and then moved back to their original state, and it will count as only one move those who have moved three times (out, back in, back out again), and

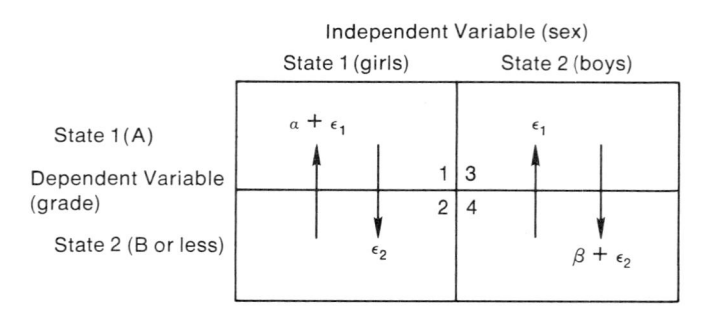

Figure 11-6

Model for data in Table 11-1, assuming opposite causal effects

so on. We can use the same reasoning that led to equation (11-1) to obtain an expression for the rate of change in number of people in one state at one time and another state at a later time, which can be used to derive an expression for the rates of change. For example, for the number of people in state 1 at both time 0 and time t,

$$\frac{dn_{10,1t}}{dt} = n_{10,2t}q_{21} - n_{10,1t}q_{12}. \tag{11-4}$$

That is, the rate of change in number of people in state 1 at two consecutive observations is a function of the number who were originally there but moved out times the probability of moving back, minus the number who are still there times the probability of moving out. Similarly, the rate of change in number of people in state 2 at one observation and state 1 at a later observation is:

$$\frac{dn_{20,1t}}{dt} = n_{20,2t}q_{21}. \tag{11-5}$$

Since $n_{10} = n_{10,1t} + n_{10,2t}$, equation (11-4) can be rewritten:

$$\frac{dn_{10,1t}}{dt} = (n_{10} - n_{10,1t})q_{21} - n_{10,1t}q_{12}. \tag{11-6}$$

To find the expected number of people moving from state 1 to state 2 in time t, one can integrate equation (11-6) over the time period 0 to t. This is done as follows.[6] First, rearrange (11-6) to

$$\frac{dn_{10,1t}}{(n_{10} - n_{10,1t})q_{21} - n_{10,1t}q_{12}} = dt. \tag{11-7}$$

Then

$$\int_{n_{10}}^{n_{10,1t}} \frac{dn_{10,1t}}{(n_{10} - n_{10,1t})q_{21} - n_{10,1t}q_{12}} = \int_{0}^{t} dt. \tag{11-8}$$

Performing the integration indicated in equation (11-8) gives[7]

$$\frac{1}{q_{12} + q_{21}} \ln \frac{n_{10}q_{21} - n_{10}(q_{21} + q_{12})}{n_{10}q_{21} - n_{10,1t}(q_{21} + q_{12})} = t. \tag{11-9}$$

Removing the absolute value signs (the value of n_{1t} will always be such as to make the lefthand expression positive) and taking antilogarithms of

---

[6]The derivations expressed in equations (11-4)–(11-14) are from pp. 131 and 137 of Coleman, *Introduction to Mathematical Sociology*. Equations (11-16)–(11-24) are derived on pp. 119–122.

[7]A formula for integrating an expression with the general form of (11-8) can be found in a standard handbook of mathematical functions.

both sides gives

$$\frac{n_{10}q_{21} - n_{10}(q_{21} + q_{12})}{n_{10}q_{21} - n_{10,1t}(q_{21} + q_{12})} = e^{t(q_{21}+q_{12})}. \tag{11-10}$$

Solving this for $n_{10,1t}$ results in

$$n_{10,1t} = n_{10}\frac{q_{21}}{q_{21} + q_{12}}[1 - e^{-t(q_{21}+q_{12})}] + n_{10}e^{-t(q_{21}+q_{12})}. \tag{11-11}$$

Similarly, integrating (11-5) and solving for $n_{20,1t}$ gives

$$n_{20,1t} = n_{20}\frac{q_{21}}{q_{21} + q_{12}}[1 - e^{-t(q_{21}+q_{12})}]. \tag{11-12}$$

These two equations can be solved simultaneously for q_{21} and q_{12} by first dividing (11-11) by n_{10} and (11-12) by n_{20}, and subtracting the latter from the former. This result and the equation formed by taking logarithms of it can both be substituted into (11-12). This, after we simplify by noting that

$$\frac{n_{10,2t}}{n_{10}} = 1 - \frac{n_{10,1t}}{n_{10}},$$

results in

$$\frac{n_{10,2t}}{n_{10}} = \frac{-q_{21}}{\ln\left(1 - \frac{n_{10,2t}}{n_{10}} - \frac{n_{20,1t}}{n_{20}}\right)} \left(\frac{n_{10,2t}}{n_{10}} + \frac{n_{20,1t}}{n_{20}}\right), \tag{11-13}$$

which, solved for q_{21}, gives

$$q_{21} = \frac{n_{20,1t}}{n_{20}} \frac{-\ln\left(1 - \frac{n_{10,2t}}{n_{10}} - \frac{n_{20,1t}}{n_{20}}\right)}{t\left(\frac{n_{10,2t}}{n_{10}} + \frac{n_{20,1t}}{n_{20}}\right)}. \tag{11-14}$$

The equation for q_{12} will be the comparable expression with the subscripts reversed appropriately, and q_{34} and q_{43} are found likewise.

Note that the data provide direct estimates for all the quantities on the righthand side of (11-14). Thus, for the example in Table 11-1, the values of the transition rates are

$$q_{21} = \frac{19}{78} \frac{-\ln\left(1 - \frac{16}{22} - \frac{19}{78}\right)}{6\left(\frac{16}{22} + \frac{19}{78}\right)} = .15,$$

$$q_{12} = \frac{16}{22} \frac{-\ln\left(1 - \frac{16}{22} - \frac{19}{78}\right)}{6\left(\frac{16}{22} + \frac{19}{78}\right)} = .45. \tag{11-15}$$

$$q_{34} = .18,$$

$$q_{43} = .02.$$

If we solve equations (11-3) using these values of q_{ij}, the results are

$\alpha = .13,$ effect toward higher grade for girls,
$\beta = -.27,$ effect toward lower grade for boys,
$\epsilon_1 = .02,$ random shock toward higher grade,
$\epsilon_2 = .45,$ random shock toward lower grade.

These transition rates cannot be partitioned as we had originally assumed (in Figure 11-6). This tells us that the model of opposite causal effects is incorrect. A closer look at the data shows why; the girls are more likely to change grade in both directions than are the boys, and the direction of change is relatively unimportant compared to this tendency.

We could interpret this to mean that both boys and girls experience equal random shocks toward lower grades but different causal effects toward higher grades.

An alternative model can be suggested (see Figure 11-7):

$$\begin{aligned} q_{21} &= \alpha + \epsilon_1, \\ q_{12} &= \beta + \epsilon_2, \\ q_{34} &= \epsilon_1, \\ q_{43} &= \epsilon_2. \end{aligned} \quad (11\text{-}15)$$

This model assumes that boys and girls are subject to the same set of random shocks toward higher and lower grades, and that there are an additional set of factors α and β that affect girls only. For this model,

$\alpha = .13, \quad \epsilon_1 = .02$ (toward higher grade),
$\beta = .27, \quad \epsilon_2 = .18$ (toward lower grade).

Which of these models is more appropriate depends on which is most consistent with a reasonable theoretical interpretation. Coleman does not provide

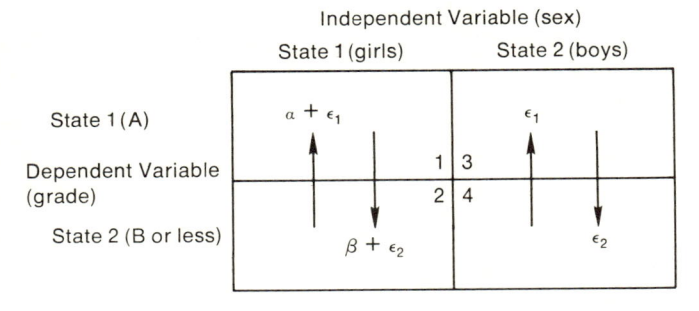

Figure 11-7

Alternative model for data in Table 11-1, assuming causal effects for girls

220 Mathematical Sociology

any techniques of statistical analysis to assess the amount of variance explained or the relative goodness of fit of different sets of assumptions.[8]

Although this is in one sense a disadvantage of the model, it is also an advantage in that it makes very clear the importance of having some theory behind the model.

Cross-sectional Data. Often sociologists theorize a process like the ones Coleman's models describe, but have only cross-sectional data with which to test the theory. Coleman shows how his general model can be used to estimate the relative effects of random and causal effect parameters from cross-sectional data, although exact estimates of transition rates and effect parameters cannot be found. To do this, an additional assumption is needed: the assumption of aggregate equilibrium.

The assumption of aggregate or statistical equilibrium is necessary for the mathematical work that follows, just as an assumption of equilibrium was necessary for the derivation of solutions for the parameters in Chapters 9 and 10, and it means basically the same thing as equilibrium meant there: that the process has continued long enough that, although individuals may change at any moment, the proportion of individuals in any state does not change over time. At aggregate equilibrium, the expected flow between states in one direction equals that in the other; if a large number of people move into a state, then a large number are available to move out, and the moves in and out cancel each other.

Note that if $t \longrightarrow \infty$, equation (11-11) becomes

$$n_{10, 1\infty} = n_{10} \frac{q_{21}}{q_{12} + q_{21}},$$

or, if we are only interested in the number in state 1 at equilibrium,[9]

$$n_{1\infty} = n_{1+2} \frac{q_{21}}{q_{12} + q_{21}}, \quad (11\text{-}16)$$

where n_{1+2} is the total number in state 1 of the independent variable. Instead of $n_{1\infty}$ we can write n_{1e} for the number in state 1 at equilibrium. Since at equilibrium the flow into one state equals the flow into the other,

$$n_{1e}q_{12} = n_{2e}q_{21}. \quad (11\text{-}17)$$

---

[8]Gudmund Hernes, "A Markovian approach to measures of association," *American Journal of Sociology*, vol. 75, no. 6 (May, 1970), pp. 992–1011, points out that for the model of interdependent variables and cross-sectional data, several of the ways of partitioning transition rates are equivalent to standard statistical measures of association for fourfold tables.

[9]Equation (11-16) is derived from (11-1) in the same way that (11-11) is derived from (11-4).

If we substitute equation (11-3) into (11-17) and its equivalent for n_{3e}, we find that

$$\epsilon_2 n_{1e} = (\alpha + \epsilon_1) n_{2e}, \qquad (11\text{-}18)$$

$$\epsilon_2 n_{3e} = \epsilon_1 n_{4e}. \qquad (11\text{-}19)$$

Equations (11-18) and (11-19) can be used to find an expression for each of the effect parameters relative to the sum of all of them, as follows. Define

$$P_{1e} = \frac{n_{1e}}{n_{1e} + n_{2e}}$$

and

$$P_{3e} = \frac{n_{3e}}{n_{3e} + n_{4e}}.$$

Then

$$P_{1e} = \frac{\alpha + \epsilon_1}{\alpha + \epsilon_1 + \epsilon_2} \qquad (11\text{-}20)$$

[by adding $(\alpha + \epsilon_1) n_{1e}$ to both sides of equation (11-19)] and

$$P_{3e} = \frac{\epsilon_1}{\epsilon_1 + \epsilon_2}. \qquad (11\text{-}21)$$

Thus,

$$\frac{\alpha}{\alpha + \epsilon_1 + \epsilon_2} = \frac{P_{1e} - P_{3e}}{1 - P_{3e}} \qquad (11\text{-}22)$$

$$\frac{\epsilon_1}{\alpha + \epsilon_1 + \epsilon_2} = \frac{P_{1e}(1 - P_{3e})}{1 - P_{3e}} \qquad (11\text{-}23)$$

$$\frac{\epsilon_2}{\alpha + \epsilon_1 + \epsilon_2} = 1 - P_{3e}. \qquad (11\text{-}24)$$

To illustrate how this can be used, consider the data in Table 11-2. This comes from a sample survey of women who had applied for welfare in ten states.[10] The interview included an employment history over a 37-month period (many welfare recipients also work) and self-esteem as measured by a set of semantic differential items. The authors hypothesize that the women who are employed will have higher self-esteem scores than those who are not, arguing that being employed, by providing a respectable role in society and decreasing feeling of dependence, enhances the self-esteem of women

---

[10] Samuel M. Meyers and Jennie McIntyre, *Welfare Policy and its Consequences for the Recipient Population: A Study of the AFDC Program* (Washington, D.C.: U.S. Government Printing Office, December, 1969). The data in Table 11-2 are adapted from Table 6.22, p. 170.

222   Mathematical Sociology

Table 11-2

Self-esteem and Months Employed for a Sample of Welfare Applicants and Recipients Who Had Worked Five Months or Less During a 37-month Period

		MONTHS EMPLOYED	
		0–2	3–5
SELF-ESTEEM	High	2114	1042
	Low	2641	729
		4755	1771

who in many other respects are in a low-status postion. Among the data that relate to this hypothesis is Table 11-2 showing self-esteem ratings for women in the sample who had worked five months or less.

We will illustrate a test for two models. The first is shown in Figure (11-8).

This model assumes that self-esteem, as measured by the instrument used, is subject to change at any time, that raising or lowering self-esteem is a result of random shocks that affect all the women equally, and that, in addition, working provides an extra push toward higher self-esteem. We also must assume that the system is in aggregate equilibrium—that is, that there is no change over time in the proportion of women in each category. The second model we will test proposes that working more and working less have equal and opposite effects on self-esteem, as shown in Figure 11-9.

The equations for this model are

$$\frac{\alpha}{\alpha + \epsilon_1 + \epsilon_2} = P_{1e} - P_{3e}, \tag{11-25}$$

$$\frac{\epsilon_1}{\alpha + \epsilon_1 + \epsilon_2} = P_{1e} \tag{11-26}$$

$$\frac{\epsilon_2}{\alpha + \epsilon_1 + \epsilon_2} = 1 - P_{1e}, \tag{11-27}$$

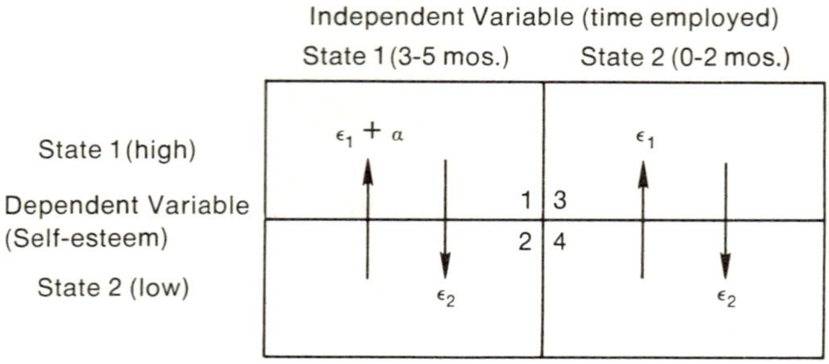

Figure 11-8

Model for data in Table 11-2, assuming one-way causal effect

discrete-state continuous time models 223

```
                    Independent Variable (time employed)
                    State 1 (3-5 mos.)      State 2 (0-2 mos.)
```

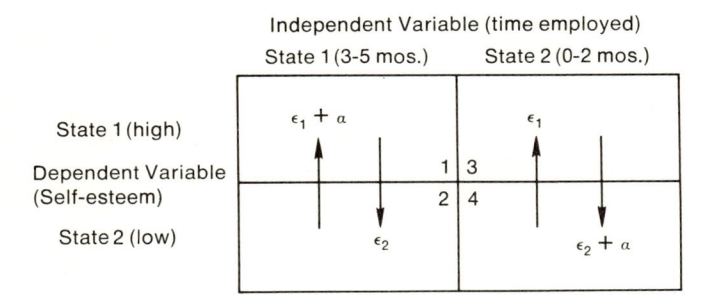

[Diagram: 2×2 table with State 1 (high) and State 2 (low) rows; arrows labeled $\epsilon_1 + a$ down into cell 1, ϵ_2 down into cell 2, ϵ_1 down into cell 3, $\epsilon_2 + a$ down into cell 4. Cells numbered 1,3 (top) and 2,4 (bottom).]

Figure 11-9

Model for data in Table 11-2, assuming equal and opposite causal effects

which are derived the same way (11-22)–(11-24) were. For the data in Table 11-2, these result in

$$\frac{\alpha}{\alpha + \epsilon_1 + \epsilon_2} = .15 \quad \text{relative effects of working (toward high self-esteem) and not working (toward low self-esteem),}$$

$$\frac{\epsilon_1}{\alpha + \epsilon_1 + \epsilon_2} = .44 \quad \text{random shocks toward high self-esteem,}$$

$$\frac{\epsilon_2}{\alpha + \epsilon_1 + \epsilon_2} = .41 \quad \text{random shocks toward low self-esteem.}$$

Using equations (11-22)–(11-24), we find

$$\frac{\alpha}{\alpha + \epsilon_1 + \epsilon_2} = \frac{\frac{1042}{1771} - \frac{2114}{4755}}{1 - \frac{2114}{4755}} = \frac{.59 - .44}{.56}$$

$$= .27 \text{ (relative effect of independent variable),}$$

$$\frac{\epsilon_1}{\alpha + \epsilon_1 + \epsilon_2} = .32 \text{ (relative random shocks toward high self-esteem),}$$

$$\frac{\epsilon_2}{\alpha + \epsilon_1 + \epsilon_2} = .41 \text{ (relative random shocks toward low self-esteem).}$$

Since the equations express the effect relative to their sum, the three results sum to 1.0.

In this case, we have some theoretical reason for choosing one version of the model over another. The authors of the report from which these data are drawn argue and present other evidence for the assumption that time on welfare without working is associated with a decrease in self-esteem, while time on welfare combined with working is associated with increasing self-esteem. The model in Figure 11-9 therefore is the appropriate one.

comments on the model

In terms of empirical adequacy, we note that the models can be applied to a variety of kinds of data, and that they "work" in the sense that they provide interesting conclusions. Coleman's book is not explicitly concerned with testing the empirical adequacy of his models in terms of statistical significance or predictive ability, so he pays rather little attention to this aspect of model testing. The models could, of course, be tested by using data from one or two points in time to predict the distribution of individuals among states at later observations.

In both the areas of theory and of data, the general model is very flexible; Coleman presents a number of variations, including testing assumptions about interdependent variables (this cannot be done with cross-sectional data), multivariate analysis, using a continuous rather than a discrete independent variable, and using several other approaches to partitioning the transition rates. As an example of an approach to the problem of assumptions about how the transition rates should be partitioned, he points out that a number of theories in sociology and psychology assume some sort of consistency process in which one combination of states is "balanced" and other combinations are not. These theories can lead to assumptions about the transition rates between states in the model of interdependent variables, if one assumes that consistency provides a causal effect toward the consistent state. Each development of the model is based on working between model and both theory and data, with the intention of building models that will help with both the analysis of data available to sociologists and the development of concepts and theories.

problems

1. How could you apply a discrete-state continuous-time model to voting behavior? Compare this application with your mover-stayer application for question 3 of Chapter 9. Which seems more appropriate? How do these applications compare with using the value-conflict model of Chapter 10 for the same problem?

2. Estimate the main effects and random shocks for the following table. Interpret your results.

		SELF-ESTEEM High	SELF-ESTEEM Low
JOB SUCCESS	High	50	10
JOB SUCCESS	Low	40	100

3. How would you apply Coleman's type of analysis to determine whether there was a tendency toward balance in interpersonal triads (Chapter 4)? What data would you need? How would you set up the necessary table?

CHAPTER 12

working with mathematical models

Perhaps the most severe problems the novice encounters in working with mathematical models involve theory construction rather than mathematics. This is because the development of models, whether they be mathematical or not, is in effect a process of theory construction.

In our discussion of individual models, we have indicated that the model is the result of a translation of sociological theory or data into mathematics, and vice versa. This translation, or mapping, is the statement of an *isomorphism* between some element of sociology and some element of mathematics. Technically, an isomorphism exists between two sets of elements if a one-to-one relationship can be established between elements of one set and those of the other, and for every relationship between elements of one set there exists a corresponding relationship between the corresponding elements of the other.

The notion of isomorphism is important to mathematics in general, and to the philosophy of science and theory construction. For example, in a discussion of the uses of logic and mathematics in science, Cohen and Nagel[1] point out: "In physics, we can see how the formula of inverse squares applies to electrical attraction and repulsion as well as to the force of gravitation. This is possible because these different subject matters have an identical formal structure with respect to the properties studied . . . . It is the isomorphism found in diverse subject matter which makes possible theoretical science as we know it today."[2] In mathematics, "a hypothesis when abstractly stated is capable of more than one concrete representation. Consequently, when we are studying pure mathematics we are studying the possible structure of many concrete situations. In this way we discover the constant or invariable factor in situations sensibly different . . . ."[3] In other words, the development of mathematical models is the search for more points at which one can describe an isomorphism between an abstract hypothesis or set of assumptions and a concrete representation.

Since one way in which science proceeds is by establishment of isomorphisms between abstract hypotheses and concrete representations, the correct statement of the isomorphism becomes an important consideration. Let us explain this in more detail. Each arrow in the translation diagram we have been using represents an assumption in a theory; the assumption is "this sociological concept is equivalent to this mathematical concept" or "this statement of relationship between sociological variables is equivalent to this mathematical equation." The rules of logic tell us that if a conclusion from a deductive system is false, then one of the assumptions from which it is derived must be false. Thus, if a prediction derived from a model is not supported by empirical test, then one of the assumptions of the model must be false; the assumptions that translate from theory or data to model must be questioned, along with the actual assumptions of the theory and/or procedures by which data were collected. If one of the translation assumptions is false, (that is, if we cannot justifiably state that the sociological concept and the mathematical concept are formally equivalent), then the predictions from the model are meaningless.

Unfortunately, there is no way of setting down rules for developing valid translation assumptions; these, like other theoretical assumptions, must be developed inductively, which is essentially a creative process. (This is part of what people mean when they refer to building models as an "art.") We can, however, suggest a set of questions that can be used as a guide in deciding what kinds of mathematical concepts and assumptions may be most appropriate for a particular sociological problem. The questions are summarized at the end of this section.

[1] M. R. Cohen and E. Nagel, *An Introduction to Logic and Scientific Method* (New York: Harcourt, Brace, Jovanovich, 1934).
[2] Cohen and Nagel, *op. cit.*, p. 139.
[3] *Ibid.*

The first step in this series of questions involves identifying the source of the model: is the source theory, data, or another model? Then, one needs to consider the potential directions of mapping and uses of the model. For example, a model developed to represent a theory may be intended for use as a guide to collecting data later. If it is assumed that a model will subsequently be used as a source in further work, it may be necessary to anticipate the demands which this further application will place on the model in addition to the immediate demands of the source from which the model is being developed.

We hope all four directions of movement to and from the model point of the theory-model-data triangle will become increasingly evident in sociological work. Data formulated more precisely in mathematical form will have implications for new data as well as implications for general theories. Theories formulated in precise mathematical form will have stronger implications for data as well as greater possible linkage to other substantive areas. A model itself should ideally be the product of repeated testing and revisions, based on mapping to and from both theory and data.

Once the source has been identified, we suggest a set of questions about the properties of the variables and characteristics of relationships in the source. Detailed specification of the properties of the variables and relationships in the mapping source may necessitate unanticipated work on the source itself before translation can proceed. A poorly delineated theory cannot provide adequate basis for developing a mathematical model; if modeling based on such a theory is attempted, it will soon become evident that the information contained in the theory is not sufficient to determine the properties of the variables or forms of relationships. An example of this is the graph representation of balance theory described in Chapter 4; the original theory did not make the status of absent (as opposed to positive and negative) relations clear enough to represent in a model without making additional assumptions. Similarly, attempting to construct a model that will adequately reflect existing data sometimes will require reanalysis of the data.

questions about variables

Order. A particularly important property of variables concerns inherent order in the variable as conceived theoretically or measured empirically. When data are concerned, this is the question of level of measurement —that is, whether nominal, ordinal, or higher mathematical properties are found. Nominal data and theoretical variables that imply only unordered categories can be referred to as "states," a term which applies equally readily to such diverse items as a mental set, an observed choice between alternatives, or a category on some variable such as religion, sex, or political preference.

No "higher-lower" or "more-less" distinction between states is implied, nor can a distance between them be assumed. The mathematics of graph theory, matrix algerba, and Markov processes are particularly well suited to handling variables that are states.

Continuity. Data resulting from ordinal or higher levels of measurement, and theoretical concepts that imply placement on continua, are usually mapped onto numbers. A property that is of concern here is whether the variable are continuous or discrete. If the operations which have produced data are examined, it will be evident whether a variable can take on an infinity of values between its limits, in which case it is continuous, or whether it can assume only specific values, in which case it is discrete. An example of a discrete ordered variable is the number of people in a group; an example of a continuous ordered variable is physical height.

Variables that are ordered but discrete can sometimes be treated as states and mapped onto points in a graph or states of a Markov model, or alternatively mapped onto numbers if one remembers that numbers when subjected to the operations of arithmetic assume continuous values (resulting in possible anomalies such as 2.2 persons). If the variables are inherently continuous, then equations expressing the usual set of functions familiar from calculus may be used, or one of the probability distributions that requires continuous variables. If the intent of the model building is to induce general relationships from data that happen to be discrete but could conceivably be measured in a continuous manner, then the distinction is not crucial. If, on the other hand, it is intended to use the model to predict future data which can only be measured in discrete form, then using continuous variables in the models would produce unnecessary inaccuracies of prediction.

When the source of the model is theory, it may not be immediately obvious whether variables should be treated as continuous or discrete. Again, the intent of the modeling may help determine what form would be most useful. It is possible for certain purposes to decide to treat inherently continuous variables as if they were discrete—for example, by dichotomizing a theoretical dimension.

An example of this sort of analysis of variables is the treatment of time as a variable in the Markov models discussed in Chapters 9, 10, and 11. In the value-conflict model, time must be treated as a discrete variable, because it is assumed that people can change their values only when they make certain behavioral decisions; in between these decisions, there is no movement between states. In the Coleman process models, in contrast, time is treated as a continuous variable, and we must assume that movement takes place constantly, not just at the times we observe the system. In the mover-stayer model time is assumed to be discrete, but this is probably not a necessary theoretical assumption, because it is quite possible that people change jobs several times in a three-month interval. As Coleman points out, the assumption that time can be mapped onto discrete intervals may be sufficiently erroneous to justify rejecting some discrete-time Markov models.

Level. A third consideration is whether a variable is unique or summary. For data, this is related to the set of methodological problems of aggregation of data, of individual vs. collective levels, contextual effects, and the "ecological fallacy." Uniqueness implies that the property pertains to a specific individual or other unit in the theory or data being modeled. Thus, an individual may have a unique political preference, attraction to a group, or social status. A summary variable pertains to a set of individual entities in the theory or data being modeled. A statistical mean, for example, is a summary variable; it requires adding over a set of unique properties and may be a better representation of some kinds of collective characteristics than would a unique property defined at the level of the collectivity.

An example of this sort of problem appear in the simulation model in Chapter 8, which relates the amount an individual wants to talk (a unique individual-level variable) to the stability of a group (a unique group-level variable) through the intervening variable of the average amount others in the group want to talk (a summary variable with individuals as the units). In a typical nonmathematical treatment of such a problem, people would be divided into "high" and "low" talkers and groups into "high" and "low" based on the talking propensities of all members. Then "high" individuals in "high" groups would be compared with "high" individuals in "low" groups, and so on. The mathematics is useful because it allows us to deal with amount of talking as something other than a dichotomized variable, and to examine its relationship with amount of talking by others in much more detail than the other treatment allows. Many mathematical models are developed specifically to deal with this problem.[4]

If both individual and group variables are included in a theory, there must be clear understanding of whether any unique variables at the group level are in any way definitionally linked to unique properties of individuals. Obviously, summary properties are so linked. If, in fact, a group property were treated in the theory as in some way summary over group members, the probable consequence of providing the model with a new, unique group-level variable rather than using a summary variable would be to overlook implied constraints on the distribution of that variable.

Implied constraints on the distribution of a summary variable are important for any model, but particularly so in models that treat change of a system over time. As individual actor variables undergo change, any sum-

[4]For example, J. S. Coleman, *The Mathematics of Collective Action* (Chicago: Aldine, 1973); also R. L. Hamblin, R. B. Jacobsen, and J. L. L. Miller, *A Mathematical Theory of Social Change* (New York: John Wiley & Sons, 1973).

mary characteristics of a group will undergo simultaneous change. To the extent that group changes feed back to or otherwise condition subsequent changes at the individual level, it is imperative that linkage between the levels be correctly incorporated into the model. If linkage is not adequate, the deduction from the model will be progressively in error as more iterations of cyclic processes are made. If there are no intentions of treating larger collectivity variables as summary forms of individual variables, then the model builder can separate his efforts into three distinct parts: relationships at the collectivity level, relationships at the individual level, and relationships between these levels.

The question of unique versus summary variables relates to an important point in the unification of knowledge in fields that are arrayed on a continuum of increasing scope. Beginning at a very basic level, one can assume that the information of biochemistry is a constituent part of biology, which in turn underlies much of individual psychology, which forms a foundation for social psychology, which can again be seen as fundamental to many broader social processes, which contribute to general cultural patterns. The same type of linkage between adjacent levels is apparent when we begin at the most general end of the continuum and note that culture influences social processes, which mold much of social-psychological patterning, and so on. The point is not one of reductionism or determinism, but that we need to explain how variables at one level affect the relationships between variables at adjacent levels of information. For example, we predict different behavior on the part of a person who normally talks a lot when he is faced with a lot of other talkative people than when he is interacting with a few nontalkative people. Much of the interrelating can be done by the treatment of properties at one level as summary variables based on an immediately adjacent level. It can also be done by treating parameters as dependent variables in a second stage of analysis, as we suggest as a general strategy for building models.

Randomness. A question intermediate between properties of variables and properties of relationships is whether the concept of randomness or unpredictability is included in the model. Models that include random variables differ from deterministic models; a random variable must conform to the rules of probability. It has a distribution of possible values for any given case rather than a single value, and random relationships, in contrast to deterministic ones, are such that the particular value of a dependent variable has a stated probability of occurring under specified conditions of the independent variables. This probability must be between 0 and 1 in value.

In developing a probabilistic model, one alternative is to think in terms of an event (such as talking or not talking in a discussion, endorsing or disagreeing with an attitude) which may or may not occur, or which may take on any of a range of values, but whose occurrence or value can be described by a probability distribution. The distribution will have properties such as range of possible values, expected mean and variance, and equations expressing the probability of occurrence of the event or of the occurrence of a certain value. Examples are the hypergeometric, binominal, multinominal, Poisson, or normal distributions. The parameters of the distribution may sometimes be treated as dependent variables in an equation describing a deterministic relationship. This happens with the probabilities of initiating acts in the model of the distribution of acts in small groups, described in Chapter 3. An alternative approach is to conceptualize randomness in a relationship (rather than in variables) in a typical linear regression equation, which treats two variables as nonrandom but describes the relationship between them as including a random "error" term. The error term, of course, has the properties of a random variable. While the mathematics is based on the same general assumptions, the translation from and back into sociological theory may be quite different if one thinks of a deterministic relationship with some "error" rather than an inherently random relationship. Most of the standard statistical methods used by sociologists make the same sort of assumption. We suggest this decision be made explicitly rather than implicitly.

Treatment of Time. Another question intermediate between properties of variables and properties of relationships is the treatment of time. For certain purposes it may be desirable to include time explicitly as a variable in the model. Such may be the case, for example, if a theory concerns changes as a consequence of maturation, length of association, or other time-based changes. The birth control model in Chapter 8 is one example. For other purposes it is preferable to treat time implicitly as a part of relationships rather than explicitly as a variable. Thus, subsequent values of a particular valuable may be defined in terms of present values plus some change-inducing inputs, but the amount of time needed to get from present to subsequent is not a variable. This type of analytical use of time may be particularly helpful for tracing developmental processes when there is no intention of relating the model to data. The White kinship models make implicit use of time, in that it must be assumed that the relationships of marriage and parenthood alternate; people must marry first, then have children who in turn must marry, and so on. The assumption that one stage must precede the next appears in the alternation of C and W matrices in the development of the more complex kinship relationships.

If time is explicitly included as a variable, as in some of the process models, it may be treated as either continuous or discrete, like other variables. The meaning of discrete treatment of time is not as strange as it might appear at first. People tend to think in convenient time units such as days, months, and so on, rather than conceiving of time as a continuous stream of infinitesimal units. Consequently, building a model which uses discrete time units is equivalent to saying that time-based changes will be considered at regular intervals rather than continuously. For modeling data such as obtained in panel studies, this makes good sense.

Continuous time is also intuitively valid, and sometime it is more convenient to use mathematically. For models that involve differential equations, continuous time is most useful. For most Markov models discrete time is assumed, although the Coleman models are designed to use continuous time. In general, although not invariably, models that involve other discrete variables will use time as a discrete variable, and models in which the other variables are continuous will also assume that time is continuous.

In some cases, implicit relationships involving time can be used to derive explicit time-based relationships. Thus, expressing the rate of change of different variables as functions of time by using differential equations allows implicit use of time in relating those variables to each other. Yet one can solve the differential equations for the explicit equations linking time to each of the other variables. The advantage of implicit use, however, lies in being able to ignore the question of just how much time is needed for a given change in the other variables, and concentrating on how those variables change jointly as time passes.

Although we have made the distinction between process models, which involve changes in variables over time, and structure models, which predict structure at a given point in time, we actually see the structure models as based on implicit process models. For any structure, if we have a theory that explains how variables are related to each other, the theory tells us that change in one variable will be followed by changes in another; thus the structure at a point in time is the result of processes that we assume have occurred. For example, the graph-theory models of balanced structures are based on a theory that says that if relationships are not balanced, they will change, or else people will feel uncomfortable. Because relationships are expected to change to balance, we predict that we will tend to find balanced structures if we look at ongoing groups. Any theory that posits a causal relationship between variables will have implicit a process model, because it will predict that changes in one variable will cause changes in another subsequently.

questions about relationships

Causality. Key properties of relationships pertain to the variables linked by those relationships and the manner in which the linkage takes place. About the variables themselves, one must ask how many of them are linked by a particular relationship (this will be relevant to the complexity of the relationship), and which has priority among the variables (this will be relevant to the form of the relationship). Most commonly, models use relationships that link only two variables, treating one as dependent upon the other. More complex forms may treat one variable as dependent upon a number of others, as in multiple regression or path analysis, or a set of variables as dependent upon a set of other variables, as in canonical analysis. Priority among variables concerns which variables are treated as independent, which as dependent, and whether any implications of causality are to be drawn from the dependence.

Many mathematical forms used to represent causal relations are in fact symmetrical; that is, the equation that links two variables can be solved for either as an unknown. While this is acceptable mathematically, it requires caution in interpreting the results in substantive terms. If we had an equation that expressed the relationship between a man's height and his ability to play basketball, for example, and we knew his basketball ability, we could solve for his height. We would *not* want to conclude that a man grows taller because he practices basketball. We would rather conclude that we can predict his height because we know the particular value of height that is likely to produce the level of skill we know he has.

Form. After we settle the question of causality in the relationships between variables, our next problem is the form of the relationships. Relationships may be linear, in which case a standard increment in the independent variable will be reflected by a proportional increment in the dependent variable anywhere in the range of the relationship. Alternatively, relationships may be nonlinear, meaning that the amount of change in the dependent variable for a standard increment of the independent variable differs over the range of the equation. In simplest form nonlinear relationships are monotonic; that is, the dependent variable continues to increase or decrease consistently throughout the entire range. Logarithmic and exponential functions are examples. Simple logarithmic or exponential relationships can be converted easily to linear relationships (see Chapter 2 for an example).

Nonmonotonic forms are exemplified by a relationship in which the dependent variable increases as the independent variable increases for part of its range, then begins to decrease—such as a parabola. A variety of standard mathematical functions describe various kinds of curves. Such nonmonotonic forms may also be cyclic or in other ways more complex. Because a general nonlinear equation includes the terms of a linear equation plus added terms, linear forms are typically used as first approximations for model building, and more complex forms are attempted if linear forms prove unsatisfactory.

Aside from a general nonlinear equation, which serves curve-fitting purposes but has little theoretical interpretability, various specific nonlinear relationships are of interest. For example, growth processes which begin slowly, accelerate, then taper off can be represented as in the diffusion models of Chapter 7. Another form is the exponential equation which was used in the income-education example of Chapter 1: $Y = a + bX^c$. Logarithmic functions, trigonometric functions, and many other nonlinear forms also exist. To choose adequately from these alternative equation forms requires two things: a knowledge of the way the curves work (which is acquired only through practice and study of other people's use of them) and a clear understanding of the type of nonlinearity which the theory or data might imply.

Both linear and nonlinear equations typically are used with continuous variables and are themselves continuous. For relationships, continuity means that a graph of the relationship would show smooth change in the dependent variable over the whole range of the independent variable. There would be no breaks in the graph, nor would there be abrupt angular changes. If discontinuous relationships are considered, it would be possible to link specific values without regard for intermediate values. For example, one can define a function $y = f(x)$, where $y = 0$ if $x > k$, and $y = 1$ if $x \leq k$, k being some constant.

The advantage of discontinuous relationships can be most clearly seen when theories deal with special configurations of variables which form discrete types in a typology. For example, a particular dependent variable might be affected if any one of a set of independent variables reached a given threshold. Alternatively, a dependent variable might depend upon special combinations of independent variables in a way which cannot be expressed in the usual continuous equations.

The main questions about relationships, then, are: Is there a causal priority among the variables? Are they to be continuous or not? If continuous, are they linear or nonlinear, and if nonlinear, what form?

Two other ideas are relevant to discussing relationships, because they are inherent in some theories. First is the notion of feedback, or some sort of reflexivity in the model. As expressed in such concepts as homeostasis, equilibrium, or a cybernetic system, changes eventually come back to haunt the place where they started. Although they set no requirement for the form of equations, such notions require that equations make a complete cycle through a set of variables so that each variable is independent in one equation and dependent in one other (or possibly more than one of either). The model builder must ask how a process such as that used by Meeker in Chapter 10 has this type of feedback built in.

If feedback loops are used, the second question becomes whether variables that will be reiteratively affected must be kept within specifiable limits. An obvious example is a probability variable. Just increasing a probability by a linear function of some other variable increase may result in pushing its value beyond 1.0, which is maximum probability. For such cases it will be necessary to use relationships which become "asymptotic"—that is, as the dependent variable approaches its logical limit, it changes by smaller and smaller amounts. Otherwise a discontinuous function will be needed, which simply stops the change at the variable limit. The diffusion models discussed in Chapter 7 use asymptotic relationships. On the other hand, some processes should be able to "explode" into astronomical values if they create an unstable system. Since feedback models are complicated and require a number of iterations to produce predictions or parameter estimates, we recommend that the model builder consider computer simulation as the first step in developing or testing one of these models if the feedback loops are particularly complex.

key questions for model building

Major Emphases:

1. What is the *source:*
   Theory?
   Model?
   Data?
2. What is the *direction*?

   Development from a theory or from data? Are there anticipated applications after the model is developed?
   Application of a model to theory building or data analysis?

Source Properties:

1. Are the properties of the source variables
   States or ordered variables? If ordered, are they continuous or discrete?
   Unique or summary?
2. Is there a random variable or relationship?
3. Is time involved? If yes, is time:
   Explicit as a variable or implicit in relationships?
   Discrete or continuous?
4. Are the properties of the source relationships:
   Assumptions of causal priority?
   Discontinuous or continuous? If continuous, linear or nonlinear, and what form?
5. Are feedback loops needed? If yes, will any relationships have to be asymptotic?

general philosophical considerations

Beyond the problem of mapping or translating assumptions, a set of philosophical issues is relevant to using mathematical models in sociology. These are somewhat harder to express because they tend to remain implicit in the work of sociologists, whether mathematical or not, rather than receiving explicit statement. We could refer to these as *assumptions of strategy* or *choice of paradigm* in development of theory and research, and they are related to general issues in sociology, not only to the construction and testing of models.

Most sociologists, whether they are aware of it or not, have a set of principles they use to determine what kind of theoretical and research activity is most appropriate. Authors of books on mathematical sociology sometimes feel constrained to explain their philosophy or strategy.[5] This, as well as recurrent criticisms by adherents of one type of model of the "triviality" of other types of models, would seem to indicate that there is no general agreement among sociologists as to the best way to proceed in terms of constructing models. (This is not to say that some models are not in fact trivial.) In part there is a lack of agreement on the theory and data aspects of the work, relating, for example, to debates between proponents of such theoretical orientations as structural-functionalism, exchange theory, symbolic interactionism, or Marxism, or between experimentalists and survey researchers. We cannot really deal with these issues here, except to point out that the assumptions one holds about the best way to collect data or the best theoretical framework will influence the kinds of assumptions he is able to make about how these matters translate into mathematical language. There are, however, some similar problems of general orientation or strategy that are particularly relevant to mathematical models, and which we will mention briefly.

One current source of controversy involves whether one should emphasize being able to include many variables at once or whether one should concentrate on equations that link two or three variables, and build a model out of these. The former view is based on the assumption that social behavior is determined by many factors operating simultaneously and interacting with each other. This kind of strategy leads to the use of such models as multivariate statistical models, path analysis, and factor analysis. While permitting the inclusion of many variables in a single model, this approach tends to force the assumption of very simple shapes to the relationships. In general, the relationships are assumed to be linear and additive.

The other approach is based on the assumption that if we know the shapes of relationships well enough to produce an equation linking two or

---

[5]For example, Hamblin *et al.*, *A Mathematical Theory of Social Change*, chap. 10; J. S. Coleman, *Introduction to Mathematical Sociology*, chap. 18.

three variables, we can combine several such equations to link more variables. For example, if we know an equation that describes status as a function of education and another describing education as a function of parental income, we can derive an equation describing status as a function of parental income. The equations linking status and education can then be used to compare different populations; if the relationships have different shapes for the different populations we will find this out, which we would not if we simply included the variables that define different populations as other variables in a multivariate model that assumes that all relationships are alike.

People who adopt the multivariate strategy tend to become impatient with models that do not include many variables at once, while people who adopt other strategies often feel that the assumptions of linearity, and so on, in the multivariate models are so simplisitc as to make the models useless. In oversimplified terms, we might say that the first strategy assumes that if we could only include enough variables the world would turn out to be linear, and the second assumes that if we would only specify the form of relationships exactly enough, we would not need to include many variables. When it is put in these terms, it appears that at some higher level the two approaches ought to complement each other; as a practical matter, however, people generally must choose one or the other.

Another issue of strategy involves the use of structure models vs. process models. Since any assumption of causality implies some sort of changes over time (that is, changes in one variable precede changes in another) the complete development of models must at some point consider how variables change over time. Once again, this is difficult to do in a model that includes many variables at once, and many of the multivariate and path models must make the assumption that the system has reached an equilibrium in which any causal effects have already taken place. We suggest that a kind of model recently attracting interest in such disciplines as genetics and biochemistry might be useful to sociologists. These models assume that the process of development of relationships between two variables may be different in the presence or absence of some constellation of exogenous variables. Thus, for example, it may take a certain level of environmental stimulation to allow the full development of a genetically determined trait.

Another dimension of strategy is whether one should develop models that utilize data already avilable (as Coleman argues we should do) or develop models that suggest new ways of collecting data (Hamblin's model does this). Still another matter of strategy is deciding whether to concentrate on explaining a particular phenomenon (as the models of distribution of acts in small groups do) or on developing models that can deal with a wide variety of phenomena at a general level (as Coleman's models do). Both of these issues must be decided partly on the basis of the characteristics of the source of the model (that is, theory or data or both), which will be related to the model builder's initial inspiration.

inspiration for the model builder

A surprising number of models of great variety exist in the literature, although they are widely scattered among various journals and collections of papers on mathematical models. Similarly, there are a number of examples of applications of models, most often related to the analysis of data. The better acquainted the person working with mathematical models is with this literature, the more likely he will be to find a model suited to his purpose. It is, of course, much easier to borrow procedures, or even entire models, than to have to develop them completely anew. Working from a model to existing theories or data sets requires, as well, extensive knowledge of a particular substantive area or access to a variety of data in that area. Whatever the intent of the mapping, there can be no substitute for thorough knowledge of what has already been accomplished by others.

The best, and most fruitful, inspiration for the model builder, however, comes from his own substantive interest. If there is something really intriguing about his area of inquiry, he will learn how to use models once he is convinced of their potential contribution, just as sociologists have learned to use statistical procedures. The inspiration for mathematical sociology, then, is primarily *sociology*, rather than mathematics. The latter is just a better tool for doing the job.

index

Abelson, R. P., 54
Abortion as birth control, 161
Absorbing state, 170, 204
Accelerating power function, 7, 28
Adjacency matrix, 56
Anderson, B., 66
Arithmetic mean, 23
Arney, W. R., 118
Aronson, E., 54
Asch, S., 204
Asymmetric interpersonal choice, 69
Asymptotic relationship, 115
Atkinson, R. C., 187
Axiomatic theory, 2

Balance, 55-74, 196, 224
   degree of, 161
Balanced graph, 58

Bales, R. F., 39, 49, 50, 164
Bartholomew, D. J., 137, 165
Bayesian analysis, 198
Beaton, A. E., 86
Berge, C., 56
Berger, J., 50, 66, 69, 204
Birth control, 161-63
Blackwell, L., 21
Blalock, H. M., Jr., 111, 113, 114
Blumen, I., 171-82
Borgatta, E. F., 39, 50
Boudon, R., 111, 113
Bower, G. H., 187
Buckholdt, D., 21
Budger, D. A., 21

Cartwright, D., 54, 56, 59, 60, 62, 63, 90
Causal analysis, 110-16, 212, 232

Chilton, R., 94
Clique, 60, 85-97, 135
Clustering, 67-72
Coalition formation, 156
Cognitive consistency, 54, 196, 224
Cohen, B. P., 59, 204
Cohen, M., 226
Coleman, J. S., 50, 129, 135, 188, 208-24, 229, 232, 237
Completely connected graph, 56
Computer simulation, 141-57
Conner, T. L., 50, 204
Continuous time, 232
   -discrete state models, 210-24
Continuous variables, 14, 228
Contraception, 162
Coombs, C. H., 94
Costner, H. L., 94, 118, 185
Cross sectional data, 220
Crothers, E. J., 187
Curve fitting, 118-26
Cybernetic system, 234
Cycle, 58
   of generations, 83

Daley, D. J., 137
Davis, J. A., 66-69, 93
Davis, K., 99
Day, R. C., 21
Decelerating power function, 25
Deficient diagonal, 176, 188
Dehumanization by mathematical models, 18
Diffusion, 128-39
Digraph, 56
Dimensional analysis, 110
Directed graph (see Digraph)
Discrete time, 231
Discrete variables, 227
Dissonance (see also Cognitive consistency), 196
Dodd, S. C., 135

Ecological fallacy, 229
Education (relation to income), 5-9
Equilibrium, 169, 200
   aggregate, 220
Esteem, 33
Expectation states, 204
Exponential function, 29
   waning, 132
   waxing, 132

Fararo, T. J., 93, 136
Farr, G., 141-57
Feedback, 234
Feller, W., 198
Ferrotor, D., 21
Festinger, L., 87

Fisek, H., 50, 164, 204
Flament, C., 56, 64, 65
Function (see Relationships)

Gamson, W., 156
Geometric mean, 23
Ginsberg, R., 185
Gompertz curve, 137
Gouldner, A., 191
Graph theory, 56-58
Gray, L. N., 42
Group (mathematical), 84
Guetzkow, H., 141
Gullahorn, J. E., 141
Gullahorn, J. T., 141
Guttman, L., 94

Hamblin, R. L., 20-36, 139, 229
Harary, F., 54, 56, 61, 63, 90
Hare, A. P., 50
Harris, T. R., 99-110, 116, 209
Hastings, D. W., 137
Hayes, D. P., 146
Heider, F., 54
Henry, N. W., 94
Hernes, G., 137
Hierarchy (in small group), 43, 69
Holland, P., 65, 71, 93
Homans, G. C., 209
Homeostasis, 234
Horvath, W. J., 50, 51, 136, 164
Hubbell, C. H., 76, 89-92

Income (relation to education), 5-9
Initiation tendency, 40
Input-output model, 76, 89
Interaction (social), 209
Interpersonal choice, 65-73, 86-93, 141-57
Interpersonal liking, 52-55, 65-73, 209
Isomorphism, 225

James, J., 155
Jordan, N., 59

Kadane, J. B., 51
Katz, L., 88, 89
Kemeny, J. G., 77, 185, 198
Kendall, D. G., 137
Keyfitz, N., 158-63
Kinship structures, 76-85
Kogan, M., 171-82
Kozloff, M., 21

Lazarsfeld, P., 94
Leadership in a small group, 43
Lee, H., 204
Leik, R. K., 41, 94, 141-57
Leinhardt, S., 65, 66, 69, 71, 93
Leontief, W. W., 86, 90

Level (of variables), 229
Lewis, G., 51
Line (in a graph), 56
Linear relationship, 7, 48, 119-27, 233
Local balance, 61
Log function, 29
Log-log graph paper, 25
Logistic curve, 134
Luce, R. D., 87, 189

Mapping, 11, 225
Marginal analysis, 99-110
Marginal productivity, 99-110
Markov process, 166
   stationary, 173
Matrix
   payoff, 189
   permutation, 80
   reachability, 63, 88
   transition, 168
   who-to-whom, 46, 48
Matthews, M., 94
Mayer, T., 118
McCarthy, P. J., 171-82
McFarland, D., 171, 182-85
McGinnis, R., 185
McGuire, W. J., 54
McIntyre, J., 221
Mead, G. H., 145
Meeker, B. F., 188, 189, 234
Meltzer, L., 146
Menzel, H., 94
Meyers, S. M., 221
Mishler, E. G., 50, 51
Mobility (occupational), 165-85
Monotonic relationship, 234
Moore, W. E., 99
Moreno, J. L., 86
Morrison, P. A., 185
Mover-stayer model (see Mobility)

Nagel, E., 226
Nerlove, S. B., 94
Net
   biased (friendship), 93, 136
   random, 93
Newcomb, T. M., 54
Nonmonotonic relationship, 234
Norman, F., 56, 62, 63, 94

Order (of a variable), 227
Origin (setting of, in power function), 26

Panel data, 215
Parabola, 119, 146
Parameter
   definition, 5
   estimation, 26, 125, 173, 178, 198, 215
Partial differential equations, 103-5

Participation (in groups), 141
Path, 56, 88
Path analysis, 110-16
Perry, A. D., 87
Point (in a graph), 56
Power function, 11, 21, 48
Preferential marriage system, 77
Prisoner's dilemma, 189
Proaction (in small groups), 44
Process models, 117
Productivity functions
   independent, 102
   interdependent, 102
Psychophysical models, 21

Race-ethnicity (relation to income), 5-9
Raiffa, H., 189
Ramage, J., 51
Random shocks, 212
Randomness, 230
Rapaport, A., 93, 135
Rate of interaction, 40
Rationality, 191
Reachability, 63
Reaction (in small groups), 44
Reciprocity, 42, 191
Recursive systems, 111
Relationships, form of, 5-9, 232-35
   causal, 110-16, 232
   exponential, 29, 132
   independent, 41, 102
   interdependent, 41, 102
   inverse, 40
   linear, 7, 48, 119-27, 233
   logarithmic, 119, 233
   parabolic, 121, 234
   power, 11, 21-29, 48-51
   stochastic, 165
Renewal process, 159
Robinson, J. G., 137
Romney, A. K., 94
Rosenberg, M. J., 54

Scales, 14, 74, 228
Scaling models, 93
Schachter, S., 121
School enrollment, 122
Schuessler, K. F., 94
Self esteem, 221
Set theory, 64
Sex (related to income), 9
Shepard, R. N., 94
Sign of a cycle, 58
Signed graph, 57
Simon, H., 209
Singer, B., 185
Smith, C. R., 21
Snell, J. L., 59, 77, 165, 198
Social exchange theory, 33

Social pressure, 151
Sociogram, 65
Sociometric choice, 65, 86
Sociometric structure, 85-93
Solomon, H., 50
Spilerman, S., 136, 165
Starbuck, W. H., 107
States (variables), 14, 74, 227
Statistical model, 3
Status (related to income), 23
Status structures, 87-89
Steel processing, 100
Stephan, F. F., 50
Stevens, S. S., 23
Stevens' Law, 23, 48
Stimulus-response model, 23
Stinchcombe, A. L., 99-110, 116, 209
Stouffer, S. A., 94
Strategy (in model building), 236-38
Stratification, 99
Straus, M. A., 37
Strauss, A., 145
Structural balance, 53-73
Structure theorem, 60
Summary variables, 229
Sunshine, M. H., 93, 136
Supervision, 100
Symmetric graph, 64

Tannenbaum, O. H., 54
Task behavior, 45
Theory construction, 225-27
Theory-model-data triangle, 9-11, 225
Thompson, G., 77, 165, 198
Time, 221
　continuous, 208-24, 232
　series, 118-22
Topology, 53
Torgerson, W. S., 94
Transitivity (of interpersonal choice), 71
Tree diagram, 77, 166, 192, 197

Vacuous balance, 59
Vacuous transitivity, 71
Value-conflict model, 187-207
Variables, 5, 227-29
　continuous vs. discrete, 228-29
　order, 227-28
　unique vs. summary, 229-30
　values vs. states, 14, 227

White, H. C., 76-85, 165, 231
Who-to-whom matrix, 46-48

Yancey, W. L., 21

Zelditch, M., Jr., 59, 66
Zetterberg, H., 2, 37